English Unlimited

B1+ Intermediate
Teacher's Pack

Theresa Clementson, Leanne Gray & Howard Smith

CAMBRIDGE
UNIVERSITY PRESS

CAMBRIDGE UNIVERSITY PRESS
Cambridge, New York, Melbourne, Madrid, Cape Town, Singapore,
São Paulo, Delhi, Dubai, Tokyo, Mexico City

Cambridge University Press
The Edinburgh Building, Cambridge CB2 8RU, UK

www.cambridge.org
Information on this title: www.cambridge.org/9780521157179

First published 2011

Printed in the United Kingdom at the University Press, Cambridge

A catalogue record for this publication is available from the British Library

ISBN 978-0-521-15717-9 Intermediate Teacher's Pack
ISBN 978-0-521-73989-4 Intermediate Coursebook with e-Portfolio
ISBN 978-0-521-15182-5 Intermediate Self-study Pack (Workbook with DVD-ROM)
ISBN 978-0-521-73990-0 Intermediate Class Audio CDs

Cambridge University Press has no responsibility for the persistence or
accuracy of URLs for external or third-party Internet websites referred to in
this publication, and does not guarantee that any content on such websites is,
or will remain, accurate or appropriate. Information regarding prices, travel
timetables and other factual information given in this work are correct at
the time of first printing but Cambridge University Press does not guarantee
the accuracy of such information thereafter.

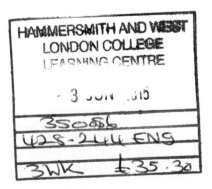

Contents

Introduction

Teaching notes

The thinking behind *English Unlimited*

The aim of *English Unlimited* is to enable adult learners to communicate effectively in English in real-life situations. To achieve this, *English Unlimited* is:

1 a **practical** course
2 an **authentic** course
3 an **international** course
4 a **flexible** course

1 A practical course

Each unit of *English Unlimited* is designed to help learners achieve specific **communicative goals**. These goals are listed at relevant points throughout the Coursebook. For example, you and your learners will see these goals at the top of the first lesson in Unit 10:

10.1 goals
- talk about memory
- talk about what you remember

All the goals are of a practical 'can do' nature, chosen to enable Intermediate learners to deal with a wide range of situations and topics in English. Of course, a substantial amount of each unit is dedicated to learning vocabulary and grammar – but the goals come first. We've identified goals which we think will be useful for Intermediate learners to work on, and then selected vocabulary and grammar to help them do this.

Where exactly do the goals come from?

The goals for the course have been taken from the **Common European Framework of Reference for Languages (CEF)**, and adapted and supplemented according to our research into the needs of Intermediate learners.

The goals in the Coursebook are based on the CEF goals but they have been reworded to make them less 'technical' and more motivating and accessible for learners and teachers.

What is the CEF?

The CEF uses 'Can Do' statements to describe the abilities of learners of English (or any other language) at different levels. The focus is on **how to do things in the language**, rather than on abstract knowledge of the language itself. For example, here are some CEF goals which describe learners' speaking abilities at the end of Intermediate:

- Can explain why something is a problem, discuss what to do next, compare and contrast alternatives
- Can give brief comments on the views of others
- Can invite others to give their views on how to proceed

The CEF originated in Europe but is used increasingly widely around the world as a guide for curriculum design and assessment. It can be used with learners of any nationality or first language.

What's the level of the course?

The CEF is divided into six main **levels**, sometimes with 'plus' levels in between. This table shows the CEF levels and how they relate to the Cambridge ESOL exams:

CEF levels		Cambridge exams
C2	'Mastery'	CPE
C1	'Operational proficiency'	CAE
B2+		
B2	'Vantage'	FCE
B1+		
B1	'Threshold'	PET
A2+		
A2	'Waystage'	KET
A1	'Breakthrough'	

English Unlimited Intermediate is based on 'Can Do' statements at the B1 and B1+ levels of the Common European Framework. It completes B1+ and prepares learners for the B2 level of competence.

2 An authentic course

Because it is based on practical goals, *English Unlimited* teaches authentic language – that is, the kind of language which is really used by native speakers and proficient non-native speakers of English in everyday situations. An important tool for identifying useful language to include in the course has been the **Cambridge International Corpus (CIC)**.

What is the CIC?

The CIC is an electronic collection of more than a billion words of real text, both spoken and written, which can be searched by computer to discover the most common words, expressions and structures of the language, and the kinds of situations in which they are used.

How has it been used in the course?

The CIC has been used throughout *English Unlimited* to ensure that, as far as possible given the level of the course, learners are taught **the most frequent and useful words and expressions** for meeting their communicative goals. For example, the course includes a focus on *It's* + adjectives in Unit 2 because the CIC suggests that this is a common way to give opinions (*It's better to talk to people face to face*).

The CIC has also been used in the preparation of **grammar** sections, both to select structures to be taught and to identify realistic contexts for presentation. For example, the CIC suggests that a common use of verb + *-ing* (Unit 6) is to 'give advice' (*Have you considered getting a new one?*).

A further use of the CIC is in the **Keyword pages** which appear in odd-numbered units. Each Keyword page focuses on one or two of the most frequently used words in English and teaches its most common meanings, as well as useful expressions based around it.

How else is English Unlimited *an authentic course?*

In addition to being informed by the CIC, *English Unlimited* contains a large amount of **unscripted audio and video material**, recorded using non-actors, both native and non-native speakers. Many other listening texts have been scripted from recordings of real conversations.

What are the benefits for learners of using 'authentic' listening material?

Listening to spontaneous, unscripted speech is the best way to prepare learners for the experience of understanding and communicating in English in the real world. We also find that authentic recordings are more motivating and engaging for learners in general.

3 An international course

In what ways is English Unlimited *'international'?*

Firstly, *English Unlimited* is an **inclusive** course, catering for learners of different backgrounds from all around the world. We have taken care to select topics, texts and tasks which will appeal to a broad range of learners. We've tried to avoid topics which learners may find uncomfortable, or simply uninteresting, and we don't assume a knowledge of a celebrity culture, but focus instead on more universal themes, accessible to all.

English is most often used nowadays between non-native speakers from different places. How does the course take this into account?

A second strand to the 'internationalism' of the course is that it includes features which will help learners become more effective communicators in international contexts.

In every odd-numbered unit there is an **Across cultures** page which focuses on a particular topic of cultural interest. The aim of these pages is to increase learners' awareness of how the values and assumptions of people they communicate with in English might differ from – or be similar to – their own. Learners who have this awareness are likely to be more sensitive and effective communicators in international environments.

Listening sections use recordings of **speakers with a range of accents** in order to familiarise learners with the experience of hearing both native and non-native speakers from a wide variety of places. Regardless of accents, care has been taken to ensure that recordings are of appropriate speed and clarity for learners at this level, and that they are error-free. All non-native speakers are competent users of English and should provide learners with strong and motivating role models to help them progress and achieve greater confidence in English.

For the purposes of language production, taught grammar, vocabulary and pronunciation follow a British English model, but by exposing learners to a wide range of accents and models, we are helping to enhance their ability to use English in real international contexts.

4 A flexible course

The next five pages show how a typical unit of *English Unlimited* is organised.

As you'll see, the first five pages are connected to each other and make up the 'core' of the unit. After that, there is the **Explore** section, two pages of activities which have a topical or linguistic link to the unit, but which can be used separately. On the last page of each unit is the **Look again** page, comprising review and extension activities, which can be done by learners either in the classroom or for homework.

This means that *English Unlimited* can be adapted not only for lessons of different lengths, but also for shorter and longer courses. For example, just using the 'core' of each unit would be suitable for a course of about 50 hours, while using all the material, including the **Explore** and **Look again** pages, would give a course length of 80 or 90 hours.

The flexibility of *English Unlimited* is further enhanced by an extensive range of supplementary materials. These include **Grammar reference and extra practice** at the back of the Coursebook, the **Teacher's DVD-ROM** containing three extra activities for each unit of the Coursebook, **Achievement and Progress tests**, and the **Self-study Pack**, which offers more than 50 hours of additional language and skills practice material in the Workbook and on the Self-study DVD-ROM.

In the rest of this introduction you'll find:
- a plan showing how a unit is organised *pages 6 to 10*
- more detailed notes on the different sections of the units *pages 11 to 15*
- information about the other components of the course *pages 16 to 21*
- more detailed information about the CEF *page 22*

We hope that you and your learners will enjoy using *English Unlimited*.

Theresa Clementson
David Rea
Alex Tilbury
Leslie Anne Hendra

How a unit is organised

3

Success

3.1 goals
- talk about a business idea
- talk about hopes, dreams and ambitions

> The course consists of 14 units, each of which has eight pages.

> **The first two pages** are a single lesson with goals based on the CEF. You can, of course, spread the material over more than one lesson if you want.
> ⏱ *about 90 minutes*

Great ideas

READING

1 You're going to read about an inventor. Which of these facts do you think are about the inventor of:
- karaoke?   • the iPod?

a He never became rich from his invention.
b He's shy and doesn't usually do interviews.
c He made people listen to music in a different way.
d He used his invention to celebrate his 59th birthday.
e He was a drummer in a band.
f He has also designed computers.

2 Work in A/B pairs. A, read the article below and B, read the article on p119 to check your ideas.

Mr Song and Dance Man

1 Karaoke is a $10 billion-a-year industry, but the man who invented it has made almost no money out of it. Inoue Daisuke came up with the idea in 1971. He could have become one of the richest men in Japan, but he didn't patent his idea and doesn't seem worried about the lost opportunity. 'I took a car stereo, a coin box and a small amplifier to make the karaoke,' says the 65-year-old in his small office in Osaka. 'Who would consider patenting something like that?'

2 In the early 1970s, Inoue was a drummer in a bar band with six colleagues, playing in local clubs in Kobe. They played for middle-aged businessmen who wanted to sing traditional Japanese songs. Inoue says, 'Out of 108 club musicians in Kobe, I was the worst! And the clients in my club were the worst singers!'

3 One day, one of his clients asked Inoue to play for him on an overnight trip. Inoue, unable to leave his job, gave him a tape of the backing music instead. That night, the businessman gave an emotional performance and karaoke (meaning 'empty orchestra') was born.

4 Inspired by this success, Inoue made 11 boxes with tapes and amplifiers, and began renting them to bars in Kobe in 1971. His plan was to make a bit of money but he never thought the idea would be so popular. In fact, karaoke was soon picked up by larger companies and through the 1980s and 1990s, it swept across Asia, the US and Europe. Then in 1999, *Time Magazine* called Inoue one of the 20th century's most influential people, saying he had completely changed nightlife. 'Nobody was as surprised as me,' he says.

5 Inoue himself only used a karaoke machine for the first time to celebrate his 59th birthday. These days, he makes a living selling a cockroach repellent for the machines. 'Cockroaches get inside the machines, build nests and eat the wires,' he says. He's very excited about his next venture. 'My dream,' he says, 'is to train Japanese pet-owners to take better care of their pets.' Friends say he is the ideas man, while his wife, who works in the same Osaka office, helps bring the ideas to life.

3 a A, complete the summary of this article; B, complete the summary on p119.

1 Inoue Daisuke invented karaoke, but he didn't …
2 He was a drummer in a band which …
3 The idea for karaoke started when Inoue gave …
4 Over the next twenty years karaoke became … Inoue was surprised whe…
5 Now, Inoue … In the future, he …

b Tell each other about your articles. How are the two men similar or differe…

22

3.1

VOCABULARY
Talking about a business idea

4 Look at the sentences from the articles. Match 1–3 with topics a–c.

a a description of the product
b the financial success of an idea
c the start of a project or invention

1 Inoue Daisuke came up with the idea in 1971.
He didn't patent his idea.

2 You can use it to store thousands of songs.
Critics said it looked fantastic and was easy to use.

3 The man … has made almost no money out of it.
He makes a living selling a cockroach repellent.

5 Complete the questions with verbs from the highlighted expressions in 4 in the correct form.

1 How did Inoue Daisuke _____ up with his idea?
2 Why didn't he _____ his invention?
3 Do you think Jonathan Ive _____ a lot of money out of the iPod?
4 What do you think is the easiest way to _____ a living?
5 Is it more important that a gadget is easy to use or _____ fantastic?

SPEAKING

6 Ask and answer the questions together.

Hopes, dreams and ambitions

VOCABULARY
Hopes, dreams and ambitions

1 What's Inoue Daisuke's dream for the future? What do you think of his idea?

2 ◀ 1.22 Listen to Aminata, Eduardo and Elisa talking about their hopes, dreams and ambitions. Match each speaker to one of the pictures A–C.

3 ◀ 1.22 Listen again. Complete sentences 1–8 with a–h.

Aminata	1	One day, I'd like to	a	taking some lessons.
	2	At some point, I'd absolutely love to	b	be comfortable in the water.
	3	I'm thinking of	c	learn to swim.
Eduardo	4	I'm considering	d	be a guitar player.
	5	My dream is to	e	doing a degree in music.
Elisa	6	My aim is to	f	live in Tokyo for a year.
	7	My ambition is to	g	train at the JKA dojo.
	8	I've always wanted to	h	go there next year.

4 Choose five of the highlighted expressions from 3. Write sentences about your hopes, dreams and ambitions.

One day, I'd like to travel around the world.

PRONUNCIATION
Schwa /ə/

5 a ◀ 1.23 Listen to sentence 1 above. What kinds of word are usually stressed? What kinds of word often have a schwa?

One day, I'd like to learn to swim.

b Mark the stressed syllables and schwa sounds in sentences 2–8 above.

c ◀ 1.24 Listen and read the script on p148 to check. Practise saying the sentences.

SPEAKING

6 Talk to your partner about your hopes, dreams and ambitions. Do you think you can both achieve your ambitions?

7 Tell the class something interesting your partner wants to do in the future.

23

> Lessons include **vocabulary** and/or **grammar**, as well as practice in **reading**, **listening** and **speaking**. Lessons always finish with a communicative speaking task.
> *See pp11–13 for details of language and skills sections.*

> Every unit has a focus on **pronunciation**.
> *See p12 for details.*

3.2

Your abilities

3.2 goals
- talk about abilities
- talk about achievements

READING

1 a What's an IQ test? Have you ever taken one?

b Read the article from an educational magazine. Which intelligence types might help with these activities?

- doing your accounts • playing tennis • writing a poem • designing a building
- staying happy • learning a song • resolving an argument

What is intelligence?
➡ Not just a high IQ

The **theory of multiple intelligences** was proposed by Howard Gardner in 1983. He believed that the traditional intelligence test (known as an IQ test) didn't acknowledge the wide variety of abilities that people have. Here is a summary of the main types of intelligence that he identified:

1 Bodily-kinesthetic People who have bodily-kinesthetic intelligence learn best by doing something physically. They are good at building and making things. They may enjoy acting or performing and are generally good at physical activities such as sports or dance.

2 Interpersonal People who have a high interpersonal intelligence learn best by working with others and often enjoy discussion and debate. They are able to co-operate in order to work as part of a group. They communicate effectively and empathise easily with others.

3 Intrapersonal Those who are strong in this intelligence are typically introverts and prefer to work alone. They are capable of understanding their own emotions, goals and motivations and learn best when concentrating on a subject by themselves.

4 Verbal-linguistic People with high verbal-linguistic intelligence have a facility with words and languages. They are typically good at reading, writing, telling stories and memorising words along with dates. They tend to learn best by reading, taking notes, listening to lectures, and through discussion and debate.

5 Logical-mathematical This area has to do with logic, reasoning and numbers. People with this ability excel at scientific thinking and investigation, and have the ability to perform complex calculations. Traditional concepts of intelligence, or IQ, reflect ability in this area.

6 Musical This area has to do with rhythm, music and hearing. Those who have a high level of musical intelligence are able to sing and play musical instruments. They can also often compose music and may learn best by listening to lectures.

7 Visual-spatial People with strong visual-spatial intelligence are typically very good at visualising and mentally manipulating objects. They have a good visual memory and are often artistically inclined. They also generally have a good sense of direction and may have good hand–eye co-ordination.

> A lawyer probably needs interpersonal and verbal-linguistic intelligences.

2 Read the article again. Which intelligences do you think are important for these jobs? Why?

- lawyer • politician • poet • engineer
- doctor • singer • DJ • social worker

VOCABULARY
Abilities

3 Look at the highlighted expressions in 1–7 in the article. Which can be followed by

a an infinitive?   b an *-ing* form?   c a noun?   d an *-ing* form or a noun?

4 a Which intelligences do you think you have? What about people you know well? Write five sentences. Explain your ideas and give examples.

I think I have musical intelligence because I'm able to learn tunes very quickly.

b Talk about your sentences together. What intelligences do most people have?

24

3.2

Your achievements

LISTENING

1 🔊 Listen to interviews with Aminata, Margot and Charlie about their achievements. What are they most proud of?

Margot

Aminata

Charlie

2 Can you answer the questions about each person? 🔊 Listen again to check.

Aminata	1 What did she want to learn? Why?	2 When did she start learning?
Margot	3 What's her book about?	4 What's she doing at the moment?
Charlie	5 What did he join?	6 What do they do together?

3 Do you think each of them found it easy to do these things? Why?

GRAMMAR
Present perfect and time expressions

4 Match the sentences from the listening with functions a or b.

1 I've had the bike for about a year now.
2 I've just written a cookery book.
3 I've learned to ride a bike recently.
4 I've always wanted to write.

a a situation or state which is still true
b a finished action which is important now

5 Match the highlighted words in 1–8 with categories a–e.

1 I've always wanted to write.
2 I've just written a cookery book.
3 I've never been able to go with them.
4 I've already written a novel actually.
5 I've learned to ride a bike recently.
6 It hasn't come out yet.
7 I've had the bike for about a year now.
8 I haven't written anything since the cookery book.

a the whole of your life until now *always* / _____
b part of your life until now _____ / _____
c something you expect to happen _____
d a short time ago _____ / _____
e something that happened sooner than expected _____

6 Notice the position of the highlighted time expressions. Then add them to the sentences in the quiz.

Find someone who:
recently
1 has won a competition ʌ. What was it? recently
2 has passed a test or an exam. just
3 has learned to drive. Why not? never
4 has done well in interviews. always
5 has achieved something today. What was it? already
6 has been married over ten years. for
7 hasn't taken a test or an exam since they left school. since
8 hasn't done what they needed to do today. yet

Grammar reference and practice, p136

SPEAKING

7 a Ask questions to find who the statements in 1–8 are true for. Find out more about each situation.

> Have you won a competition recently?

> Actually, I've never won a competition.

b In pairs, tell each other what you found out.

25

⏱ *The last four pages of a unit will take about 45 minutes each.*

The fifth page is the heart of the unit, the **Target activity**. Learners prepare for and carry out an **extended task** which is designed to combine and activate language taught in earlier lessons in the unit. *See p13 for details.*

Target activities **review goals** from the earlier lessons of the unit.

Model recordings are used to demonstrate the task.

Task vocabulary sections provide learners with **useful language** for the task.

Learners are encouraged to **take time to prepare** ideas and language.

Target activities have a **clear outcome**.

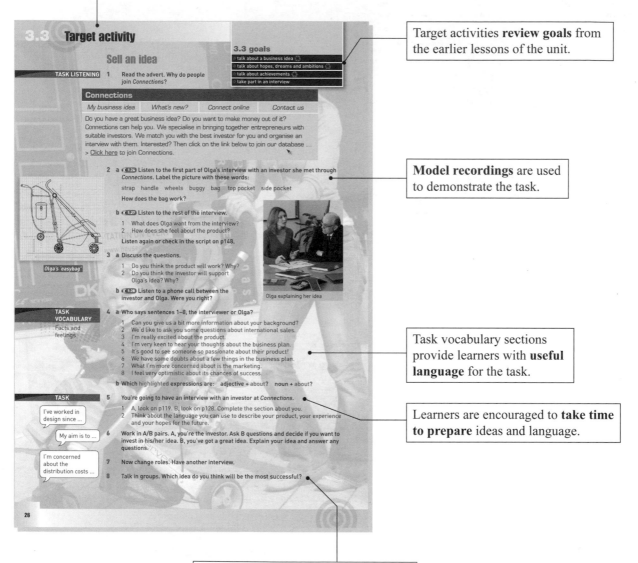

3.3 Target activity

Sell an idea

3.3 goals
- talk about a business idea
- talk about hopes, dreams and ambitions
- talk about achievements
- take part in an interview

TASK LISTENING
1 Read the advert. Why do people join *Connections*?

Connections

| My business idea | What's new? | Connect online | Contact us |

Do you have a great business idea? Do you want to make money out of it? Connections can help you. We specialise in bringing together entrepreneurs with suitable investors. We match you with the best investor for you and organise an interview with them. Interested? Then click on the link below to join our database ...
> Click here to join Connections.

2 a 🎧 Listen to the first part of Olga's interview with an investor she met through *Connections*. Label the picture with these words:

strap   handle   wheels   buggy   bag   top pocket   side pocket

How does the bag work?

Olga's 'easybag'

b 🎧 Listen to the rest of the interview.
1 What does Olga want from the interview?
2 How does she feel about the product?
Listen again or check in the script on p148.

3 a Discuss the questions.
1 Do you think the product will work? Why?
2 Do you think the investor will support Olga's idea? Why?

b 🎧 Listen to a phone call between the investor and Olga. Were you right?

Olga explaining her idea

TASK VOCABULARY
Facts and feelings

4 a Who says sentences 1–8, the interviewer or Olga?
1 Can you give us a bit more information about your background?
2 We'd like to ask you some questions about international sales.
3 I'm really excited about the product.
4 I'm very keen to hear your thoughts about the business plan.
5 It's good to see someone so passionate about their product!
6 We have some doubts about a few things in the business plan.
7 What I'm more concerned about is the marketing.
8 I feel very optimistic about its chances of success.

b Which highlighted expressions are: adjective + about? noun + about?

TASK

I've worked in design since ...

My aim is to ...

I'm concerned about the distribution costs ...

5 You're going to have an interview with an investor at *Connections*.
1 A, look on p119. B, look on p128. Complete the section about you.
2 Think about the language you can use to describe your product, your experience and your hopes for the future.

6 Work in A/B pairs. A, you're the investor. Ask B questions and decide if you want to invest in his/her idea. B, you've got a great idea. Explain your idea and answer any questions.

7 Now change roles. Have another interview.

8 Talk in groups. Which idea do you think will be the most successful?

26

The **Explore** section is made up of activities which extend and broaden the topics, language and skills taught in the core part of each unit. On the first page is **Across cultures** or **Keyword** in alternate units. On the second page is either **Explore writing** or **Explore speaking**.

Odd-numbered units have **Across cultures** pages which give learners the chance to think about and discuss how cultures differ – or are similar – around the world. *See p13 for details.*

Odd-numbered units have **Explore writing** pages which enable learners to write a range of different text types. *See p14 for details.*

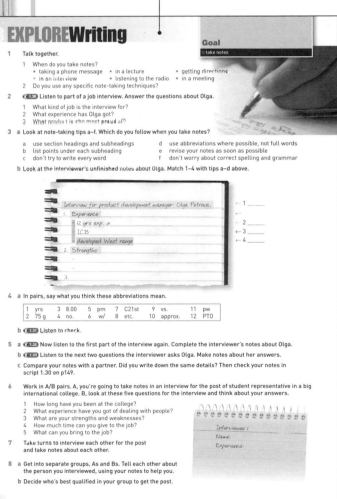

Even-numbered units have **Keyword** pages. Each one focuses on one or two common English words, teaching and practising the main meanings and useful expressions. *See p14 for details.*

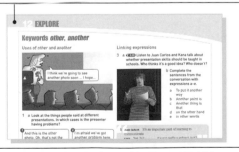

Even-numbered units have **Explore speaking** pages dedicated to developing learners' speaking skills and strategies. *See p14 for details.*

The last page of each unit, **Look again**, is a series of short classroom activities for reviewing and extending the language from the unit. *See p15 for details.*

Review activities include **vocabulary** and **grammar** from the unit.

Spelling and sounds activities help learners make connections between English spellings and how to pronounce them.

Notice activities draw out further useful language from the unit's reading or listening texts.

At the end of each unit is a **Self-assessment** for learners to complete.

Can you remember? activities review a language point from the previous unit.

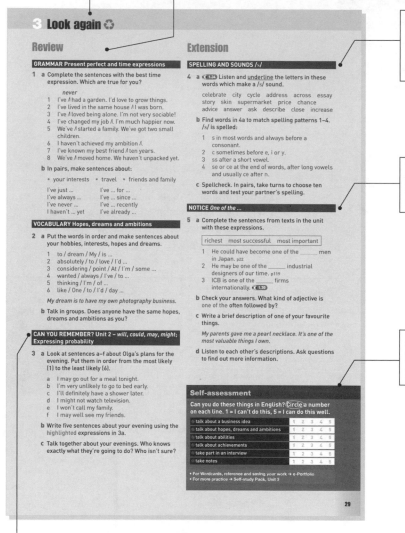

3 Look again ♻

Review

GRAMMAR Present perfect and time expressions

1 a Complete the sentences with the best time expression. Which are true for you?

never

1 I've ∕ had a garden. I'd love to grow things.
2 I've lived in the same house ∕ I was born.
3 I've ∕ loved being alone. I'm not very sociable!
4 I've changed my job ∕. I'm much happier now.
5 We've ∕ started a family. We've got two small children.
6 I haven't achieved my ambition ∕.
7 I've known my best friend ∕ ten years.
8 We've ∕ moved home. We haven't unpacked yet.

b In pairs, make sentences about:

• your interests • travel • friends and family

I've just …	I've … for …
I've always …	I've … since …
I've never …	I've … recently
I haven't … yet	I've already …

VOCABULARY Hopes, dreams and ambitions

2 a Put the words in order and make sentences about your hobbies, interests, hopes and dreams.

1 to / dream / My / is …
2 absolutely / to / love / I'd …
3 considering / point / At / I'm / some …
4 wanted / always / I've / to …
5 thinking / I'm / of …
6 like / One / to / I'd / day …

My dream is to have my own photography business.

b Talk in groups. Does anyone have the same hopes, dreams and ambitions as you?

CAN YOU REMEMBER? Unit 2 – *will, could, may, might*; Expressing probability

3 a Look at sentences a–f about Olga's plans for the evening. Put them in order from the most likely (1) to the least likely (6).

a I may go out for a meal tonight.
b I'm very unlikely to go to bed early.
c I'll definitely have a shower later.
d I might not watch television.
e I won't call my family.
f I may well see my friends.

b Write five sentences about your evening using the highlighted expressions in 3a.

c Talk together about your evenings. Who knows exactly what they're going to do? Who isn't sure?

Extension

SPELLING AND SOUNDS /s/

4 a ◀ 1.34 Listen and <u>underline</u> the letters in these words which make a /s/ sound.

celebrate city cycle address across essay story skin supermarket price chance advice answer ask describe close increase

b Find words in 4a to match spelling patterns 1–4. /s/ is spelled:

1 s in most words and always before a consonant.
2 c sometimes before e, i or y.
3 ss after a short vowel.
4 se or ce at the end of words, after long vowels and usually ce after n.

c Spellcheck. In pairs, take turns to choose ten words and test your partner's spelling.

NOTICE *One of the …*

5 a Complete the sentences from texts in the unit with these expressions.

| richest | most successful | most important |

1 He could have become one of the _____ men in Japan. p22
2 He may be one of the _____ industrial designers of our time. p119
3 ICB is one of the _____ firms internationally. ◀ 1.30

b Check your answers. What kind of adjective is one of the often followed by?

c Write a brief description of one of your favourite things.

My parents gave me a pearl necklace. It's one of the most valuable things I own.

d Listen to each other's descriptions. Ask questions to find out more information.

Self-assessment

Can you do these things in English? Circle a number on each line. 1 = I can't do this, 5 = I can do this well.

talk about a business idea	1 2 3 4 5
talk about hopes, dreams and ambitions	1 2 3 4 5
talk about abilities	1 2 3 4 5
talk about achievements	1 2 3 4 5
take part in an interview	1 2 3 4 5
take notes	1 2 3 4 5

• For Wordcards, reference and saving your work → e-Portfolio
• For more practice → Self-study Pack, Unit 3

29

A more detailed look at the features of *English Unlimited*

Vocabulary

English Unlimited provides learners with **a wide variety of vocabulary**, chosen to meet each unit's communicative goals. In most units, there are three or four vocabulary sections in the first two lessons and Target activity, and vocabulary is also presented and practised on **Keyword**, **Across cultures**, **Explore writing** and **Explore speaking** pages.

Vocabulary includes:

- **words** like *dented, torn*
- **collocations** like *have a word, have a feeling*
- **stems** like *It's no use ...*
- **fixed expressions** like *so far, such as.*

The focus on longer items as well as single words will enable learners to express themselves more fluently, naturally and effectively.

The course provides a balance of:

- **more frequent vocabulary**, selected and checked using the Cambridge International Corpus (CIC);
- **topical and functional items** which learners need in order to achieve particular goals. For example, natural events words (e.g. *a flood, a hurricane*) are not especially frequent statistically, but are obviously necessary for the fulfilment of the goal 'talk about natural phenomena'.

Taught vocabulary is generally drawn from texts which learners have already read or listened to as part of a skills section of a lesson. In other words, vocabulary is **placed in clear contexts** which help learners work out what it means, and how it's used.

Grammar

Each unit of the course teaches the grammar essential to achieving the **communicative goals**.

The points of the grammar syllabus have been selected and placed in particular units to help learners meet these goals. For example, real and unreal conditionals are focused on in Unit 9 because they are useful for making suggestions and discussing consequences.

Before focusing on grammar explicitly, learners are first exposed to grammar **in context** through reading and listening texts. Then meaning and form are highlighted using **a 'guided discovery' approach**, which actively involves learners in finding out about the grammar for themselves while also providing plentiful support and opportunities for you to monitor and assist:

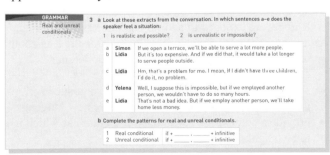

Thorough **controlled practice** is provided to check learners' understanding of the language and provide initial practice, while maintaining and developing the topic of the lesson:

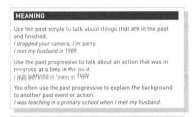

Lessons end with a speaking task (or, occasionally, a writing task) which gives learners the chance to use the language of the lesson, including the grammar, in **freer practice**.

Grammar reference

In each grammar section, you'll see a label like this ...

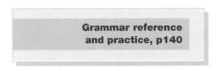

... which directs learners to a **Grammar reference section** at the end of the book, accompanied by **extra practice exercises**.

Each Grammar reference section sets out the **meaning, form and pronunciation** of the point in question, using simple language and a range of examples:

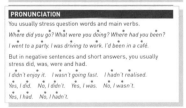

The extra practice exercises can either be done in class as the need arises, or set as homework.

Pronunciation

There is one pronunciation section in each unit.

These sections have both **receptive and productive aims**:
- to help learners understand natural spoken English;
- to build confidence by isolating and practising specific, manageable features of spoken English;
- to help learners speak more intelligibly.

Note that although native-speaker voices are used to model features of pronunciation, the primary goal of these sections is **intelligibility** and not (necessarily) achieving a native-like accent.

Pronunciation sections address areas which will be useful for all Intermediate learners to work on, regardless of their first language: **the schwa sound**, **sentence stress** (including **contrastive stress** and **emphatic stress**), **intonation**, **groups of words** (or tone units) and **linking** (including **consonant–vowel linking** and **common pairs of words**).

Each pronunciation section is based on **a short extract** drawn from a listening sequence. Learners are encouraged to **notice** a language feature and then **practise** it:

Key pronunciation areas may be touched upon **two or three times** during the course rather than being 'one-offs', thereby building learners' familiarity and confidence. Interest is maintained by slightly increasing the level of challenge on each occasion. For example, the focus on sentence stress above is from Unit 2, while the sequence shown below is from Unit 3 and deals with the schwa sound, with a review of sentence stress:

Learners can also practise the **individual sounds** they have problems with, using the phonemic chart on the Self-study DVD-ROM. In addition, on the e-Portfolio **Word list**, learners can check their pronunciation of words and expressions against British and American English recordings.

In addition to the dedicated pronunciation sections, you'll often see the symbol **P** in Vocabulary and Grammar sections. This symbol indicates points in the lesson at which it would be useful to do some **drilling** of new language.

Listening

There is usually at least one major listening section in the first two lessons of each unit, and other listening activities occur frequently on pages such as **Target activity**, **Across cultures** and **Explore speaking**.

A wide range of recordings, both **authentic** and **scripted**, is used, including monologues (for instance, on radio shows and in presentations), conversations between friends and colleagues, conversations in service situations and phone calls.

Authentic recordings are unscripted and feature both native and non-native speakers from a variety of backgrounds. These provide exposure to a range of accents and to features of real spoken English, such as vague language and hesitation devices.

Scripted recordings are based on real-world recordings and corpus data to guarantee the inclusion of natural expressions and features of English. They are often used to contextualise functional language, such as expressions for making a complaint or resolving a dispute.

Texts are exploited using **a range of tasks** designed to develop specific listening skills, build confidence and prepare learners for less-graded authentic texts. For example, this sequence includes:
- listening for gist (2);
- listening for specific information (3);
- an opportunity for learners to respond to the recording in a natural way (4).

Reading

Units usually have at least one major reading section in the first two lessons. Smaller reading texts are used in some **Target activities** and can be found in **Across cultures** and **Explore writing** pages.

A wide range of text types is used, both **printed and electronic**: newspaper, magazine and online articles, web postings and blogs, interviews, advertisements, reviews and personal correspondence.

Reading texts:
- are drawn from sources around the world in order to appeal to as many learners as possible;
- are authentic, or based on authentic texts, ensuring that learners are exposed to natural language and preparing them for the experience of reading outside the classroom;
- recycle known language in order to build learners' confidence in reading;
- are slightly above learners' productive language level, so that learners have opportunities to notice new language;
- provide a context for vocabulary and grammar which is to be taught.

Texts are exploited using **a range of tasks** appropriate for the level and text type. For example, this sequence includes:

- a prediction task (1);
- reading for gist (2);

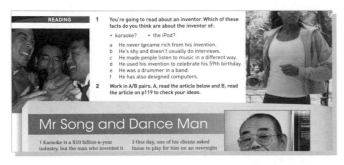

- reading in detail (3a);
- a jigsaw reading task which provides an information gap (3a) and motivates learners to speak (3b);
- an opportunity for a natural, personal response to the text (3b).

For further reading practice, the Self-study Pack contains seven **Explore reading** pages, each of which focuses on a different real-life reading scenario.

Target activity

The Target activity is **an extended speaking task**, which **recycles some or all of the goals, vocabulary and grammar of the previous two lessons**. It is the conclusion of the first five, topically linked pages of the unit.

As part of the task preparation, the Target activity also provides further listening or reading skills development, and further language input. Target activity pages have **three sections**.

Task listening and **Task reading** sections have three objectives: they provide a model for the task which learners do later on, they provide a context for the vocabulary which is presented afterwards, and they provide further receptive skills development:

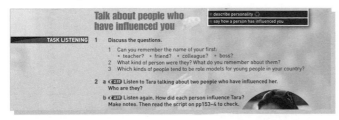

The **Task vocabulary** is drawn from the listening or reading above, and focuses on useful language for the task to follow:

In the **Task** section, learners are given the chance to think about the ideas and the language they want to use before they begin, meaning that they will be able to focus on accuracy as well as fluency when they do the task itself:

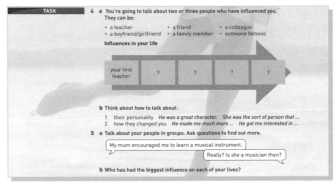

You can support your learners during task preparation by encouraging them to look back at the relevant vocabulary and grammar sections from the preceding lessons.

Across cultures

More and more people around the world are learning English in order to live, work, study and travel in other countries. The increasingly global nature of business, travel, education and personal relations in today's world means that **intercultural awareness** is an area of growing interest and need for learners everywhere. The Common European Framework of Reference for Languages (CEF) identifies intercultural awareness as a key sociolinguistic competence (chapter 5.1.1–3). Learners who are interculturally competent are more sensitive and effective communicators in international situations.

To this end, the **Across cultures** pages are intended to help learners to:

- communicate better with people from a range of cultural backgrounds;
- be more aware of the kinds of differences and similarities that can exist both between and within cultures;
- reflect on aspects of their own and other cultures in an objective, non-judgmental way;
- contribute to an exchange of ideas about cultures by drawing on their own observations and experiences.

The course has seven **Across cultures** pages in **odd-numbered units** (alternating with Keyword). Each looks at a particular topic from an intercultural perspective:

Unit	
1	Intercultural experiences
3	Attitudes to success
5	Saying no
7	Roles in life
9	Dealing with conflict
11	Attitudes to family
13	Rules and risk

Across cultures pages are structured like an ordinary lesson. They typically include a brief lead-in, a listening or reading text for further skills development, and some language input to support learners in a final speaking stage where they talk about their own and other cultures.

Listening stages usually use **authentic recordings** of people talking about their own countries and cultures. These are intended to engage learners' interest and promote discussion, rather than representing the only 'truth' about a given culture. Indeed, learners with experience of the same culture are encouraged to agree, disagree and add further information.

Keyword

The **most frequent words** in English tend to have a number of different meanings and to occur in a range of patterns and expressions. Each even-numbered unit of the course has a self-contained Keyword page which focuses on one of these words, clarifies its **key meanings** and **useful expressions** as identified by corpus research, and practises them.

The meanings and expressions of the keyword are often illustrated using examples from the current unit and previous units:

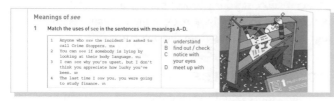

They are often contextualised in listening or reading texts:

This is followed by meaning checks and freer practice:

Explore writing

Explore writing pages occur in **odd-numbered units** (alternating with Explore speaking).

This page is dedicated to improving learners' writing skills through a sequence of activities which build towards a practical, purposeful writing task. As with Explore speaking, the page will have a topical link with the rest of the unit.

Specifically, Explore writing pages will help learners to:

- **write a range of text types** appropriate to the level, e.g. an email giving information or making offers and promises, a web posting explaining an argument, a book review for a website;
- **understand genre-specific conventions**, e.g. appropriate language for a factual report or a book review and referring back in letters or emails;
- **develop micro-skills** such as taking notes, writing summaries and writing cohesively using a range of linkers;
- **develop confidence** in writing by planning and discussing ideas with peers, talking about and improving texts together, and building from shorter to longer texts.

Each page contains one or more models of the text type learners will produce at the end of the lesson. The sequence of exercises will usually require learners to:

- **read the model texts** for meaning;
- **notice** specific language features in the texts;
- **practise** using the new language in writing;
- **plan** a piece of writing, e.g. learners may be asked to generate ideas in pairs or groups, then organise their ideas into paragraphs;

- **write** their own texts;
- **read** each other's texts and **respond** where possible (either orally or in writing);
- work to **improve** their own or each other's texts.

You can, of course, set some of the later stages of the writing process as homework if you prefer.

In many cases, the goals for these pages refer to both traditional and electronic media (e.g. 'referring back in emails or letters'), meaning that the language is appropriate for either format. You can choose to ask your learners to write either on paper or on computer if the facilities are available.

Explore speaking

Explore speaking pages occur in **even-numbered units** (alternating with Explore writing).

Explore speaking is a complete, free-standing page which aims to equip learners with **skills and strategies for improving their spoken interaction** in a wide range of situations. It addresses real-life, immediate needs of Intermediate learners, such as:

- ask for clarification and clarify what you're saying;
- say you don't understand, ask for help and explain something;
- describe objects you don't know the name of;
- use vague language to describe things;
- refer to an earlier topic or conversation.

Other pages help learners to be more confident and take interaction further, for instance:

- add comments to say how you feel;
- give yourself time to think;
- manage a discussion;
- interrupt politely.

Each Explore speaking page includes:

- **a listening text** containing the target language. The listening, which generally links to the topic of the unit as a whole, provides a clear context for the target language;
- **the listening script** on the same page. This enables learners to see and study the target language right away without having to flick to the back of the book;

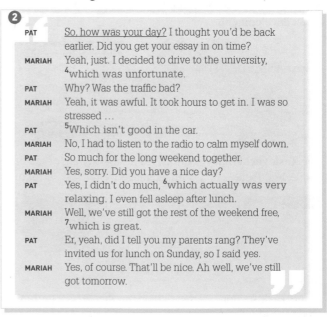

- activities in which learners **notice the target language** in different ways, such as categorising expressions according to their function;
- **controlled practice exercises** which build familiarity and confidence with the target language;
- **a freer practice task**, such as a role play, which gives learners the chance to use the target language in a real-life situation.

Look again

The Look again page is divided into two columns, **Review** and **Extension**. Although some sections can be set as homework, the page is intended as a series of communicative activities for learners to do in class. The Look again page also includes a final **Self-assessment** for the unit.

Review

The **three Review activities** will help learners to recycle language from both the current and previous unit:

1 Vocabulary – provides further communicative practice of a key area of functional or topical language from the unit.

2 Grammar – provides further communicative practice of the key grammar point in the unit.

3 Can you remember? – recycles a key language focus from the preceding unit to help learners reactivate and better retain the language.

Extension

The **two Extension activities** focus on useful aspects of language, extending learners' knowledge beyond what is taught in the main body of the unit.

4 Spelling and sounds – this section is intended to meet the need of learners and teachers for a systematic approach to English spelling.

It takes a 'sounds to spelling' approach in the belief that the most useful guide for Intermediate learners is to help them spell words when they hear them. It looks at spelling patterns for different consonant and vowel sounds, such as /f/, /s/, /k/, /ɔː/, /uː/ and /ɔɪ/.

Spelling and sounds will help learners to:
- become aware of sound / spelling correlations, helping to improve both spelling and pronunciation;
- learn general rules for spelling in manageable amounts;
- develop accuracy in spelling and therefore confidence in writing;
- revise words encountered in the current and previous units.

5 Notice – this section further exploits reading and listening texts from the unit by briefly looking at and practising a useful and regularly occurring language feature, e.g. expressions with *off* and *on*, the use of synonyms in texts and expressions with *and*, such as *on and on* or *over and over*.

Self-assessment

Each unit concludes with a Self-assessment box for learners to complete either in class or at home. Many learners find it useful and motivating to reflect on their progress at regular intervals during a course of study.

For teachers, the Self-assessment will be a valuable means of gauging learners' perceptions of how much progress they've made, and of areas they need to work on further. Self-assessments can also be useful preparation for one-to-one tutorials in which the learner's and teacher's perceptions of progress are compared and discussed.

The Self-study Pack

About the Self-study Pack

English Unlimited Intermediate Self-study Pack offers a wealth of activities for learners to **reinforce what they have learned in class**. It has been designed to offer **flexibility and depth** to your English teaching, whatever the specific needs of your learners. The Workbook and Self-study DVD-ROM provide a wide range of language and skills practice activities to accompany each unit of the Coursebook, so you can:

- set homework tasks based on the Coursebook lessons;
- supplement your lessons with further language and skills practice;
- use authentic video activities in class, or get learners to watch in their own time.

Your learners can:

- consolidate their knowledge of language and skills taught in class;
- practise and check their pronunciation;
- learn and practise essential speaking skills;
- create tests on specific language areas quickly and easily, which allows learners to focus on either grammar-based or vocabulary-based questions or both from any unit or combination of units;
- check their progress and get feedback on their level of English and any specific areas of difficulty;
- record and listen to themselves speaking in everyday conversations, using the audio materials.

In the Workbook

English Unlimited Intermediate Workbook contains:

- activities which practise and extend the vocabulary and grammar taught in the Coursebook units;
- further reading and writing skills practice;
- numerous opportunities in each unit for learners to personalise what they are learning to their own interests and situations.

The first two pages of each unit consist of **vocabulary and grammar practice activities** to consolidate and reinforce what has been taught in the Coursebook, which can either be used in class or set for homework. **Over to you** activities suggest ways for learners to practise and personalise the language and skills they have learned in a more open way.

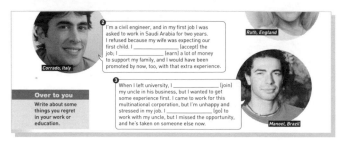

My English, in odd-numbered units, profiles learners from around the world, offering your learners a different perspective on learning English and encouraging them to reflect on their own learning.

Time out, in even-numbered units, offers a fun way for learners to practise and remember vocabulary sets.

Explore reading, in odd-numbered units, offers practice in reading, understanding and responding to a range of everyday texts, such as journalistic articles, leaflets, web pages, reviews and instruction manuals.

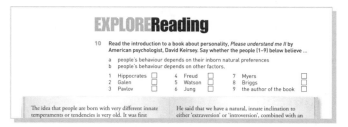

Explore writing, in even-numbered units, gives learners key pointers on structure and language, to enable them to produce a wide range of written texts, such as emails, reviews, letters and adverts. Taken alongside the Explore writing pages in odd-numbered units of the Coursebook, this means that there is a dedicated writing lesson for every unit of the course.

The last page (or sometimes two pages) of each unit has a set of activities that link up directly with the authentic video on the Self-study DVD-ROM. Learners have the chance to watch and listen to real people from around the world, talking about topics connected to the unit.

On the Self-study DVD-ROM

The *English Unlimited Intermediate Self-study DVD-ROM* offers your learners over 300 interactive activities which they can use to practise and consolidate what they have learned in class, while providing a number of easy ways to check their progress at every step of the course.

Just click on the icon for each unit and the learners will find a wide range of engaging and easy-to-use activities, from picture matching and drag-and-drop categorisation to cloze exercises. Learners are also able to record themselves, practising pronunciation or taking part in conversations, and compare their recordings with the original audio. If learners have used their e-Portfolio from the Coursebook, they are able to save their conversation recordings direct to their e-Portfolio.

Each unit's activities practise and extend the vocabulary, grammar, pronunciation and Keyword areas focused on in the Coursebook. Learners can also generate tests quickly and easily, using the Quick check test question bank. They can choose which units they want to test and how many questions they want the test to consist of, and Quick check will randomly select from the 700 questions in the bank.

Learners can also keep track of their progress as they work through the course with the Progress page, which shows which exercises they have attempted and their scores. Learners can therefore quickly see the language areas where they need to do more work and can retry the relevant exercises.

In addition to language practice, each unit of the Self-study DVD-ROM also contains Explore speaking and Explore listening activities. Explore speaking trains learners to notice key speaking skills, such as reacting when people say sorry or using *I suppose* to agree tentatively, and then incorporate these techniques into their own spoken English. Explore listening activities expose learners to useful everyday listening texts, such as a podcast, a sales pitch or a news broadcast.

In most language courses, it is rare for learners to get the chance to listen to themselves in conversation, but if there is a microphone available, this can be done easily using the recorded dialogues on the DVD-ROM. Learners listen to the dialogues, take a closer look at the language used, and then have the opportunity to record themselves and play back to hear how they sound in the conversations. If they have installed the e-Portfolio from their Coursebook, they can save this conversation directly to the My work section. Learners can also record and listen to themselves during any exercise, for example, to practise pronunciation.

In every unit of the Self-study DVD-ROM, you will also find video, which can be used with the whole class or by the learners themselves outside class, using the last page (or two) of each unit of the Workbook, or just watching them to get extra exposure to real language. At Intermediate level, there are two types of authentic video:

- 11 sets of **Interviews** including topics such as: *A proud moment*, *Reunions* and *Making presentations*.

- three short **Documentaries**, each starring one or two experts in their field discussing engaging topics. The three documentary subjects are:
  - *The chef manager*
  - *The hairdressing entrepreneurs*
  - *The runner*

These videos on the Self-study DVD-ROM are available in full-screen version with optional subtitles, or inset alongside an onscreen transcription. In the full-screen version, subtitles can be easily toggled on and off, so learners can find extra support for any part of the video if they need it.

The e-Portfolio

The *English Unlimited Intermediate e-Portfolio* is an interactive DVD-ROM which learners can use as a progress check, a reference tool and a store of written and spoken texts. It contains useful features to help reinforce learning and record and encourage progress. Learners click on one of the four icons on the start-up menu to start using these features.

Self-assessment

The **Self-assessment** feature allows learners to reflect on their own progress through the course. They do this by choosing a number between one and five to assess how well they feel they can complete each communicative goal from the Coursebook units. This encourages learners to take responsibility for their own progress and also motivates them by giving a visual record of the goals which they feel they are able to achieve. These rankings are recorded and can be revised when learners feel they have made improvements.

Word list

The **Word list** feature gives learners a comprehensive reference tool for checking the spelling, meaning and pronunciation of the words and expressions presented in the Coursebook. Learners can search by Coursebook unit or by topic group. Clear definitions show how each word or expression is used in the Coursebook, and both British and North American pronunciation guides allow learners to listen and compare with their own pronunciation.

The Word list also allows learners to enter and save new information about each word or expression. They can make notes on a word or expression, or add an example sentence which they have heard or read. New words that learners discover for themselves can also easily be added to the list, giving learners the chance to extend and personalise the Word list.

My work

The **My work** feature gives learners a convenient repository in which they can build a portfolio of their work as they progress through the course. Divided into **Reading and writing** and **Speaking and listening** folders, My work allows learners to import recorded examples of speaking and written work directly from the Self-study Pack or to import documents and files directly from their computer.

Developing a bank of their own written and spoken work provides another opportunity for review over a longer term and can be exceptionally motivating for learners. My work also offers a simple solution for English courses in which the production of coursework counts towards a learner's end-of-course grade.

Word cards

The **Word cards** feature encourages the review of words and expressions from the Coursebook. A series of words and expressions can be generated randomly by unit or topic, with the number of 'cards' set by the learner. Cards are then dragged and dropped into categories based on how well the learner can recall the word. A learner can check the meaning of the word by turning over the card. There is also the option for learners to include new words which they have added in the Word list. This is a fun and easy-to-use way of reinforcing vocabulary acquisition.

The Teacher's Pack

We understand that no two teachers or classes are alike, and that the role of a Teacher's Pack accompanying a language course is to cater for as diverse a range of pedagogical needs as possible. The materials in this Teacher's Pack serve to enhance the flexibility of *English Unlimited* to meet the needs of teachers who:

- are teaching courses of different lengths;
- want to supplement the Coursebook materials;
- have different class sizes and types;
- are teaching in different parts of the world;
- are addressing different assessment needs;
- want to use video materials in the classroom.

English Unlimited Intermediate Teacher's Pack offers a **step-by-step guide to teaching** from the Coursebook, **three sets of photocopiable activity worksheets per unit** to extend and enrich your lessons and a **complete testing suite**. The Teacher's Pack consists of the **Teacher's Book** and the **Teacher's DVD-ROM**.

In the Teacher's Book

Teacher's notes

In the Teacher's Book, there are more than 100 pages of teacher's notes (pp23–124) to accompany the Coursebook material. These notes are a comprehensive and easy-to-follow guide to using the *English Unlimited Intermediate Coursebook*, and have been written with a broad range of class types and teaching styles in mind.

Each unit's notes take you smoothly through the different stages of the Coursebook lessons. Answers are clearly highlighted, and the Individual, Pair and Group work symbols show at a glance what interaction is suggested for each stage.

On most pages, there are instructions for alternative activities, clearly boxed, to offer greater variety and interest. There are also suggestions throughout for adapting activities to stronger and weaker classes, multi-lingual and monolingual classes, and to different class sizes and environments.

On the Teacher's DVD-ROM

A teacher-friendly resource

English Unlimited Intermediate Teacher's DVD-ROM offers a large suite of language and skills practice, assessment and video materials in an easy-to-use package. It also contains unit-by-unit PDF files of the Teacher's Book.

It is designed to offer flexibility to teachers who may want to use materials in digital and paper format. So you can:

- display activity worksheets and tests on a screen or whiteboard as well as distributing paper copies to learners. This is useful if you want to: demonstrate an activity; go through answers with the whole class; zoom in on an area of a worksheet; display Progress or Achievement tests as learners attempt them, or when you go through the answers;
- display answers to Progress tests, so that learners can mark their own papers;
- print out just the unit of the Teacher's Book that you are using, rather than carrying the book around;
- display answer keys to Coursebook exercises from the Teacher's Book;
- watch videos with your learners.

Photocopiable activities

There are 42 photocopiable activity worksheets on the Teacher's DVD-ROM (three for each unit), ready to print out and use straight away. These offer extra vocabulary, grammar and pronunciation practice, extra reading and writing work, role plays and games which further activate the language that learners have been introduced to in the Coursebook, and build their fluency, confidence and communication skills.

Each activity is accompanied by a page of clear, step-by-step instructions, with answer keys and extra teaching ideas. At the end of each unit of the Teacher's notes, there is a page to help you find the activities you need, and there are also boxes in the unit notes which suggest when particular activities might be used.

Progress and Achievement tests

The *English Unlimited* testing suite consists of 14 unit-by-unit Progress tests and three skills-based Achievement tests to motivate your learners and give you and them a clear idea of the progress that they are making. These and other methods of assessment are discussed in detail on pp20–21.

Videos

The video from each unit of the Self-study Pack is also included on the Teacher's DVD-ROM, as this is easily adaptable for use in class, either using the video exercises from the Workbook, or just for extra listening practice and class discussion. The 11 Interviews and three Documentaries are each linked topically to the unit, and so they offer extension and consolidation of the work done in the Coursebook, as well as giving learners the chance to listen to authentic, spontaneous speech from a range of native and non-native English speakers. The subtitles toggle on and off, so you can easily show any sections of text which learners find difficult to understand.

The book on the disk

English Unlimited Intermediate Teacher's DVD-ROM also contains the whole Teacher's Book in PDF format, so that you can print out the unit or section that you want, instead of carrying the book around with you.

There are also CEF tables, which show how *English Unlimited Intermediate* completes CEF levels B1 and B1+ by mapping the relevant 'can do' statements from the CEF to specific pages and tasks in the Coursebook.

Assessing your learners with *English Unlimited*

There are many ways of assessing learner progress through a language course. For this reason *English Unlimited* offers a range of testing and assessment options, including progress tests, skill-based achievement tests, assessment using the e-Portfolio, self-assessment and continuous assessment.

Tests on the Teacher's DVD-ROM

There are two types of test available as PDFs on the Teacher's DVD-ROM: Progress and Achievement tests.

Progress tests

There is one Progress test for each of the 14 units of the course. These assess the learners' acquisition of language items taught in the main Coursebook material. Each test carries 40 marks and includes questions assessing grammar and vocabulary items taught in the unit. These are not intended to be 'high stakes' tests but rather quick checks that will help the teacher and learner judge which language points have been successfully acquired and understood, and which areas individual learners or the whole class may need to study again.

We suggest that each test should take no more than 30 minutes in the classroom. Tests can be copied and distributed to each learner and taken in class time. The tests are designed for quick marking with the provided Answer Key. Teachers may choose to mark tests, or, alternatively, learners can mark each other's work. A mark can be given out of 40. If particular problem areas are identified, learners can be directed to do extra work from the Self-study Pack.

Achievement tests

There are three Achievement tests, designed to form the basis of formal learner assessment.

- **Achievement test 1** can be taken after Unit 4.
- **Achievement test 2** can be taken after Unit 9.
- **Achievement test 3** can be taken after Unit 14.

These tests are based on the four skills: Reading, Listening, Writing and Speaking.

Reading tests

Each test is based on a short text and we advise allowing no more than 15 minutes for each test. As with the Coursebook texts and Listening tests, there may be a few unfamiliar items in the text, but the tasks are graded so unknown items should not hinder the learners' ability to answer the five questions. The teacher may mark the tests or it may be acceptable for learners to mark each other's work.

Listening tests

The audio tracks for these are found at the end of the three Class Audio CDs. Achievement test 1 is track 54 on CD1; Achievement test 2 is track 48 on CD2; Achievement test 3 is track 40 on CD3.

We suggest carrying out tests under controlled conditions, with the recording played twice. Each test should take no longer than ten minutes. As with the Coursebook audio, there may be a few unfamiliar language items in the listening text, but tasks are graded to the level of the learner, so unknown items should not hinder the learners' ability to answer the five questions. The tests are simple and quick to mark. They can be marked by the teacher or it may be acceptable for learners to mark each other's work.

Writing tests

Learners are set a writing task based on themes from the Coursebook and the teacher assesses work using the Writing assessment scales provided. Tasks are designed to simulate purposeful, real-life, communicative pieces of writing. The teacher should endeavour to identify the band the work falls in for each category. This marking scheme can give learners a profile of the strong and weak points of their written work, helping them improve their writing skills over the length of the course.

If the tests are to be used under timed conditions in class, 40 minutes should be allowed for the learners to produce their texts – planning and redrafting may be encouraged by the teacher at the outset.

Another way is to set the tasks as assessed writing assignments to be done as homework. In these cases, the teacher should interpret the band scales according to the time available and the availability of dictionaries and other reference materials.

The option chosen will depend on your learning environment. A timed test may help you assess learners under equal conditions, but can be a rather artificial, pressured environment. Written homework assignments are less controlled, but could be a better way of encouraging learners to work at their writing and feel satisfied with a polished piece of written work. The Explore Writing tasks in the Coursebook and Self-study Pack may also be used as assessed assignments and marked using the assessment scales.

Speaking tests

These are designed to be carried out by an assessor, who may be the learners' regular teacher, or another teacher in the institution. Learners do the tests in pairs. The ideal environment is for the test to take place in a separate room from the rest of the class, who can be engaged in self-study work while the testing is taking place. It is best if seating is set up as a 'round table' if possible, rather than the assessor facing both learners across a desk, so as not to suggest an interrogation! Each test takes ten minutes.

The assessor should be familiar with the Speaking assessment scales for the Speaking tests before the test and have a copy of the Mark Sheet for each learner with their names already filled in. Screen the Mark Sheets from the learners.

The assessor will need the Teacher's Notes, which provide a script of prompts for the test. Each test is in two parts. In the first part (six minutes), the assessor puts the learners at ease with warm-up questions, before asking the learners in turn a selection of questions from the Notes, based on themes from the Coursebook. The assessor may depart from the script to elicit further responses, maintaining a friendly, encouraging manner. The assessor may begin to note down some marks based on the scales for each learner.

In Part 2 (four minutes), learners are provided with prompts for a communicative task, which they carry out between themselves. Learners may need some encouragement, or to have the instructions explained more than once.

During this section, the assessor should withdraw eye contact, making it clear that the learners should talk to each other, listen closely and revise the marks from Part 1, gradually completing the grid.

The assessor should not correct learners at any point during the test.

Filling in the Mark Sheets

Once all four papers of the Achievement tests have been carried out, the teacher can provide marks for each learner. This includes analytical marks for the Speaking and Writing tests, and an average mark out of five for each one; and marks out of five for the Reading and Listening tests. This gives the learners a snapshot of their performance in the four skills. The learners should be encouraged to reflect on what they found easy or difficult, and given strategies to improve performance in different skills. The marks can be used as the basis for course reports or formal assessment.

Self-assessment

Assessment is not just about tests. Self-assessment encourages more reflective and focused learning. *English Unlimited* offers a number of tools for learner self-assessment:

- Each unit of the Coursebook ends with a self-assessment grid in which learners are encouraged to measure their own progress against the unit goals, which in turn are based on the can-do statements of the Common European Framework of Reference for Language Learning.
- Progress with the activities on the Self-study DVD-ROM can be analysed in detail on the Progress screen.
- The Self-study DVD-ROM also contains Quick check tests, using a bank of 700 multiple-choice questions. Learners select which units they want to be tested on and how long they want the test to be – new tests will be randomly generated each time.

Using the e-Portfolio

Portfolio-based assessment is a useful tool for both self-assessment and formal assessment, particularly for teachers seeking an alternative to traditional timed writing tests. The e-Portfolio allows learners to:

- assess their progress against can-do statements and revise their assessments later in the course depending on progress made;

- build up a personal e-Portfolio of written work associated with the course. The learner may then select their best work, as an alternative to tests, or at the end of the course to be provided as a Portfolio. This may include word-processed documents, project work and even audio files. Some of the Explore writing tasks may lend themselves well to portfolio work, and in some classrooms, learners may be asked to record personal audio files based around speaking tasks in the Coursebook. The satisfaction of producing a polished *spoken* text is a rare one in a language course, but if the learner or the centre has access to a microphone, it is relatively easy to do.

Written texts and audio in a learner's e-Portfolio may be assessed using the same analytical scales as the Writing and Speaking Achievement tests. You can find more information about the e-Portfolio on p18.

Continuous assessment

Finally, some teachers and institutions may prefer to dispense with tests and adopt a form of continuous assessment. This can be demanding on the teacher's time but perhaps no more so than the marking load created by frequent formal tests. The important thing is to explain the system to learners early in the course, and regularly show them their Mark Sheets to indicate how they are getting on. How actual assessment is carried out may differ between institutions, but here are some guidelines and ideas:

- It is possible to assess learners using the Speaking assessment scales regularly through the course. The Target activities, where learners are involved in more extended discourse, offer an opportunity for this.
- Tell learners when their speaking is being assessed and the teacher can monitor particular groups.
- Learners should be assessed several times during the course or they may rightly feel they were let down by a single bad performance, even if the assessment is not 'high stakes'.
- An atmosphere of gentle encouragement and striving for improvement should always accompany this kind of assessment. Some learners can get competitive about this, which can have a negative effect on class atmosphere and demotivate less confident learners.
- The Explore writing tasks can be used for continuous written assessment, using the Writing assessment scales.

A final word

Testing and assessment can be a vital tool for teachers and learners in assessing strengths and weaknesses, building awareness and encouraging improvement. But it can be frustrating for a learner to feel that they are being assessed too often, at the expense of actually learning, and whilst there are certainly learners who like being tested, there are many others who certainly don't!

English Unlimited aims to help learners communicate in real-life situations, and the testing and assessment tools provided should be used with that purpose in mind. Testing and assessment should never take precedence over learning, but serve as useful checks on the way to increasing confidence, competence and fluency.

The Common European Framework of Reference for Languages (CEF)

A goals-based course

English Unlimited is a practical, goals-based course for adult learners of English. The course goals are taken and adapted from the language-learning goals stated in the Common European Framework of Reference for Languages (CEF).

The goals of the CEF are divided into a number of **scales** which describe abilities in different kinds of communication. We've chosen the scales which we felt to be the most useful for adult general English learners at Intermediate level. These are:

Speaking
Describing experience
Addressing audiences
Conversation
Informal discussion
Goal-oriented co-operation
Transactions to obtain goods and services
Information exchange
Interviewing and being interviewed
Compensating
Monitoring and repair
Turntaking
Co-operating
Asking for clarification

Writing
Creative writing
Reports and essays
Correspondence
Note-taking
Processing text

Listening
Overall listening comprehension
Understanding conversation
Listening to announcements and instructions
Listening to audio media and recordings

Reading
Overall reading comprehension
Reading correspondence
Reading for orientation
Reading for information and argument

Where the goals are met

As you'll see in the example unit on pp6–10, goals are given for the two lessons at the start of each unit, for the Target activity, and on the Explore speaking and Explore writing pages. They are also listed in the Self-assessment, which learners do at the end of the Look again page.

Listening and reading goals are not usually given on the page, as they are addressed repeatedly throughout the course. The CEF tables on the Teacher's Pack DVD-ROM show which parts of the course deal with the listening and reading goals.

Find out more about the CEF

You can read about the CEF in detail in *Common European Framework of Reference for Languages: Learning, teaching, assessment* (2001), Council of Europe Modern Languages Division, Strasbourg, Cambridge University Press, ISBN 9780521005319.

1 Media around the world

1.1

Goals: talk about entertainment media
talk about habits
express preferences

Core language:

VOCABULARY	Habits and preferences
GRAMMAR	Talking about the present
PRONUNCIATION	Common pairs of words 1

Entertainment and you

LISTENING

1 　Focus learners' attention on the TV logos to introduce the topic of TV. Learners read the questions. Check they understand the types of programme listed. Learners then discuss the questions in pairs. Feedback as a class.

> **Optional language presentation**
>
> Brainstorm more words and expressions around the subject of TV and radio. For example, you could extend the list of programme types, writing words on the board as learners call them out, e.g. *documentaries, soap operas, gardening programmes.* Draw attention to the appropriate collocations for different types of programme, e.g. *reality* **shows,** *gardening* **programmes,** etc. This extra language will all be useful to learners during the lesson.

2 a *Listening for main idea.* Learners look at the photos and logos and guess which of the TV channels the people watch (nationality and age are obvious clues). Then play recording **1.1.** Feed back as a class. Don't comment on their answers at this stage, as this will pre-empt the listening.

> 1 *Yasir watches Al Dawri & Al Kass Sport channel.*
> 2 *Aiko watches Fuji Television Network.*
> 3 *Carmen watches CincoShop.*
> 4 *Juan watches MTV Latinoamerica.*
> 5 *Aiko watches BBC World News.*

　b *Listening for detail.* Learners read through the questions and think about possible answers. Then they listen again to answer the questions.

> 1 *Yasir* 2 *Aiko* 3 *Juan* 4 *Juan* 5 *Aiko* 6 *Carmen*
> 7 *Yasir*

3 　/ 　*Speaking: Personalisation.* Find out if learners have the same opinions as their partner(s), and compare ideas as a class.

> **Alternative for multilingual classes**
>
> Pair or group learners with people from different parts of the world. In feedback, ask what learners found out about TV and radio in other parts of the world. This may lead to a class discussion about cultural differences.

> **Note: 'Quiet' learners**
>
> If you have a number of reticent or under-confident learners, it's helpful to let them discuss their opinions in pairs or small groups. Monitor while learners are talking in order to spot people who find it difficult to express themselves in front of others. Rather than putting them with chatty confident learners who will dominate the conversation, group them with similar learners to give them time to build confidence in expressing their ideas. Once they are more comfortable talking in groups, they will probably be happier to contribute to class discussions, but this may take some time.

VOCABULARY Habits and preferences

4 *Focus on expressions.* Learners look at the three sets of expressions. Ask if they can answer question 1 before looking for the expressions in the script. Learners then find the expressions in the conversations and answer the questions. Go through the answers as a class and check that learners understand:
- that *I'll* is used to talk about current habits, not the future
- what a noun, an *-ing* form and an infinitive are.

> 1 　1 *b* 　2 *c* 　3 *a*
> 2a *I hardly ever watch TV.*
> 　*I tend to record the shows I like and watch them later.*
> 　*I tend to listen to the radio a lot.*
> 　*If there's something good on, I'll watch it on the Al Kass Sport Channel.*
> 2b *I used to look forward to it all day on Mondays.*
> 3 　+ noun: *I'm a big fan of, I'm really into, I prefer … to …, I'm not a big fan of, I'm not keen on, I find … really …, I can't stand*
> 　+ -ing form: *as above*
> 　+ infinitive: *I tend to, hardly ever, I'll, I used to, I'd rather*

> **Language note:** *prefer, rather*
>
> Make sure learners understand how to use the expression *I'd rather* by asking how it could continue (*I'd rather watch documentaries … **than** reality shows*). Contrast this with *I prefer radio **to** TV.* Check this by putting a few contrasting items on the board and asking learners to state their preferences using the two forms, e.g. *football/baseball on TV; sport on TV/radio; films on TV/in the cinema,* etc.

> **Optional extra**
>
> For question 3, make three lists on the board for a–c. Elicit examples from 1–3 for each list, e.g.
>
> | + noun | + -ing form | + infinitive |
> |---|---|---|
> | *I'm a big fan of **all sports.*** | *I can't stand **watching** the ads.* | *I tend to **record** the shows I like.* |

WRITING AND SPEAKING

5 a *Writing: Personalisation.* To give learners some ideas, write a sentence about yourself on the board, e.g. *I can't stand watching reality TV shows.* Ask what learners like watching on TV and find out who likes listening to the radio. Learners write five sentences using the expressions from **4.** As they do this, go round and check, and give help if necessary.

b 👥 / 👥👥 *Speaking: Personalisation.* Learners focus on the two questions and talk together about their sentences. In feedback, find out if learners like the same programmes, and ask a few people to tell you something about their partner's habits and preferences.

Anything good on TV?

LISTENING

1 a *Pre-listening discussion.* Learners discuss the questions. Find out what some learners do if they don't want to watch the same programmes as other people they live with.

b *Listening for detail.* Focus learners on the three questions, then play recording **1.2**. Learners answer the questions and compare their ideas in pairs. Check if they need to hear the recording again. Before you check the answers, ask what they think Paul and Rebecca's relationship is.

> 1 Rebecca wants to read her book.
> 2 Paul wants to watch TV.
> 3 Paul wants to watch a film at eight o'clock. Rebecca is going out with her friend, Carole.

GRAMMAR Talking about the present

2 *Focus on meaning and form.* Make sure learners know that the sentences are from the conversation they have just listened to. Learners complete 1–3. Remind learners that:
– with present simple, we make questions and negatives with *do* (or *does*) + infinitive.
– present progressive is formed with *am / is / are* + *-ing*; we make questions by changing the word order; we make negatives by adding *not* (or *-n't*).
– present perfect is formed with *have / has* + past participle; we make questions by changing the word order; we make negatives by adding *not* (or *-n't*).

> *1 C   2 B   3 A*

3 a 👤 / 👥👥 *Practice.* Learners complete the questions using the verbs in brackets.

b Play recording **1.3** so learners can listen to check their answers.

> 1 Do; prefer   2 Are; reading   3 Have; read   4 Are;
> following   5 Do; like   6 Have; heard   7 Have; seen

Then learners write three more questions of their own using each of the present tenses. Go round and check while they are writing and help as necessary.

> **Note: Grammar practice**
> You could do the grammar practice on p134 at this point.

 You could use photocopiable activity 1A on the Teacher's DVD-ROM at this point.

PRONUNCIATION Common pairs of words 1

4 a *Focus on connected speech.* Draw learners' attention to the red words and play recording **1.4**, one sentence at a time. Learners repeat the red words after hearing each sentence. Then they practise saying the complete question.

b Learners practise on their own. Make sure they don't answer the questions yet.

> **Optional extra**
> Write the red words on the board and, after playing each sentence, write the phonemic script for each word pair:
> 1 /dju:/ 2 /əju:/ 3 /həvju:/ 4 /wədʒu:/ 5 /kənju:/
> Explain where learners can find the phonemic script in their coursebooks and in bilingual dictionaries. This is a good moment to find out if learners have vocabulary notebooks and to encourage them to write down new language from the lessons, including any words they find difficult to pronounce.

SPEAKING

5 a 👥 / 👥👥 *Speaking: Personalisation.* Learners ask and answer the questions from **3a**, including their own questions from **3b**. Go round while they are talking and make a note of good and problematic language for a feedback session after **5b** or at the beginning of the next lesson.

b *Round-up.* Ask a few learners to tell the class something interesting they found out about their partner(s).

> **1.2**
>
> **Goals:** talk about information media
> evaluate ideas
> make recommendations
>
> **Core language:**
> GRAMMAR   Talking about facts and information
> VOCABULARY   Evaluating and recommending

Fact or fiction?

READING

1 a Discuss the sources for getting information as a class. Extend the list if possible.

b Find out how learners feel about the different sources.

> **Alternative**
> *Books closed.* Build up a list of information sources on the board. Then find out which ones learners trust and why.

> **Alternative: 'Authentic texts' option**
> If you can get up-to-date examples of some of the information sources in the list, bring them into class. Pass them round and ask learners what sort of information you can find in them and which ones (or similar texts) they read. Ask them if they trust all/some/any of the information they read in the sources and to explain why they do or don't trust it.

2 *Reading for main idea.* Learners read the first sentence of the text and say what they know about Wikipedia. Learners match the summaries to the paragraphs.

> *a 2   b 3   c 4   d 1*

3 👥 *Reading for detail.* Learners read the questions and find the answers in the article. Check as a class, and encourage learners to explain their opinions in **4**.

> 1 Mike Scott's fan checked his page regularly and changed facts back if he noticed changes. He did this because he wrote the original page and was a big fan.
> 2 Terry Millstone thinks Wikipedia is quite dangerous because anyone can change or add facts, e.g. to a political rival's online biography.
> 3 Stephen Glass made up facts in 27 of the 41 articles he wrote for The New Republic *magazine*.
> 4 Learners' own answers
> 5 The writer is not sure what we should believe, but feels that the Internet may not be a good place to get reliable facts (para. 2, line 2; para. 3, line 1; whole of para. 4). However, he also mentions that printed materials may not be reliable sources either (para. 3).

GRAMMAR Talking about facts and information

4 👥 *Guessing meaning from context.* Do an example with the class. In feedback, check pronunciation.

> 1 reliable   2 inaccurate   3 accurate   4 scandals
> 5 a fake   6 made up   7 trust (verb)   8 trust (noun)

SPEAKING

5 a 👤 *Preparation.* Learners read the questions and ask you about any words they are unsure about. They then complete the questions and prepare their answers.

> 1 inaccurate   2 a fake   3 trust   4 scandals
> 5 reliable; accurate   6 made ... up

b 👥 *Speaking: Personalisation.* While learners discuss their answers together, walk round and monitor their use of the new language.

Round-up. Ask a learner from each group to tell the class something interesting they found out, and feed back on any good or problematic language use from their discussions.

It's a good way to ...

VOCABULARY Evaluating and recommending

1 *Focus on expressions.* Ask what you can use the adjectives for (e.g. to give opinions, advice, recommendations). Check understanding of *popular*. Learners complete the sentences with the adjectives from the article.

> Is it a <u>good</u> place to get reliable facts?
> Wikipedia has become a <u>popular</u> way to do research.
> There's never been a <u>worse</u> time to get accurate information.
> Is it a <u>better</u> idea to trust what we read in magazines, newspapers and books?

Optional extra

Brainstorm more adjectives that go with the expressions, e.g. *awful, great, sensible, fantastic.*

Language note: Frequency

Place, way, time and *idea* are extremely frequent words (all in the top 300 words in English), with *time* coming in at 90 and *way* at 118. Enabling learners to use these words will help them express their opinions about many different topics because the words themselves are extremely transferable.

2 Do this quickly with the whole class.

> 1 really   2 Before a/an: quite   After a/an: really

Alternative for stronger groups: Closed books

Write the sentence on the board, but gap *really* and *quite*. Ask learners which word goes where, and which is stronger.

3 a 👤/👥 Remind learners of the functions (recommending, evaluating) and ask for another example for the first one. Then learners write their sentences. Walk round and help as necessary.

b Get several examples from strong learners and write them on the board. Ask the class to decide whether to add *quite* or *really* to the sentences and to decide where it goes in the sentences. 👤 Learners then choose some sentences of their own and do the same.

c 👥/👥👥 Learners discuss their ideas.

 You could use photocopiable activity 1B on the Teacher's DVD-ROM at this point.

SPEAKING

4 a 👤 *Preparation.* Learners choose one of the things from the list, e.g. websites. Ask for a recommendation, then find out if other people agree. Learners choose four or five things to recommend for their chosen topic and to prepare their ideas. Walk round and offer help as necessary.

b 👥 *Speaking: Personalisation.* Learners make their recommendations and respond to each other's ideas.
Round-up. Find out if anyone disagreed with the recommendations different people made and why.

1.3 Target activity

Goals: express preferences ♻
evaluate ideas ♻
describe a book or TV show

Core language:

TASK VOCABULARY	Describing books and TV shows
1.1 VOCABULARY	Habits and preferences
1.1 GRAMMAR	Talking about the present
1.2 VOCABULARY	Evaluating and recommending

Describe a book or a TV show

TASK LISTENING

Explaining objectives

Explain to learners that the Target activities in the Coursebook give them an opportunity to recycle all the language that they've learned so far in the unit but to use it in a new, practical way (you can point out the goals to show them what they are going to do). Explain that they will do a longer speaking task at the end of the lesson, but first they will listen to somebody doing a similar task and focus on some new useful language to help them when they do the task later.

1 a *Pre-listening discussion.* Focus learners on the pictures of books and TV shows. In pairs, learners guess what they're about. Ask a few learners for their ideas, but don't say whether they're right or not, as they will listen to check their own ideas in **b**.

b *Listening for main idea.* Learners read the two questions, then play recording **1.5**.

> 2 Carmen didn't like A Hundred Years of Solitude *because she found it boring. She didn't finish the book.* Aiko enjoyed The West Wing *because it's very entertaining, but found it a bit difficult to understand.* Rebecca really enjoyed Born on a Blue Day *because it's an interesting book about an interesting person.* Yasir liked Chef Ramzi *because the meals he's tried making have been good.*

2 ▦ / ▦ *Speaking: Personalisation.* Learners discuss their own opinions of the books and shows. Encourage them to give reasons for their opinions.

TASK VOCABULARY Describing books and TV shows

3 a ▦ *Focus on expressions.* Look at the example with the class, then tell learners to complete the sentences in pairs. Play recording **1.6** for them to check their answers.

> 1 *It's by someone called Gabriel García Márquez.*
> 2 *It's quite a well-known book.*
> 3 *It's about this family who have all these problems.*
> 4 *People say it's amazing.*
> 5 *I found it boring.*
> 6 *It's based on Márquez's own life.*
> 7 *It has Martin Sheen in it.*
> 8 *It looks at his life.*
> 9 *It's a really interesting book.*
> 10 *Basically, it shows you how to cook great meals.*

b Do this as a class. Contextualise the expressions by asking which book or programme each one was about, and if it can be used to talk about the other one or not. While you are doing this, check learners know how to say *well-known* and *basically,* and let them practise saying the expressions.

> 1 a TV show: 7, 10
> 2 a book: 1
> 3 both: 2, 3, 4, 5, 6, 8, 9

Alternative for weaker groups

▦ If learners need more support with the new language, tell them to choose a well-known book or TV show and to write three or four sentences about it with the language in **3a** but *not* to write the name of the show or book. Then they change partners, listen to each other's sentences and guess what book or TV show their partner is talking about.

TASK

4 *Preparation.* Tell learners to choose a book or TV show they know well and have strong opinions about (they don't have to be positive opinions). This activity will work better if they don't choose something everyone knows about already, so there is a genuine information gap in **5**. Learners shouldn't write sentences, but encourage them to make notes about content and think about what language from the unit they need in order to express their ideas.

5 ▦ *Speaking.* Learners say as much as they can about their book or programme and ask each other more questions. When everyone in the group has finished speaking, learners should choose the one they would most like to read or watch.

6 *Round-up.* Find out the favourites from each group. Give learners time to write down ideas they're interested in.

Optional extra

Ask one person from each group to write down everyone's recommended books and TV shows as they're read out. Let them check names and spelling with their groups at the end. Then ask for a volunteer from each group (the same or a different person) to produce a tidy version of the list at home to make a class poster of recommended things to see and read.

1 Explore

Across cultures: Intercultural experiences

Goals: raise awareness of cultural differences
talk about experiences of adapting to different cultures

Core language:
VOCABULARY   Changes

LISTENING

1 ▯ / ▦ Learners read the questions and take a few minutes to think about and note down experiences they've had and differences that they have noticed in different places. Help learners with ideas if necessary. Depending on where learners have been, you could ask about differences in concrete things like greetings, clothing, hospitality, traffic and transport, and food. For help with question 1, you could ask, e.g. *Was there anything you didn't understand? Did anything go wrong? How did you / other people deal with it?* Then learners talk together.

Round-up. Ask a few learners for the most interesting experiences from their groups, and find out how many learners have had similar experiences.

2 *Listening for main idea.* Ask learners where Federico is from and where they think he is in the picture. Ask why they think he was in Egypt for a year. Focus on the questions, then play recording **1.7**. Learners discuss the answers in pairs, then feed back as a class.

> *During the day, Federico appreciated the hospitality, but he didn't feel comfortable. At the end of the day, he felt awful when he realised he'd upset Manu.*

3 *Listening for detail.* Play recording **1.7** again, then learners discuss the questions in pairs. Play all or part of the recording again if necessary. Then check as a class.

Alternative for stronger groups

Tell learners to read the questions in pairs and try to answer them as far as they can before you play the recording again. They listen to check their answers.

Intercultural note

In the listening task, Federico feels uncomfortable spending the whole day with his Egyptian colleagues; he needs to spend some time alone in order to relax. Manu, on the other hand, is upset that Federico wished to spend time alone; he feels that his hospitality has been rejected. We see that there has been a cultural misunderstanding. Ask your learners to think about which person, Federico or Manu, they empathise with to a greater degree, and about how they would feel and what they would do if they were in the same situation. Ask them whether they think that it is culture or personality (or something else) which influences how people behave in these kinds of social situations.

Some commentators on culture, such as Gert Hofstede et al. (2002), believe that cultures around the world can be described as broadly 'individualist' or 'collectivist'. In collectivist societies, people tend to spend more of their time in large groups of family, friends, neighbours or colleagues, as Manu, in the task, is accustomed to doing. Federico, living in Buenos Aires, is used to a life in which independence and freedom to do as you please are more important than responsibilities towards groups such as family or neighbours. It is interesting to note, however, that Federico's individualist character may be more connected with being from the city than with being from Argentina. You could present these ideas to your learners, asking them if they think these labels, 'individualist' and 'collectivist', are useful ones for describing cultural difference and whether they serve to explain the misunderstanding between Manu and Federico. A more detailed description of this and other cultural dimensions can be found in *Exploring Culture*, by Gert J. Hofstede, Paul B. Pedersen, Geert Hofstede (Intercultural Press, 2002).

4   *Listening for main idea.* Ask learners to predict how Federico might feel six months later and what cultural difference he might talk about. Then play recording **1.8**. Give learners a minute to talk through their ideas with a partner, then feed back as a class.

Get learners' reactions to Federico's feelings about his experience and also their opinions about his hosts' actions and responses. Find out how they think he changed. This will lead into the vocabulary.

He says that Egyptians are very hospitable and welcoming and spend a lot of time in big groups. But Federico comes from a big city in Argentina and wasn't used to spending so much time with other people, in groups, so he didn't feel comfortable at first, although he got used to this after some time.

VOCABULARY Changes

5   *Focus on expressions.* Learners read and categorise the sentences from the listening.

1 C   2 A   3 B

6 a *Writing: Personalisation.* If possible, write a sentence on the board about a change relating to you or someone you know using an expression in **5**. Then learners write sentences. Go round and help as necessary.

   b *Speaking.* Learners discuss their ideas. In feedback, find out who has had similar experiences.

SPEAKING

7 a *Preparation.* Make sure learners understand what is meant by *personal space, hospitality, work–life balance, sense of humour,* and the difference between *employer* and *employee*. Give them a few moments to think about the three questions on their own. Encourage them to think of examples from their experience and to take notes if they want to.

   b *Discussion: Personalisation.* Learners discuss their ideas. Monitor use of the new language and other useful vocabulary for discussing cultural experiences.

   Round-up. Ask a few learners for their ideas on the three points. See if other learners agree, and why or why not. Put examples of useful and incorrect language on the board from learners' discussions and go through it with the class.

Alternative for multilingual classes

Group learners carefully for the final discussion activity. Try to put learners together who come from different parts of the world (see *Intercultural note* on this page for ideas) in order to raise awareness of their cultural similarities and differences. Walk round and monitor their discussions, keeping an eye on how they handle their differences. Finding out about learners' attitudes at this stage will help inform how you approach subsequent Across cultures sections.

Explore writing

Goal: write a book review for a website

Core language:

Adverb and adjective collocations
which clauses (non-defining)

1   *Pre-reading discussion.* Discuss the question as a class. Find out how many learners read travel books and reviews, what for and where (e.g. online or in newspapers and magazines).

2   Focus learners on the picture of the travel book. In pairs or as a class, learners predict information about the book.

3 a *Reading for main idea.* Learners read to find out whether it confirms their predictions in **2**.

   b *Reading for detail.* Check learners understand how to interpret a five-star rating system by asking, e.g. *What do five stars mean? What about one star?* Then tell them to check p118 for the number of stars in each review. Ask why the first reviewer liked the book (*it's written by travellers for travellers and is very inspiring*), and what the second reviewer was unhappy about (*it included inaccurate information*). Draw attention to the photo of Tashkent and find out if anyone has been there or knows anything about it.

> *L A Seadan: 5 stars*
> *Aliya Bakaev: 3 stars*

Option for stronger groups

The reviews are rich in descriptive language and expressions for describing the book and personal responses to it. Focus on some of the language which learners could find helpful when writing their own reviews, e.g.
adjectives: *colourful, easy to read, disappointed*
verb phrases: *captures the mood, fascinates, browsed through it, get some inspiration from.*

Option for weaker groups

There are a lot of useful sentence frames in the reviews that learners can use to create their own reviews with minimal changes, e.g. *This is a/an … book; If you are interested in …, then this book is definitely (not) for you; It …, which means that …; It is written by …; It's really …; After reading it, …; It contains …; This book isn't …, but it is … .* You could go through the reviews with the class either on an OHT or projected onto the board, highlighting the transferable expressions. Learners can come back to this when they write their reviews.

4 Learners read the reviews for the adjectives which go with the adverbs. Make sure learners understand *stunning*. Model the collocations so learners can practise saying them with the correct word stress and intonation.

> *absolutely amazing / stunning*
> *especially clever / helpful*
> *completely different / wrong*
> *really easy to read / nice*

Language note

Point out that *amazing* and *stunning* are 'extreme' adjectives, i.e. they already mean *very …,* so we can't use *very* with them, but that *very* could go with all the other adjectives except for *wrong* and that *really* can go with all of them, except for *wrong*.

5 Do question 1 with the class. Ask learners to read the second review again and call out the *which* clauses as they find them. Write them on the board and check understanding of *refreshing*. Learners categorise the clauses as a or b.

> *1 a Expression 2 adds extra information.*
> *b Expressions 1 and 3 say what the writer feels or thinks.*
> *2 a which means that you see a completely different part of the world every time you turn a page*
> *b which is very unusual in my experience*
> *3 You put the comma (,) before <u>which</u>.*

Language note

The highlighted expressions are non-defining relative clauses, which are very frequent in reviews of this type, both for adding extra (non-essential) information and for adding comments about the writer's personal response, e.g. *which is refreshing.* Comment clauses are actually the most frequent of all spoken relative clauses. There is a further focus on comment clauses in Explore Speaking on p20.

6 a *Writing sentences: Practice.* Learners choose one or two books to write sentences about. Encourage them to use two adverb–adjective collocations from 4 and two *which* clauses, to practise the target language.

b 👥 *Speaking.* Learners read their partner's sentences or read out their sentences to each other and talk about the recommended books. In feedback, find out how many learners would like to read each other's books.

7 a *Writing.* Learners choose a book to review (it can be the same as the one above or a different one). Tell them to take about five minutes to plan their reviews and make notes about both positive and negative things to say. Remind them to use the language from 4 and 5, as well as using any additional language from the reviews that they focused on with you. Then learners write their reviews. Tell them other learners are going to read their reviews to encourage them to write legibly and accurately.

b *Reading and reacting.* Learners read each other's reviews in groups, or you could put reviews up around the walls and learners walk round and read them.

Round-up. Ask a number of learners which book they would most like to read. If possible, take a class vote on the most popular book reviewed.

Alternative: Book prize

Find out if learners are aware of any book prizes or awards in their countries and what they know about them. Then tell them they are going to judge each other's books from the reviews and decide on how many stars they deserve. Give a time limit of five minutes or so, then call out each book in turn and find out how many learners have given it five stars. The winning book is the one that most learners give five stars to.

You can devise your own 'prize' for the winning reviewer.

 You could use photocopiable activity 1C on the Teacher's DVD-ROM at this point.

1 Look again

Review

GRAMMAR Talking about the present

1 a Focus learners on the board game and ask them how they think it is played. Elicit an example question from the class, then learners continue to complete the questions in pairs. As they do this, go round and help as necessary.

> *2 Have you seen any good films recently?*
> *3 Are you studying anything at the moment?*
> *4 What do you usually do on Friday nights?*
> *6 Have you changed anything in your life this year?*
> *8 What are you doing at work or college at the moment?*
> *10 Are you learning anything new at the moment?*

b Learners read the instructions. Make sure every group has a coin, then learners agree which side is one space and which is two. Encourage learners to ask follow-up questions when they land on a square. Check they've understood the instructions. Walk round while learners are playing the game and help with any problems. Stop the game when at least one learner from each group has reached the FINISH.

Round-up. Ask someone from each group to tell you something new they found out about another person. Deal with any common language problems that learners had while they were playing the game.

VOCABULARY Habits and preferences

2 a *Preparation: Find someone who.* Elicit a question for item 1, i.e. *What games did you use to play as a child?* Check understanding by asking a different learner to form a question for item 2. Go round while learners are writing their questions and help if necessary.

Option for weaker groups

Go through the questions one by one, eliciting them from different learners and writing them on the board. Tell learners to choose one of the questions to ask everyone (or until you stop the activity). Learners can report back on their question in groups or to the class (i.e. how many learners played the same games as them, and what other kinds of game people played).

---

b *Speaking: Asking and answering.* Point out that the objective is different in different questions, and ask which questions are finding out if people share the same habits (1, 2, 6) and which are finding out if people have different habits (3, 4, 5). Encourage learners to find out more information by asking follow-up questions. Put a time limit on the activity, or stop after learners have talked to four or five people. Feed back any problems in the use of the target language at the end.

Extension

SPELLING AND SOUNDS /f/

3 a Explain that this section focuses on the connections between how words sound and how they are spelled. Ask how /f/ can be spelt in English, giving a few examples from the list. Then play recording **1.9** or say the words yourself while learners underline the letters that make a /f/ sound. Give learners a chance to practise saying the words.

---

*official different afford off stuff
film often after
yourself surf
telephone pharmacy photograph
laugh cough enough*

Optional extra

Find out how individuals feel about their English spelling; this will help show you who might need extra support with these sections and how to group learners for the activities. Point out the interactive phonemic chart with audio on the Self-study DVD-ROM, which learners can use to practise pronunciation of particular sounds that they find difficult.

---

b The words are grouped in order to help guide learners to notice the spelling patterns which are highlighted. Point this out if necessary. In feedback, build up more examples on the board and encourage learners to add to their lists.

---

*1 film, often, after, yourself, surf
2 official, different, afford, off, stuff
3 laugh, cough, enough
4 telephone, pharmacy, photograph*

---

c Encourage learners to choose a range of spelling patterns and to choose words which they find more challenging to test their partner. When they have both written down their partner's words, let them check their spelling together.

Optional extra: Learner training

If you haven't already done this, ask learners where and how they record new language. Encourage them to keep a vocabulary notebook and to add to it in each lesson. Point out that a spelling section for words they have particular problems with will help them learn those words. You can encourage this by suggesting a five-minute warmer at the beginning of lessons or at the end of each unit in which learners use their notebooks to test each other or construct quizzes around the language they've covered in previous lessons. You can keep a vocabulary box in the class to supplement this, or as a substitute for notebooks if not all learners have them in class.

NOTICE *and*

4 a 👥 Learners read the sentences and categorise the expressions with *and*. Find out if any of the expressions are familiar to learners and if there are similar expressions in their language(s).

---

*Expressions in sentences 1, 3 and 4 add emphasis.
Expressions in sentences 2 and 5 are verb + and + verb.*

---

b *Writing sentences.* Learners complete the sentences, then discuss their ideas with a partner. Ask a few learners to tell the class their and their partner's ideas for one sentence.

Self-assessment

To help focus learners on the self-assessment, go through each goal and ask for a few examples of the language they have learned, prompting as necessary. Then ask learners to circle the numbers on each line. Walk round and see how learners feel about their progress. Try to encourage anyone who is feeling under-confident at this stage and point out the opportunities for extra practice given under the self-assessment box. This is a good moment to go through all these options with the class, explaining where they can find things and how to use them.

Unit 1 Extra activities on the Teacher's DVD-ROM

Printable worksheets, activity instructions and answer keys are on your Teacher's DVD-ROM.

1A Media board game

Activity type: Speaking and listening – Board game – Groups

Aim: To practise talking about the media

Language: Talking about the present / Habits and preferences – Use at any point from 1.1.

Preparation: Make one copy of the worksheet for every group of three to four learners (enlarge to A3 size if possible). You will need counters and dice.

Time: 30–40 minutes

1B Evaluating and recommending

Activity type: Speaking and writing – Whole-class mingle – Individuals/Pairs

Aim: To give recommendations and evaluate ideas/advice

Language: Evaluating and recommending – Use at any point from 1.2.

Preparation: Make one copy of the worksheet for each learner.

Time: 20–30 minutes

1C Which film?

Activity type: Reading, speaking and writing – Reading comprehension, Vocabulary deduction, Writing a film review – Pairs/Individuals

Aim: To practise using language for talking and writing about films

Language: Adverb + adjective, Relative clauses, Film vocabulary – Use at any point from Explore writing.

Preparation: Make one copy of each worksheet for every pair of learners. Cut each worksheet to make four film reviews from Worksheet 1 and two activities from Worksheet 2 …

Time: 40–45 minutes

Unit 1 Self-study Pack

In the Workbook

Unit 1 of the *English Unlimited Intermediate Workbook* offers additional ways to practise the vocabulary and grammar taught in the Coursebook. There are also activities which build reading and writing skills and a whole page of listening and speaking tasks to use with the Interview video, giving your learners the opportunity to hear and react to authentic spoken English.

- **Vocabulary:** Habits and preferences; Talking about facts and information; Evaluating and recommending; Describing books and TV shows
- **Grammar:** Talking about the present
- **My English:** Learning English through the media
- **Explore reading:** Description of a TV series
- **Interview:** Different ways of life – Inmaculada and Alex

On the DVD-ROM

Unit 1 of the *English Unlimited Intermediate Self-study DVD-ROM* contains interactive games and activities for your learners to practise and improve their vocabulary, grammar and pronunciation, and also their speaking and listening, with the possibility for learners to record themselves, and a video of authentic spoken English to use with the Workbook.

- **Vocabulary and grammar:** Extra practice activities
- **Pronunciation:** Common pairs of words
- **Explore speaking:** What's it about?
- **Explore listening:** A film podcast
- **Video:** Different ways of life

2 Good communication

2.1

Goals: talk about methods of communication
express opinions

Core language:

VOCABULARY	Expressing opinions
	It's + adjectives
PRONUNCIATION	Sentence stress

Keeping in touch

LISTENING

1 *Pre-listening discussion.* Learners look at the pictures of different forms of communication and ask what the people are doing (surfing the Internet, sending an email, checking messages – possibly on a BlackBerry). Then learners discuss the question. Learners feed back as a class and say which methods of communication they prefer and why.

2 *Listening for main idea.* Learners look at the photos of the four people from the two conversations. They read the questions. Play recording **1.10**. Let them discuss their ideas in pairs before checking as a class. Check understanding of the following words and expressions:

Conversation 1: *a waste of time, totally addicted / incredibly addictive, voyeuristic, virtual friendship*

Conversation 2: *straight away, pillow, miss something, the buzz (of work)*

> **Paula and Megan:** *Their conversation is about social networking sites. They think it's a waste of time (but both use it a lot).*
> **Graham and Deniz:** *Their conversation is about using mobile phones with Internet/email for work. Deniz thinks it saves her a lot of time. Graham doesn't agree.*

3 *Listening for detail.* Learners read the sentences 1–10 and answer any they can. Then play recording **1.10** again so they can check their answers. Let them discuss their answers in pairs, before checking as a class.

> **Paula and Megan:** *1 F 2 T 3 T 4 T 5 F*
> **Graham and Deniz:** *6 T 7 F 8 F 9 T 10 F*

Optional extra: Vocabulary

There are a number of useful verb + noun collocations for talking about social networking sites and technology in general.

Conversation 1: *check profiles, post pictures, be / get back in touch with somebody*.

Conversation 2: *keep up with something, take breaks, screen calls/emails*.

Write these expressions on the board and ask learners to read the recording script and try to work out their meaning with a partner. Check as a class.

---

4 / *Speaking: Discussion.* Learners discuss the questions in pairs or groups.

Round-up. Find out how learners feel about social networking sites and about being in constant mobile contact with colleagues, friends and family.

> 1 *Learners' own answers*
> 2 *Graham and Deniz have different lifestyles. Deniz spends most of her time working, whereas Graham thinks it's important to have time off and enjoy life (e.g. they say you need to take breaks from work; It's not good for you. Couldn't they wait till the morning? I reckon you must get tired. I don't have that problem.).*
> 3 *Learners' own answers*

VOCABULARY Expressing opinions

5 a *Focus on meaning.* Learners read through the sentences and try to remember who said what.

> 1 *Graham* 2 *Graham* 3 *Graham* 4 *Deniz* 5 *Paula*
> 6 *Deniz*

b *Focus on expressions.* Focus learners on the highlighted parts of the sentences, then tell them to categorise the expressions.

> 1 *a: 1, 2, 5, 6   b: 3, 4*   2 *a: 3   b: 6   c: 5*

> You could use photocopiable activity 2A on the Teacher's DVD-ROM at this point.

PRONUNCIATION Sentence stress

6 a Learners read the sentence. Point out the stress marks, then play recording **1.11** or say the sentence yourself. Learners repeat it.

b Ask learners why the stressed words in the sentence they've just listened to carry stress (because they're the most important words. We stress the words which carry meaning, such as nouns and verbs, rather than the 'grammar' words such as prepositions and articles). Break down the sentence into parts of speech to check learners understand the instructions and can discuss which words are stressed with a partner, i.e. *I* (subject: noun) *'d say* (main verb) *it must* (modal verb) *be impossible* (adjective). Learners say the sentences out loud to each other and decide which words are stressed together.

c Learners read the sentences in the script on p147. Play recording **1.12** or say the sentences yourself. Learners can repeat the sentences either one at a time or when they've heard all the sentences.

Alternative: Books closed

Dictate sentences 1–6 to the class or use recordings **1.11** and **1.12**. When learners have written the sentences, let them check with a partner. Ask a learner to call out the first sentence for you to write on the board. Then ask them which words in sentence 1 are stressed. Learners discuss in pairs, then say (or play) the recording of sentence 1 again. Then proceed as in **6b**. For **6c**, repeat the sentences for learners to check their ideas. Then let them check their answers in the script on p147.

SPEAKING

7 a *Writing sentences.* Draw learners' attention to the four topics. Elicit one or two opinions from the class about the topics or give an opinion of your own to start learners thinking. Walk round while they are writing and help as necessary.

> **Optional extra**
>
> Ask if there are other similar topics around technology that learners feel strongly about. Write them on the board and tell learners to choose three topics (from the board or book) that they feel most strongly about. Then they write their sentences.

b 👥 / 👥👥 *Discussion: Personalisation.* Learners find out whether they share the same opinions. Monitor use of the new language while they are talking and make a note of problems for feedback at the end.

Round-up. Ask a few learners to summarise their group's opinions on a topic. Feed back on learners' use of language during the activity.

It's good to talk

VOCABULARY *It's* + adjectives

1 👤 Learners complete the sentences from Deniz and Graham's conversation. They can check their own answers in the script on p147.

> **1** *tiring* **2** *difficult* **3** *amazing*

> **Language note: *It's***
>
> We often use this structure to talk about how we feel about something. The true subject of the sentence comes later (*being on call, to relax, how much I miss*), but starting the sentence with *to* or *how much* sounds awkward (*To relax is difficult*), so we turn it round and start with *It's*. It's not unusual to start a sentence with an *-ing* word (e.g. *Being on call all the time is tiring.*); both structures are possible. However, there is very little difference between *to* and *-ing* within the *It's ...* structure, although the *-ing* form is generally more informal. Both forms are possible with the examples here: *It's tiring to be on call; It's difficult relaxing.*

2 a 👤 *Practice.* Draw attention to the example, then learners continue working individually. This gives you a chance to check if anyone is having problems. Check as a class.

> **2** *It's easy to stop seeing your old friends.*
> **3** *It's important to keep in contact with your family.*
> **4** *It's stressful when you don't have much free time.*
> **5** *It's boring spending a lot of time alone.*

b 👥 / 👥👥 Learners discuss their sentences. In feedback, find out whether they agree with the sentences and each other, and encourage them to give reasons for their opinions.

> **Optional extra**
>
> In **2b**, listen to how learners handle the language of agreeing and disagreeing and put useful expressions on the board after their discussions, e.g. *I (don't) agree with you. I disagree. I think so / I don't think so.* Remind learners to add these to their vocabulary notebooks or to the class vocabulary box, along with other language from the lesson.

SPEAKING

3 a 👤 *Preparation.* Ask what the woman in the picture is doing. Then check learners understand and know how to say *chatting, surfing, tidying up, dressing up, complicated, queues* and *window shopping*. Ask one learner which one thing from the list is the biggest waste of time for them and why. This will recycle *waste of time* (which learners should remember from the first listening). Suggest they choose one thing from each list to tick.

b Learners add an idea of their own to each list.

4 👥 *Speaking: Discussion.* Make sure learners understand they should agree on three things only from their lists. Put a time limit on their discussions (three or four minutes should give them plenty of time). Walk round and note down good and incorrect examples of language use to feed back after the activity.

Round-up. Check that all the groups agreed on three things and find out if different groups chose the same or different ideas. Do a feedback session on the language that learners used during their discussions.

> **2.2**
>
> **Goals:** talk about using the Internet
> speculate about the present and future
>
> **Core language:**
>
> | | |
> |---|---|
> | VOCABULARY | Using the Internet |
> | | Expressing probability |
> | GRAMMAR | *will, could, may, might* |

Online friendships

VOCABULARY Using the Internet

1 👥👥 *Focus on expressions.* Learners discuss the questions. Give them a chance to help each other with the highlighted expressions or work out what they mean from the context or with dictionaries. Walk round and help if necessary.

Check understanding of the highlighted expressions and check pronunciation of *socialising* /ˈsəʊʃəlaɪzɪŋ/.

> **Alternative: Weaker groups**
>
> Go through the questions one at a time with the class, checking understanding of the new words and expressions as you go along. Talk about each sentence with the class, getting opinions from different learners and encouraging a range of learners to contribute to the discussion.

> **Optional extra: Books closed**
>
> After **1**, test the verb–noun collocations in the expressions. Learners close their books. Write the verbs (in infinitive form) on one side of the board and the nouns on the other side in random order. Learners match them in pairs (but don't write anything down yet). Elicit the collocations randomly from different learners around the class until you're sure that everybody is confident in using them. This will help with fluency. Remind learners to use their vocabulary notebooks to record the collocations either immediately or after the lesson: **spend / online; go to / specific sites; have / a blog or web page; post / a comment; be / on a social networking site; socialise / online**

READING

2 a 👥 *Pre-reading discussion.* Ask what people use social networking sites for (if this hasn't been covered in the previous discussion). Then focus learners on the title of the article and the second question, which will help them to understand the title. Ask them to come up with a few ideas in pairs.

b *Reading for main idea.* Learners read the article individually, then check with their partner whether it mentions their ideas from **2a**.

3 👥 *Reading for detail.* Ask who Dr Tyagi is and explain that 1–5 are views expressed by him in the article. Learners read the article again carefully to find the reasons he gives for his opinions. Do the first one together by asking *Where does he say that young people 'have an unrealistic view of the world'?* Then ask what reasons he gives (see below). Learners continue in pairs.

> 1 Because they've only known a world where they can use the Internet.
> 2 Social networking sites have encouraged that idea. It's a world where everything moves fast and changes all the time.
> 3 Because everything happens so quickly on social networking sites.
> 4 Because they won't learn about body language, facial expressions or hear people's voices (which are clues to understanding a conversation).
> 5 Because online, people often don't know about the wealth, race or gender of the person they're communicating with.

> **Alternative for weaker groups**
>
> Go through the questions one at a time, asking learners to find the view expressed in each question in the article and underline it. Then give them time to read the surrounding sentences carefully to isolate the reason given. Tell learners to check the reason with a partner first, before checking as a class. Then move on to the next question.

SPEAKING

4 👥 *Discussion.* Walk round while learners are talking and monitor their use of the new language.

Round-up. Find out if anyone strongly disagreed with the opinions in the article and why. Ask a few learners for their ideas on **2** and **3**. Check what benefits the article mentions of using the Internet and brainstorm other benefits from the class. Feedback on language used in the discussion if you have time, or save it for a later lesson.

Speculating

GRAMMAR *will, could, may, might*

1 a 👤/👥 *Focus on meaning.* Learners read the sentences and categorise them. Learners can do this in pairs, or categorise them individually, then check with a partner.

> a this will certainly happen: 1 and 2
> b maybe this will happen: 3–7

b Play recording **1.13** or say the sentences yourself, so learners can check their own answers. Give them an opportunity to repeat the sentences, but focus on the target structures, not the other parts of the sentences.

> **Note: Grammar practice**
>
> You could do the grammar practice on p135 at this point.

VOCABULARY Expressing probability

2 *Focus on expressions.* Learners read the sentences, answer questions 1–4 individually, then check in pairs. Point out to learners that they should focus on the highlighted expressions to answer the questions, though the context will help them work out the meaning.

> **1** B **2** A, C, D **3** E **4** F, G

> **Language note: *likely***
>
> *may well*, *definitely* and *probably* are adverbial expressions, whereas *likely* is an adjective and is followed by *to*. You could draw attention to these differences in use by putting these words on the board: *likely, unlikely, definitely, probably.*
>
> Then ask some focusing questions, e.g. *Which words come before them? Which words come after them?* This will guide learners to notice that there are two different patterns here, and should help them to use the expressions accurately.

3 👤/👥 *Preparation.* Ask learners what they think the picture is suggesting. Then look at the example and sentence 2 together, and find out a few learners' views on how likely these are in the future. Write a few learners' views on sentence 2 on the board and find out who disagrees with it and why. Then learners continue to prepare their sentences individually or in pairs.

> **Alternative for stronger groups**
>
> Suggest learners make notes in preparation rather than write sentences, i.e. they can write *definitely* or *unlikely*, etc. for each one. Give them enough time to work out how to say their sentences (individually or in pairs) before they discuss their ideas in **4**.

> **Alternative for weaker groups**
>
> Learners write sentences with the words in 1–10. Do a couple together and write them on the board. Then let them continue in pairs. Change pairs for the discussion in **4**. If you have time and learners need more practice, let them go back to their first partner and explain what their other partner thought about the ideas.

SPEAKING

4 👥/👥 *Discussion.* Point out that learners should say *when* (and *if*) the things will happen. Monitor the groups to see how they are handling the new language. Note down useful and incorrect examples of language for a feedback session.

2.3 Target activity

Goals: talk about methods of communication ♻
      express opinions ♻
      speculate about the present and future ♻
      speculate about consequences

Core language:

TASK VOCABULARY	Speculating about consequences
2.1 VOCABULARY	Expressing opinions
2.2 GRAMMAR	*will, could, may, might*
2.2 VOCABULARY	Expressing probability

Discuss an issue

TASK READING

1 *Pre-reading discussion.* Check learners know what an *intranet system* is, then learners discuss the questions in pairs. In feedback, find out who sends and receives the most emails in the class, and who checks their emails the most and least often at home and at work.

> **Optional extra**
>
> Put some of the figures from the extract on the board, e.g. *5,000,000,000,000, 15,000,000,000, ¼, 30*. Tell learners to read to find out what they refer to. Get some reactions to the figures from learners; this will help them with the discussion in **2**.

2 *Reading for main idea.* Focus learners on the book cover and check understanding of *survival*. Ask what kind of book they think it is and what the extract might be about. Then learners read the extract and answer the questions in pairs.

TASK LISTENING

3 a *Listening for main idea.* Focus learners on the picture of the two men and find out what they remember about Graham from his conversation with Deniz. Check understanding of *firm* (= company) and ask what kind of work the two men do (business advice). Learners read the two questions. Then play recording **1.14** and ask learners to discuss their ideas in pairs. Check if learners need to hear the recording again to answer the second question. Don't go through the answers yet, but check understanding of *ban* and the difference between *intranet* (an internet site that is internal-access only) and *Internet*.

> 1 Their firm has decided to ban the intranet (internal email) for one day a week.
> 2 It will waste a lot of time; everything will take longer; it might help them to get things done quicker (instead of emailing for days); people will talk to each other; it will cause problems.

b Learners check their answers in the script. This will give them an opportunity to read it through quickly and notice the language in **4a**.

TASK VOCABULARY Speculating about consequences

4 a 👥 *Focus on expressions.* Learners read the sentences and decide which are for and against the ban. Don't go through the answers; let learners listen to check in **4b**.

> 1 against 2 against 3 for 4 against 5 for 6 for
> 7 for (or neutral)

b Find out if learners had any problems with any of the expressions, and let them repeat the expressions after recording **1.15** or after you. They may well find *It'll* difficult to say, so give them plenty of opportunity to practise it on its own and in the expressions.

TASK

5 a *Preparation: Content.* Learners read the situation. Divide the class into two groups (A and B) and check both groups understand what to do. Encourage learners to get into the group they agree with (but this may not be possible). Walk round and help with ideas if necessary.

b *Preparation: Language.* Once learners know what they want to say, tell them to think about how to express their ideas. Draw attention to the examples and remind them that they can use language from anywhere in the unit to support their argument. Encourage them to make notes of expressions they could use.

6 👥 *Speaking.* Decide on the size of the groups (anything between two and five should be fine) and make sure there are representatives from both A and B groups. Walk round while they are talking and make a note of language use for a feedback session.

7 *Speaking.* Find out if anyone has changed their mind about the ban.

Round-up: Ask what the best reasons were for and against the ban.

> You could use photocopiable activity 2B on the Teacher's DVD-ROM at this point.

2 Explore

Keywords: *so, such*

Goals: use *so* and *such* appropriately in a range of expressions

Core language

so + adjective or adverb
such + noun phrase
Expressions with *so* and *such*

1 *Listening for main idea.* Focus learners on the picture and the context. Ask them how old they think Sylvia is and to predict what has changed her life. Learners read the three questions, then play recording **1.16**. Learners discuss their answers in pairs. Then check as a class. Find out if learners know people like Sylvia or if technology is a problem for any elderly people they know.

> 1 She recently got a computer and internet connection.
> 2 It's very easy to use, and she can be in constant contact with her daughter, who lives in Hong Kong.
> 3 She wants to get an internet phone so she can call her daughter and grandchildren for free.

2 a *Focus on meaning.* Do this with the whole class.

> a 3 and 4 b 1 and 2

b *Focus on form.* Again, you could do this as a class or ask learners to do it in pairs, then play recording **1.16** again for them to check as a class. Encourage learners to say sentences 3 and 4 out loud to a partner to work out where the strong stress is.

> 1 a *so* is followed by an adjective or adverb
>   b *such* is followed by a/an + (adjective) + noun.
> 2 *so* and *such* are stressed.

3   *Practice.* Do the first one together and remind learners that the first four sentences are in recordings they've already listened to. Learners continue in pairs. Check as a class.

> 1 I'm <u>so</u> busy!
> 2 It saves <u>such</u> a lot of time.
> 3 So many of us are wasting <u>so</u> much time looking at it.
> 4 I find a lot of channels really irritating because there are <u>so</u> many ads.
> 5 I didn't realise it was <u>such</u> a long way.
> 6 It took <u>such</u> a long time to get there that we missed the party.

4 *Practice: Writing.* Demonstrate what learners have to do by focusing on the example or making up a sentence of your own using the sentence frame. Learners continue individually, then compare with a partner. Walk round while they're writing and help as necessary.

Expressions with *so* and *such*

5 a   Do the first one together, then learners can continue substituting the underlined words in pairs.

> 1 or so 2 such as 3 and so on 4 so far

b *Practice: Speaking.* Learners cover the expressions and help each other to remember them.

> **Alternative: Test each other**
>
> Learner A closes their book. Learner B reads the sentences 1–4 (in any order) and Partner A tries to remember the expressions. Learner B can prompt as necessary. Then change roles.

6 a *Preparation: Content.* Draw learners' attention to the prompts and ask them to think of something that changed their life, with Sylvia's script from **1** as a model. Encourage them to make a few notes about why and how it changed their life. Walk round and help with ideas if necessary.

b *Preparation: Language.* Point out that learners can make their stories more interesting and dramatic by using *so* and *such*, as in the examples 1–5. Give them a few moments to think about how to use them in their stories. Walk round and help as necessary.

7   /   *Speaking.* Learners tell their stories in pairs or groups. If someone really couldn't come up with an idea, put them with a pair who have stories. Listening to other people's stories may remind them of something that's happened to them. Monitor for use of *so* and *such* and do a feedback session at the end.

Round-up. Ask one or two learners for a memorable story that they heard in their group.

> **Optional extra**
>
> After learners have told a partner their story, they change pairs and learners tell a new partner the story they have just heard. Ask a few learners to retell the story for the class. The original story-teller should check the facts. Make sure learners are happy for their stories to be made public in this way first.

Explore speaking

Goals: ask for clarification
        clarify what you're saying

Core language:
Questions and expressions asking for clarification
Expressions to clarify what you're saying

1 a *Listening for main idea.* Focus learners on the picture and ask them what they remember about Eric from the Target activity, i.e. he works for a management consultancy; Graham is a colleague; he was against the intranet ban, etc. Learners read the question, then play recording **1.17**. Learners check in pairs before checking as a class.

> Conversation 1: a colleague (2)
> Conversation 2: a stranger (3)
> Conversation 3: a friend (1)

b *Listening for detail.* Let learners discuss the questions first, then play recording **1.17** again so they can check their ideas. Don't go through the answers yet.

> 1 They're talking about employees being distracted from work by personal emails.
> 2 They're talking about a problem with the trains and Eric's ticket.
> 3 They're talking about internet relationships and Eric's experience of falling in love online.

c Learners check their own answers in the three conversation scripts. This will help them to notice the new language. Check they understand everything before moving on.

2 a *Focus on meaning.* Check understanding of *clarify* (= make clear) and *clarification* (= explanation). Learners categorise the highlighted expressions in the conversations.

> 1 Do you mean …?; Are you saying …?; What I don't get is …
> 2 what I'm trying to say is …; I'm saying …; how can I put it …

b *Vocabulary expansion.* Learners add more expressions to the categories in **a**.

> 1 What exactly do you mean?; So you're saying …?
> 2 What I meant to say was …; No, I was trying to say …

c Learners check their own answers by listening. Use recording **1.18** to model the expressions or say them yourself and ask learners to repeat.

3 *Practise speaking.* Learners practise the conversations using different expressions. Walk round and check they are using appropriate expressions and ask a few learners to demonstrate each conversation at the end.

4 *Preparation.* Learners choose one of the questions to talk about. Walk round and help with ideas and vocabulary if necessary.

5 a *Speaking.* Learners talk about one of the questions and practise using the expressions. When they're ready, tell them to change roles and talk about a different question. Walk round and monitor use of the new expressions. Do a brief feedback session focusing on any common problems.

b Learners work with a new partner and do the same thing again.

c Learners change partners again and have more conversations.

Round-up. Ask a few learners about their partner's opinions.

> You could use photocopiable activity 2C on the Teacher's DVD-ROM at this point.

2 Look again

Review

VOCABULARY *It's* with adjectives

1 a Get an example from someone in the class. Learners continue. Walk round to see if anyone is having problems. Encourage them to go back to the relevant section of the unit if they are.

b / *Discussion.* Learners say their sentences to each other. Encourage learners to respond and find out more information by asking questions. At the end, find out if there were any disagreements.

GRAMMAR *will, could, may, might*

2 a Remind learners that they can use *likely, definitely, probably* and *may well* to express their ideas. Elicit some examples about one of the sentences using different adverbs with *likely* and write them on the board.

b / Learners compare their ideas. In feedback, ask different learners to say what they think about each of the sentences. Encourage this to develop into a class discussion.

CAN YOU REMEMBER? Unit 1 – Talking about the present

3 a Learners read Paul and Rebecca's conversation. Ask if they can remember anything about them (*They argued about TV in Unit 1*). Ask what forms learners can use to talk about the present (*present simple, present progressive, present perfect*). Learners complete the conversation by putting the verbs in brackets in the correct form.

> *2 you're talking   3 I haven't read   4 I'm watching*
> *5 Have you seen   6 I don't know   7 I'm not making*
> *8 I'm just looking*

b Play recording **1.19** and check whether learners had any problems.

Extension

SPELLING AND SOUNDS /tʃ/

4 a Focus learners on the words, then say them or play recording **1.20** while learners underline the /tʃ/ sound in each word. The words are grouped to help learners notice the patterns in 1–3 in **b**.

> *chair, chance*   *question, suggestion*
> *achieve, exchange*   *tuna, Tuesday*
> *each, touch*   *cultural, future*
> *kitchen, watch, catch*

> **Alternative for weaker groups**
>
> Show the words on an OHT or interactive whiteboard and ask learners to call out the letters which make the /tʃ/ sound. Underline the different patterns in different colours. Go through **b** as a class, circling or highlighting relevant letters for 1–3 in each word on display.

b The underlining and grouping in **a** will help guide learners to notice the patterns.

> *1 in all positions   2 short vowel   3 tch, tion, tu*

c Learners think of more words with the spelling patterns.

> *Possible answers*
> *1 chin, purchase, teach   2 fetch, itch*
> *3 stretch, digestion, tube*

d Say the words or play recording **1.21**. Learners write the words they hear. They check their own answers when everyone is finished. Encourage them to record words they found difficult in their vocabulary notebooks.

NOTICE Adjective–noun collocations

5 a Learners read the sentences. Remind learners that they have seen or heard all the sentences before and see if they can remember the context. Then they complete the collocations in pairs or individually before checking in pairs.

> *1 real world*   *4 real friendship*
> *2 quick decisions*   *5 a huge waste of time*
> *3 facial expressions* *6 urgent emails*

b Learners do the matching and write questions individually. With weaker classes, you may want to point out that with some words there is more than one possible collocation. They then work in pairs to ask and answer each other's questions. You may want to check their collocations and questions for accuracy before they do this.

> *Suggested answers*
> *online conversation/chat/relationship*
> *demanding job*
> *private conversation/messages/chat*
> *quick meal/chat*
> *delicious meal*
> *personal messages/relationship*

Self-assessment

Go through the list of goals, eliciting language from the unit for each one. You may need to remind learners of the contexts for the goals and let them look back through the unit if necessary. Then they circle the appropriate number for each goal. Walk round while they are doing this and talk to learners about their progress. Remind learners about the extra practice opportunities under the box, and ask where they can find things.

Unit 2 Extra activities on the Teacher's DVD-ROM

Printable worksheets, activity instructions and answer keys are on your Teacher's DVD-ROM.

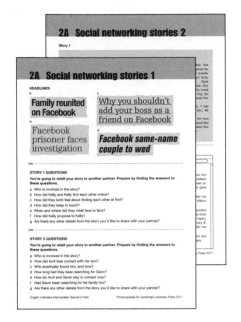

2A Chain discussion

Activity type: Speaking – Discussion card game – Groups

Aim: To practise phrases for expressing opinion; to talk about communication; to develop fluency

Language: Expressing opinion – Use at any point from 2.1.

Preparation: Make one copy of the worksheet for each group. Cut up each worksheet to make one set of eight Expressing opinion cards and 16 Topic cards.

Time: 20 minutes

2B Consequences?

Activity type: Speaking – Debate – Groups/Pairs

Aim: To speculate about possible consequences; to discuss an issue; to practise language for giving opinions

Language: Speculating about consequences and giving opinions – Use at any point from the Target activity, p18.

Preparation: Make one copy of the worksheet for each group of learners. Cut up each worksheet to make a set of ten BANNED! cards.

Time: 20 minutes

2C Social networking stories

Activity type: Reading, speaking and vocabulary – Individuals/Pairs

Aim: To extend reading practice around the theme of social networking; to practise retelling a story; to discuss an issue

Language: Past tenses to retell a story – Use at any point from 2.1.

Preparation: Make one copy of Worksheets 1 and 2 for each pair. Cut up each worksheet to make three activity sections and two stories.

Time: 40 minutes

Unit 2 Self-study Pack

In the Workbook

Unit 2 of the *English Unlimited Intermediate Workbook* offers additional ways to practise the vocabulary and grammar taught in the Coursebook. There are also activities which build reading and writing skills and a whole page of listening and speaking tasks to use with the Interview video, giving your learners the opportunity to hear and react to authentic spoken English.

- **Vocabulary:** Expressing opinions; *It's*; adjectives; Using the Internet; Expressing probability; Speculating about consequences
- **Grammar:** *will, could, may, might*
- **Time out:** Quiz: Animal communication
- **Explore writing:** Website profile
- **Interview:** Communication and technology – Alan and Aurora

On the DVD-ROM

Unit 2 of the *English Unlimited Intermediate Self-study DVD-ROM* contains interactive games and activities for your learners to practise and improve their vocabulary, grammar and pronunciation, and also their speaking and listening, with the possibility for learners to record themselves, and a video of authentic spoken English to use with the Workbook.

- **Vocabulary and grammar:** Extra practice activities
- **Pronunciation:** Sentence stress
- **Explore speaking:** Using emphasis
- **Explore listening:** A change at work
- **Video:** Communication and technology

3 Success

3.1

Goals: talk about a business idea
talk about hopes, dreams and ambitions

Core language:

VOCABULARY   Talking about a business idea
                           Hopes, dreams and ambitions
PRONUNCIATION   Schwa /ɔ/

Great ideas

READING

1   *Prediction.* Ask learners what the people in the pictures are doing and check understanding of *karaoke*, *iPod* and *inventor*.

👥 / 👥👥 Learners read and predict what the statements are about. Don't go through the answers, as learners will read to check in **2**.

> a karaoke   b the iPod   c the iPod   d karaoke
> e karaoke   f the iPod

2   *Jigsaw reading.* Explain the jigsaw reading to learners, i.e. that pairs will read different articles and each learner will only check ideas about the article they have read. Learners can check with a partner who has read the same article. If necessary, do a very quick class check of the statements in **1**.

3   a   👥 *Reading for detail.* Learners look at the first summary (for paragraph 1) and complete it in pairs by reading their paragraph in the article again. Check learners' ideas for both articles, then let them continue in pairs. Walk round and help as necessary, but don't check answers as a class.

> **Karaoke text**
> 1 Inoue Daisuke invented karaoke, but he didn't ... get rich from the idea.
> 2 He was a drummer in a band which ... played for middle-aged businessmen who wanted to sing traditional songs in local clubs in Kobe.
> 3 The idea for karaoke started when Inoue gave ... a tape of a backing band to a businessman, who gave a performance on an overnight trip.
> 4 Over the next 20 years, karaoke became ... very popular in Asia, the US and Europe. Inoue was surprised when ...Time Magazine called him one of the 20th century's most influential people.
> 5 Now, Inoue ... makes a living selling cockroach repellent for machines. In the future, he ... wants to train Japanese pet owners to take better care of their pets.
> **iPod text**
> P1 Ive invented ... the iPod and the ... iMac computer, but he is ... rather shy and doesn't usually do interviews.
> P2 The iPod made it possible for people ... to carry their music collections in their pockets for the first time.
> P3 Ive's aim is ... to create beautiful gadgets that can be used without looking at the instruction booklet.
> P4 Ive loves it when ... people tell him their iPod stories.

b   *Speaking.* Learners use their summaries to explain the main points of their articles to their partner. In feedback, get learners' views on the men's similarities and differences.

> **Alternative for weaker groups**
> Put learners in groups (two As, two Bs) to talk about their articles, so pairs can help each other explain and understand.

> **Alternative for stronger groups**
> Once learners have written their summaries, tell them to cover the article during the speaking stage.

> **Optional extra**
> Use the topics to prompt a class discussion. Write these questions on the board and talk about them as a class:
> 1 What do you think are the main reasons for the iPod's success?
> 2 What do you think about karaoke? Have you tried it?

VOCABULARY Talking about a business idea

4   *Focus on expressions.* Learners match each pair of sentences with a topic. In feedback, ask learners to try to paraphrase the expressions to check understanding, e.g. *came up with* = first had.

> 1 c   2 a   3 b

5   👤 Tell learners to cover **4** and complete the questions with verbs from the expressions. They can check their own answers.

> 1 come   2 patent   3 made   4 make   5 looks

SPEAKING

6   👥 / 👥👥 *Discussion.* Learners talk about the questions in pairs or groups.

Hopes, dreams and ambitions

VOCABULARY Hopes, dreams and ambitions

1   Remind learners about Inoue Daisuke's dream for the future or refer them back to the final paragraph in the karaoke article. Get some reactions from the class.

> He'd like to train Japanese pet owners to take better care of their pets.

2   *Listening for main idea.* Focus learners on the pictures A–C and ask what the people are doing and if they know how to do each activity. Elicit the words *rock music*, *drown*, *train/training* using the pictures (note *train* in **3**). Play recording **1.22**. Learners match the speakers to three of the pictures.

> A Eduardo   B Aminata   C Elisa

3   *Focus on expressions.* Tell learners to read the beginnings and ends of the sentences and match them up. Then play recording **1.22** again so learners can check their ideas.

Language note: infinitive or -ing

The exercise highlights some useful verb + infinitive or -ing patterns:
like / love / want to + infinitive; *is to* + infinitive; preposition (e.g. *of*) + -ing; considering + -ing.
Draw learners' attention to these patterns.

Optional practice

Write the patterns above on the board. Tell learners to cover 1–8 and test each other in pairs on possible ways to complete the endings a–h, e.g. *I'd like/love to learn to swim*; *I'm considering learning to swim*.

Alternative for stronger groups

Focus learners on the semi-fixed expression: *My (aim/dream/ambition) is to* + infinitive, and see if learners can come up with some more examples, e.g. *My idea/plan/goal/... is to ... .* Learners can use these expressions in **4**.

4 *Writing: Personalisation.* Learners write sentences about their own hopes, dreams and ambitions. To demonstrate, write an ambition of your own on the board.

Alternative: Truth and lies

Replace **4** (above), **6** and **7** (below) with the following game: demonstrate by telling learners about three of your ambitions, hopes and dreams, but say that one is a lie. They guess which one is a lie in pairs, then each pair can ask you a question to check their ideas. Tell them how many guessed right at the end. Learners write four or five sentences of their own with one or two lies. Then they play the guessing game in groups.

 You could use photocopiable activity 3A on the Teacher's DVD-ROM at this point.

PRONUNCIATION Schwa /ə/

5 a *Focus on stressed syllables and schwa sounds.* Play recording **1.23** or say sentence 1 in **3**. Elicit or teach what the schwa symbol means and demonstrate the difference between a strong and weak *to* (as in the example sentence). Talk about the questions together using the example to help.

> *Nouns, verbs, adjectives and adverbs are usually stressed. Grammar words, such as prepositions, auxiliary and modal verbs and articles, often have a schwa.*

b 👥 Encourage learners to say the sentences out loud to each other and to work out which syllables are stressed in the longer words. Point out that *in* (despite being a preposition) cannot have a schwa because of the *i* sound.

> 2 At some point, I'd absolutely love to learn to be
>   comfortable in the water.
> 3 I'm thinking of taking some lessons.
> 4 I'm considering doing a degree in music.
> 5 My dream is to be a guitar player.
> 6 My aim is to go there next year.
> 7 My ambition is to live in Tokyo for a year.
> 8 I've always wanted to train at the JKA dojo.

c Play recording **1.24** so learners can listen and read the sentences to check their answers. Stop the recording after each sentence so learners can repeat it.

SPEAKING

6 *Speaking: Personalisation.* Encourage learners to cover their sentences from **4** while they talk to a partner. Monitor and note down useful or incorrect language learners use during their discussions for a feedback session later.

7 *Round-up.* Find out about the ambitions of different learners from their partners. Encourage the class to ask questions and to find out more about each other.

3.2

Goals: talk about abilities
talk about achievements

Core language:

VOCABULARY	Abilities
GRAMMAR	Present perfect and time expressions

Your abilities

READING

1 a Discuss the question as a class and find out if any learners have taken an IQ test and what they felt it tested.

b *Reading for main idea.* Focus learners on the list of activities and the question. They read the article, then discuss their ideas with a partner. Check understanding and pronunciation of the types of intelligence, especially *kinesthetic* /kɪnəsˈθetɪk/, *visual* /ˈvɪʒuəl/ and *spatial* /ˈspeɪʃəl/. Then check ideas as a class.

> *Possible answers*
> *doing your accounts: logical-mathematical*
> *playing tennis: bodily-kinesthetic*
> *writing a poem: verbal-linguistic, musical*
> *designing a building: bodily-kinesthetic, possibly logical-mathematical/visual-spatial*
> *staying happy: intrapersonal*
> *learning a song: musical*
> *resolving an argument: interpersonal*

2 Give learners time to read the article again and think about the jobs individually before discussing their ideas in pairs. Check understanding of these words and expressions: *extrovert/introvert*, *empathise easily with others*, *self-aware*, *reasoning*, *complex (calculations)*, *visualising*, *manipulating*. Ask one or two learners for their ideas in feedback.

> *Possible answers*
> *politician: interpersonal, verbal-linguistic*
> *poet: verbal-linguistic, intrapersonal*
> *engineer: logical-mathematical, bodily-kinesthetic, possibly visual-spatial*
> *doctor: interpersonal*
> *singer: musical, bodily-kinesthetic*
> *DJ: musical, interpersonal*
> *social worker: interpersonal*

VOCABULARY Abilities

3 *Focus on expressions.* Focus learners on the first highlighted expression in the article and the options a–d, then ask learners to identify the pattern. They continue in pairs.

are good at: b	excel at: d
are able to: a	have the ability to: a
have a facility with: c	have a good: c
are capable of: b	

4 a *Writing sentences.* Learners write sentences about their abilities and skills. Point out that they should explain their ideas and give examples. Walk round and help as necessary.

b 👥 / 👥 *Speaking: Personalisation.* Learners talk about their ideas together. Monitor use of the target language and note useful examples for a feedback session later.

Round-up. Ask several learners if they share intelligences with their partner or group, and find out which intelligences a lot of people share.

Your achievements

LISTENING

1 *Listening for main idea.* Focus learners on the pictures and ask what they can remember about Aminata (she wants to learn to swim). Ask learners to read the instructions and see if they can predict the achievements from the pictures. Then play recording **1.25**.

> Aminata: has learned to ride a bike
> Margot: has written a cookery book
> Charlie: has learned to play the drums

2 👥 Learners try to answer the questions together before listening again to recording **1.25** to check.

> 1 She wanted to learn to ride a bike because her friends all ride bikes.
> 2 a year ago
> 3 cookery
> 4 She's helping to run a restaurant.
> 5 a samba band
> 6 go on tour

3 👥 / 👥 *Speaking.* Learners talk about the three people's achievements.

Round-up. Find out if anyone in the class has had similar experiences and how easy or difficult it was to learn to do these things.

> **Language note: Learning skills**
>
> Notice the expressions that Aminata uses to talk about learning a skill:
> *I've learned to ride a bike recently. I've had the bike for about a year now. It took me about (a month) to learn.*
> For skills that we can learn, we can also use this expression:
> *I (don't) know how to ride a bike.*

GRAMMAR Present perfect and time expressions

4 Give learners a few minutes to look at the sentences and categorise them in pairs, before checking as a class.

> 1 a 2 b 3 b 4 a

5 *Focus on time expressions.* Do this with the class, explaining any problems as you go along. Model the sentences for the class and draw attention to the stressed adverbs in 1–6 and the contrasting weak form of *for* /fə/ in 7. Quickly check that learners remember the difference between *for* and *since* by putting a few time expressions on the board and eliciting the correct word, e.g. *(since) 1999*, *(for) three years*, *(for) ages*, *(since) I was born.*

> a always; never
> b for; since
> c yet
> d just; recently
> e already

6 Learners look at the position of the time expressions in the sentences in **5**. You could do this by writing the adverbs on the board and telling learners to close their books. Say each sentence without the adverb (e.g. *I've wanted to write*) and elicit the correct position from the class. Learners can repeat the correct sentences for extra practice. Then they add the time expressions to the quiz and compare with a partner, before checking as a class.

> 2 has <u>just</u> passed a test or an exam.
> 3 has <u>never</u> learned to drive.
> 4 has <u>always</u> done well in interviews.
> 5 has <u>already</u> achieved something today.
> 6 has been married <u>for</u> over ten years.
> 7 hasn't taken a test or an exam <u>since</u> they left school.
> 8 hasn't done what they needed to do today <u>yet.</u>

> **Note: Grammar practice**
>
> You could do the grammar practice on p136 at this point.

 You could use photocopiable activity 3B on the Teacher's DVD-ROM at this point.

SPEAKING

7 a Learners ask you a few questions from the quiz in **6** to demonstrate the activity. Encourage them to find out more details by asking you follow-up questions. Learners then walk round asking their questions. When they find someone for whom a statement is true, they should find out more details, take a note of the person's name and information, then move on to the next question. Remind learners to take notes, or they may not have much to say in **b**. While learners are talking, walk round and monitor use of the present perfect and the adverbs. Stop the activity when most learners have reached the final question (and hopefully found someone to say yes to each one).

b 👥 Learners compare the information they have gathered from the activity.

Round-up. Ask a few learners to tell the class what they have found out about each other.

3.3 Target activity

Goals: talk about a business idea ♻
talk about hopes, dreams and ambitions ♻
talk about achievements ♻
take part in an interview

Core language:

TASK VOCABULARY	Facts and feelings
3.1 VOCABULARY	Talking about a business idea
3.1 VOCABULARY	Hopes, dreams and ambitions

Sell an idea

TASK LISTENING

1 Learners read the advert for Connections and answer the question. Check understanding of *entrepreneur* (= someone who makes money by starting a business, usually involving financial risk) and *investor* (= someone who puts money into a business or organisation).

> *People who want to start a business join so they can meet investors who might put money into their business.*

2 **a** *Listening for detail.* Focus learners on the picture and the words. Let them discuss what they know in pairs, then play recording **1.26** so they can label the picture as they listen. Check as a class. (The easiest way to do this is to project the image on the board, if possible.) Then ask how the bag works.

> *The bag sits behind the buggy. The straps clip over the handles. There's a top pocket for valuables and a side pocket for the baby's things. The main compartment is for your shopping. You can also use it without the buggy because it has its own wheels.*

b Read the questions, then play recording **1.27** (the rest of the interview with Olga). Learners discuss the questions in pairs. Find out if they want to listen again, or let them check their ideas in the script.

> 1 *Olga wants £100,000 investment for marketing and materials in return for a 33% stake in her company. She'd also like support and help with the marketing and the business plan.*
> 2 *She is really excited about the product and she feels very optimistic about its chances of success.*

3 **a** *Discussion.* Learners discuss the questions. Find out what they think about the product and ask for their predictions for question 2, with their reasons.

b Play recording **1.28** so learners can check their predictions. Find out who guessed correctly.

Extension: Compound nouns

In addition to *side pocket* and *top pocket* in **2a**, describing the *easybag*, these compound nouns are also in scripts **1.26**, **1.27** and **1.28**: *mobile phone, supermarket trolley, plastic bags, product development, business plan, international sales, design expert.*
Write one word from each compound noun on the board (e.g. *mobile, trolley, plastic, development, plan, sales, expert*) and tell learners to mine the script to complete the expressions.

Optional extra

Find out if learners have any reality TV shows about entrepreneurs or business ideas, e.g. *Dragon's Den* or something similar, in their own countries. Encourage learners to share their ideas about such programmes and to talk about interesting products they remember seeing.

TASK VOCABULARY Facts and feelings

4 **a** 👥 *Focus on expressions.* Learners read the sentences from the interview and remember who said them. This will help them process the meaning of the expressions.

> 1 *interviewer*
> 2 *interviewer*
> 3 *Olga*
> 4 *Olga*
> 5 *interviewer*
> 6 *interviewer*
> 7 *Olga*
> 8 *Olga*

b 👥 Ask learners for one example of adjective + *about* and noun + *about*, then they continue in pairs.

> adjective + about : *3, 5, 7, 8*
> noun + about: *1, 2, 4, 6*

TASK

5 *Preparation.* Learners read about their product and decide how to talk about it. Remind learners that they can look back at previous lessons for useful language.

Alternative for weaker groups

Learners can work in A/A and B/B pairs to work out how to express their ideas.

6 👥 *Interview.* Before learners start, tell investors to listen carefully to the entrepreneur's explanation and to ask questions about their idea, especially if anything is unclear. Learners conduct their interviews. Monitor the interviews and take a note of good and problematic language for a feedback session.

Option: Language feedback

On the board, write examples of useful language used by learners and incorrect or unclear language used from the unit. In pairs, learners decide which examples are incorrect and try to improve them together. Then go through them with the class. Then learners change roles and do the second interview.

7 👥 Learners change roles and do a second interview.

8 👥 *Round-up.* Divide learners into As and Bs. Learners briefly explain their two ideas to the group, who then decide which one is likely to be the most successful. Ask a learner from each group to briefly explain the idea they chose to the class. You could take a class vote on the best idea.

3 Explore

Across cultures: Attitudes to success

Goal: raise awareness of different cultural attitudes to success

Core language:
VOCABULARY   Attitudes to success

LISTENING

1 Learners look at the pictures and read the questions. Ask them to predict how Mariama and Remco feel about success or being successful. Then play recording **1.29**.

> 1 She doesn't feel comfortable.
> 2 He wants to play to a high level.
>   He wants to win all the time.

2 *Listening for main idea.* Learners read the sentences and think about their answers. Then play recording **1.29** again.

> 1 T 2 F 3 T 4 F

VOCABULARY Attitudes to success

3 a Learners decide who says the sentences. They can check their own ideas in the script on p149 or go through it quickly as a class. Check pronunciation of the adjectives *competitive*, *comfortable*, *confident* and *arrogant*.

> Interviewer: 1, 7 Mariama: 2, 3, 4 Remco: 5, 6

> **Language note: Pronunciation of o**
>
> These adjectives contain three different sounds for the letter *o*, two stressed forms and a schwa: /ʌ/ = c*o*mfortable, /ɒ/ = c*o*nfident, /ə/ = c*o*mpetitive, arr*o*gant

> **Option: Pronunciation activity**
>
> Write the following phonemic symbols on the board: /ʌ/, /ɒ/, /ə/. Model the sounds and ask learners in pairs to match the *o* sounds in the adjectives to the correct symbols. Learners then say the words and identify the stressed syllables. Ask why *competitive* and *arrogant* have a schwa (because the *o* is unstressed). You could elicit more examples of each pronunciation of o from the class, e.g. *odd*, *mother*, *photographer*.

b Learners can work in pairs first (using dictionaries if necessary), or do it as a class.

> 1 confident: certain about your ability to do things well
>   arrogant: believing that you are better or more important than other people
> 2 that you will do whatever is necessary to win
> 3 playing by the rules: following them
>   bending the rules: changing the rules to suit a person or situation

SPEAKING

4 a *Preparation.* Learners prepare to talk about the quiz questions. Walk round and help as necessary.

b *Asking and answering questions.* Learners ask and answer the quiz questions. When they finish, talk about the two round-up questions as a class.

Explore writing

Goal: take notes

Core language:
Note-taking
Understanding and using abbreviations

1 Give learners a minute to think about their ideas individually before talking in pairs. Feed back as a class and put a list of learners' note-taking techniques on the board.

2 *Listening for main idea.* Ask learners what they can remember about Olga (Target activity). Learners read the questions, then play recording **1.30**. Learners discuss their answers in pairs, before checking as a class or in the script on p149.

> 1 product development manager
> 2 She started out in finance, then moved to the development side about ten years ago. She's been at ICB for five years and helped develop a range of children's accessories.
> 3 a drinks 'pod'

3 a Tell learners to read the tips with a partner and tick the ones they usually follow. In feedback, find out if there were any tips learners disagreed about, and why.

b Focus learners on the notes about Olga, then they do the matching. They can work individually, then compare ideas in pairs.

> 1 a 2 d 3 b 4 c

4 a Ask learners what *yrs* means (*years*) and highlight its use in the notes about Olga. Point out that although some abbreviations are very common, there are often several different ways to abbreviate a word. Learners guess what the abbreviations mean in pairs. Don't go through the answers, as this will pre-empt **b**.

> 1 years
> 2 75 grams
> 3 eight o'clock
> 4 number
> 5 after midday
> 6 with
> 7 21st century
> 8 and so on (etcetera)
> 9 against (versus)
> 10 approximately
> 11 per week
> 12 please turn over

b Play recording **1.31** so learners can check their answers. Check for any problems before moving on.

> **Optional extra**
>
> Learners can take turns to test each other by choosing five abbreviations from **4a**. They say the five full words to their partner, who writes down the abbreviations, e.g. A: *number* B: *no*. Then they swap roles. Learners can check their abbreviations at the end.

5 a *Listening for detail.* Draw learners' attention to the incomplete notes about Olga in **3b**. Play recording **1.32** so learners can complete the notes.

> – 12 yrs exp. in finance then development
> – ICB: 5 yrs
> – developed West range w/ R West – cleaning products

b Learners listen to the rest of the interview (recording **1.33**) and make notes.

> Possible answers
> Strengths:
> – international exp.
> – worked w/ R West
> Most proud of:
> drink 'pod': 75g; new material – keeps temp. same from
> 0–100°C. Good for sports, work, school

c Learners compare their notes. Then they check their own answers in the script.

6 *Preparation.* Focus learners on the context and give them a moment to prepare answers to the five interview questions. Walk round and help as necessary.

7 *Note-taking.* Learners ask each other the questions and take notes on their partner's answers. Remind learners that they should not try to write everything down and to remember to use the tips and abbreviations from the lesson.

8 a *Speaking.* In groups of three or four, learners use their notes to explain their previous partner's answers.

b *Round-up.* Groups decide on the person who should get the post. Ask groups to say who they chose and why.

> You could use photocopiable activity 3C on the Teacher's DVD-ROM at this point.

3 Look again

Review

GRAMMAR Present perfect with time expressions

1 a Learners decide on the best time expressions to complete the sentences. They can do this individually, then talk about the sentences with a partner, or work in pairs, discussing each sentence as they complete it.

> **Alternative for stronger groups**
>
> *Books closed.* Dictate the sentences as they're written. Learners work in pairs to complete them with appropriate time expressions, then discuss them as above.

> 2 I've lived in the same house <u>since</u> I was born.
> 3 I've <u>always</u> loved being alone.
> 4 I've changed my job <u>recently</u>.
> 5 We've <u>already</u> started a family.
> 6 I haven't achieved my ambition <u>yet.</u>
> 7 I've known my best friend <u>for</u> ten years.
> 8 We've <u>just</u> moved home.

b Point out the ideas and prompts, then demonstrate the activity with a confident learner.

VOCABULARY Hopes, dreams and ambitions

2 a Learners use the prompts to write about their hobbies, interests, hopes and dreams. Walk round and help as necessary.

> 1 My dream is to …
> 2 I'd absolutely love to …
> 3 At some point I'm considering …
> 4 I've always wanted to …
> 5 I'm thinking of …
> 6 One day I'd like to …

b Learners discuss their hopes, dreams and ambitions in groups.

Round-up. Find out if anyone shares the same hopes for the future.

> **Option: Mingling**
>
> Tell learners to write their sentences (neatly) on a piece of paper. Collect their sentences, shuffle them and tell learners to take someone else's paper. They read the sentences, guess who the person might be, then walk round and ask questions to find the writer. If a few people find the writer immediately, they can hand in their paper and take a different one.

CAN YOU REMEMBER? Unit 2 – *will, could, may, might*; Expressing probability

3 a Elicit the most likely sentence (*c*), then learners continue individually before comparing with a partner. Check quickly as a class.

> a I may go out for a meal tonight. (3)
> b I'm very unlikely to go to bed early. (5)
> c I'll definitely have a shower later. (1)
> d I might not watch television. (4)
> e I won't call my family. (6)
> f I may well see my friends. (2)

b Learners write sentences saying what they are likely / not likely to do that evening. Walk round and help as necessary.

c Learners talk together. In feedback, ask a few learners from different groups what others are going to do.

Extension

SPELLING AND SOUNDS /s/

4 a Write *celebrate* on the board and say it (or, for more of a challenge, say the word but don't write it). Ask learners which letter makes the /s/ sound (*c*). Then play recording **1.34** (or say the words yourself) while learners underline the letters which make a /s/ sound.

> *celebrate, city, cycle, address, across, essay, story, skin, supermarket, price, chance, advice, answer, ask, describe, close, increase*

b Elicit the words for the first spelling pattern, then learners continue in pairs.

> 1 story, skin, supermarket, answer, ask, describe
> 2 celebrate, city, cycle
> 3 essay, address, across
> 4 close, increase, price, advice, chance

c Learners test each other on the words from the section, then check together.

NOTICE *One of the ...*

5 a Point out to learners that they have seen or heard all these expressions in reading and listening texts in the unit. Learners complete the sentences individually, then compare with a partner.

> *1 richest   2 most important   3 most successful*

b Learners check their answers using the page references. Do the question as a class.

> *a superlative adjective*

c Give learners a moment to think of something they're fond of, then to write a few sentences describing it using *one of the*.

d Learners listen to each other's descriptions, then ask questions to find out more.

Self-assessment

Go through the list of goals, eliciting language from the unit for each one. You may need to remind learners of the contexts for the goals and let them look back through the unit if necessary. Then they circle the appropriate number for each goal. Walk round while they are doing this and talk to learners about their progress. Remind them about the extra practice opportunities under the box, and ask where they can find things.

Unit 3 Extra activities on the Teacher's DVD-ROM

Printable worksheets, activity instructions and answer keys are on your Teacher's DVD-ROM.

3A My hopes and dreams

Activity type: Speaking – Making conversation – Pairs

Aim: To practise talking about hopes, dreams and ambitions

Language: Hopes, dreams and ambitions – Use at any point from 3.1.

Preparation: Make one copy of the worksheet for each learner.

Time: 20 minutes

3B Present perfect pictures

Activity type: Speaking and grammar – Card game – Groups

Aim: To use the present perfect to talk about unfinished actions or situations and finished actions that are important now

Language: Present perfect and time expressions – Use at any point from 3.2.

Preparation: Make one copy of the worksheet for every group of three or four learners. Cut up the worksheet to make one set of eight Sentence-starter cards and one set of 12 Picture cards.

Time: 20 minutes

3C Entrepreneurs

Activity type: Writing and listening – Note-taking – Pairs/Groups

Aim: To practise making notes

Language: Note-taking – Use at any point from Explore writing.

Preparation: Make one copy of the worksheet for each learner and one copy of the Teacher's sheet (or one copy of the Teacher's sheet for each pair).

Time: 40 minutes

Unit 3 Self-study Pack

In the Workbook

Unit 3 of the *English Unlimited Intermediate Workbook* offers additional ways to practise the vocabulary and grammar taught in the Coursebook. There are also activities which build reading and writing skills and a whole page of listening and speaking tasks to use with the Interview video, giving your learners the opportunity to hear and react to authentic spoken English.

- **Vocabulary:** Talking about a business idea; Hopes, dreams and ambitions; Abilities; Facts and feelings
- **Grammar:** Present perfect and time expressions
- **My English:** Using the present perfect
- **Explore reading:** Article: Billy Bragg
- **Interview:** A proud moment – Saadia and Clare

On the DVD-ROM

Unit 3 of the *English Unlimited Intermediate Self-study DVD-ROM* contains interactive games and activities for your learners to practise and improve their vocabulary, grammar and pronunciation, and also their speaking and listening, with the possibility for learners to record themselves, and a video of authentic spoken English to use with the Workbook.

- **Vocabulary and grammar:** Extra practice activities
- **Pronunciation:** Schwa /ə/
- **Explore speaking:** Respond to statements
- **Explore listening:** Selling a product
- **Video:** A proud moment

4 What happened?

4.1

Goals: talk about accidents and injuries
explain how something happened

Core language:

VOCABULARY   Accidents and injuries
Saying how something happened

Accident-prone

SPEAKING

1 a 👤 Write on the board: *Do you take a lot of risks?*
Check learners understand the meaning of *risk*.
Draw attention to the picture and ask if it shows
risky behaviour; elicit a few more examples from the
class to introduce the quiz. Then tell learners to read
through the statements and ask about any problem
vocabulary before they answer the questions. Check
understanding of *unplug*, *travel insurance* and *break
the speed limit*. Then learners do the quiz and read
through the analysis on p118 when they are ready.

   b 👥 *Discussion.* Focus learners on the two questions
before they get into groups. Learners discuss the quiz
together, then move on to talk about people they know
who take risks.

   Round-up. Find out if most learners agreed with the
quiz and why / why not. Find out if anyone scored
highly and if so, what kind of risks they take and why.
You could also ask if anyone is very risk-averse and if
they can explain why. Ask a few learners about people
they know who take a lot of risks and if they have a lot
of accidents as a result. This will lead into the reading.

READING

2 a *Pre-reading discussion.* Focus learners on the list of
points and check understanding of *upbringing* (= the
way a child is treated and taught how to behave by its
parents) and *adolescence*. Learners then discuss how
the points can make people have more accidents. Find
out who is left-handed in the class, and if they think
this has any connection to having accidents.

   b *Reading for main idea.* Learners read the article quite
quickly to check their ideas. Let them compare with
a partner before checking as a class. Make sure they
understand *clumsy* (= someone who is not careful
so often damages, breaks or knocks into things) and
accident-prone (= someone who often has accidents).

3 a 👥 Use the unfinished sentences to focus learners on the
main points in the article. Learners talk in pairs to see
what they can remember. Don't go through the answers
yet, as this will pre-empt the reading task in **b**.

> **Alternative**
>
> *Books closed.* Read out the unfinished sentences to learners
> one at a time. They talk about each one in pairs. Continue as
> above.

   b *Reading for detail.* Learners read the article again
carefully to check their ideas. 👥 Then they compare
with a partner. In feedback, ask learners to explain the
ideas in more detail, e.g. ask why or what happens as
a result of each fact.

> 1 Parents are usually stricter with their first child.
> 2 Adolescents are often clumsy because their bodies
>   are growing very quickly.
> 3 Watching too much TV affects children's physical co-
>   ordination skills and awareness of physical risk.
> 4 Watching cartoons doesn't help children to
>   understand how the world works.
> 5 The world is designed for right-handed people.

I dropped it!

LISTENING

1 *Listening for main idea.* Learners look at the pictures
and say what they think has happened in each one.
Then play recording **1.35**. Learners match each
conversation to one of the pictures. Let them compare
in pairs before checking as a class.

> 1 B   2 E   3 D   4 A   5 C

VOCABULARY Accidents and injuries

2 a *Focus on expressions.* Learners try to complete the
sentences from the conversations using the verbs in
the box. Point out that they will have to choose the
correct form of the verbs. Then play recording **1.35**
again, stopping after each conversation to check
meaning and pronunciation. At the end, ask learners
how to spell the past form of *drop*, *slip* and *trip*.

> 1 dropped; I've broken it
> 2 banged my head
> 3 broke my wrist
> 4 slipped; fell over
> 5 cut my finger
> 6 tripped over

> **Alternative for weaker groups**
>
> Learners read the sentences and discuss possible answers
> with a partner, but they don't try to complete the gaps before
> listening. Reassure them that you will explain any new words
> after they have listened to the conversations again and have
> completed the expressions.

   b *Vocabulary expansion.* Learners use the new language
to talk about accidents and injuries and what often
causes them.

VOCABULARY Saying how something happened

3 a Point out the three highlighted stems which can
be used to explain a problem or accident. Learners
complete the stems individually before comparing
with a partner, or in pairs.

> 1 c   2 a   3 b

b *Vocabulary expansion.* Learners extend the language by completing the stems with a range of endings. Point out the patterns that follow each expression (*on the way to* + noun; *of* + *-ing*; *was trying to* + infinitive).

> 1 I was on the way to: the shops; the airport.
> 2 I was in the middle of: cooking dinner; having a shower.
> 3 I was trying to: change a light bulb; open a bottle.

c Look at the example and ask learners to think of different outcomes. Then they write sentences for the situations in **b**. If learners work alone, you will be able to see if they understand how to use the stems correctly. Walk round and help as necessary.

SPEAKING

4 a *Preparation.* Tell learners to think about their own experience of minor accidents and about how to express their ideas. Walk round and help with ideas and vocabulary as necessary. If any learners really can't think of any incidents to talk about, tell them to listen to their classmates in **b** and ask questions and to see whether other people's experiences jog their memory.

b *Speaking: Personalisation.* Learners tell each other about their experiences. Monitor while they're talking and take a note of language use for a feedback session at the end.

Round-up. Ask a learner from a few groups for the best stories and find out who is the most accident-prone in the class.

> 💿 You could use photocopiable activity 4A on the Teacher's DVD-ROM at this point.

4.2

Goals: talk about natural events
describe a dramatic experience
say how you feel about an experience

Core language:

VOCABULARY	Natural events
	Adverbs for telling stories
GRAMMAR	Narrative verb forms
PRONUNCIATION	Groups of words 1

The power of nature

VOCABULARY Natural events

1 a Focus learners on the pictures and events and match them as a class. Check pronunciation as you go along.

> A an earthquake
> B a tsunami
> C the northern lights
> D a volcanic eruption
> E a hurricane
> F an eclipse

> **Alternative**
>
> *Books closed.* If you can project the images onto the board, elicit or teach the words for the events. Learners can then do the matching exercise quickly in pairs.

b 👥 / 👥 *Discussion.* Learners discuss in pairs whether or not any of the events have happened in their countries. Pairs then join other pairs to exchange their stories.

LISTENING

2 *Listening for main idea.* Learners read the questions, then listen to recording **1.36**. Let them compare with a partner before checking as a class. Check understanding of the following words and expressions before they listen again:
Fran's story: *landlady, roof, canals of water, subsided*
António's story: *packed with people, headed down to* ... *, total (eclipse), eerie, atmosphere, odd, glad, missed*

> *Fran: tsunami; scary*
> *António: solar eclipse; interesting but strange/eerie*

3 👥 *Listening for detail.* Learners read the questions. Give them a moment to discuss answers with a partner before playing recording **1.36** again. Stop after Fran's story and let learners compare their answers. Then do the same with António's story. Ask if learners need to hear it again. Go through the answers.

> *Fran*
> * *She lived 200 metres from the sea, but the water didn't come into her street.*
> * *There were canals of water in the streets; it subsided quickly.*
> * *She didn't have to move from her home.*
> * *Her parents were visiting her at the time. They were able to contact family at home.*
> *António*
> * *It was full of people.*
> * *It was the middle of a working day.*
> * *The sky changed colour very slowly.*
> * *They didn't see the eclipse; he wishes they had.*

> **Language note: *actually***
>
> *Actually* appears a number of times in Fran's and António's stories with two different meanings:
>
> Fran and Astrid
> *I was actually living within two hundred metres of the sea* ...
> (= in fact, in reality)
> *Erm, just, I was actually at home when it happened.* (= in fact, in reality)
> *A: Your family probably was very worried for you.*
> *F: Well, my parents were actually visiting me at the time* ... (= to correct or contradict what someone has said)
> António
> *It wasn't actually a total eclipse.* (= in fact, in reality)
>
> Ask learners to search for *actually* in the scripts and then explain what it means. Tell them to listen out for it or notice it in texts that they hear or read in English.

GRAMMAR Narrative verb forms

4 a *Focus on meaning.* Learners match the examples from the stories with their uses.

> 1 B   2 A   3 C

You could illustrate the correlation between the three forms by drawing a timeline on the board like this (A = *was living*; B = *hit*; C = *had been*):

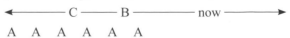

b *Focus on form.* Learners do the matching. Point out that *hit* is irregular.

> A: past progressive   B: past simple   C: past perfect

Elicit the negative and question forms of the three tenses using Fran's sentences, i.e.

I wasn't living ... The tsunami didn't hit. There hadn't been ...

Where were you living? When did it hit? Had there been an earthquake?

5 a *Practice.* Learners choose the correct verb forms in one of the stories. Walk round and help learners who are having problems.

> 1 Did you have to   2 stayed   3 found out   4 had been
> 5 had caused   6 were actually visiting   7 headed
> 8 started   9 went   10 were selling   11 were walking
> 12 had gone

b 👥 Learners check their ideas in pairs, before reading the scripts to check.

Note: Grammar practice

You could do the grammar practice on p137 at this point.

💿 You could use photocopiable activity 4B on the Teacher's DVD-ROM at this point.

Describing an experience

VOCABULARY Adverbs for telling stories

1 a *Focus on adverbs.* Give learners a few minutes to look at the questions and sentences in pairs, then do the questions as a class. Model the adverbs for the class. Ask learners which syllable is stressed in each word and give them a chance to repeat the adverbs (*imme̲diately, su̲ddenly, slo̲wly, qui̲ckly, o̲bviously, unfo̲rtunately, ama̲zingly, lu̲ckily*). This will help when they do the pronunciation activity in **2**.

> 1 A
> 2 • when you don't expect it, quickly: <u>suddenly</u>
>   • without waiting, at once: <u>immediately</u>
> 3 B
> 4 a surprise: amazingly   good news: luckily
>   a bad thing: unfortunately   clearly true: obviously

b Point out that adverb position can vary. Look at the first sentence together and help learners to try putting the adverb in different places in the sentence, e.g. *Immediately they headed down to the sea. They headed down to the sea immediately.* Explain that the position in this case makes the sentence more dramatic. Point out that the position of *amazingly* in

sentence 7 is quite unusual, but again the position increases the dramatic effect of the sentence.

> *beginning or end: immediately, suddenly, obviously, unfortunately, amazingly, luckily*
> *before the verb: immediately, suddenly, obviously, unfortunately, slowly, quickly*
> *end: slowly, quickly*

Language note: Adverb position

The fact that adverbs can go in several different positions in English may not in itself cause learners problems, but in some languages *different* positions from those in English sentences are also possible, which can cause confusion. For instance, in English, an adverb cannot come between the verb and object (as in French), e.g. *She drove badly the car.* This is a common mistake, so it's worth pointing out that this word order is not possible.

💿 You could use photocopiable activity 4C on the Teacher's DVD-ROM at this point.

PRONUNCIATION Groups of words 1

2 a Model the first sentence and point out the division between the two groups (//). You could say the sentence with unnatural groups to exemplify how the groups make speech easier to understand, e.g. *Obviously I'd // have liked my kids to // see it too.* Play recording **1.37** so learners can read and hear the sentences.

b Learners practise the sentences either on their own or with a partner. Alternatively, stop after each sentence and ask learners to repeat.

SPEAKING

3 *Preparation.* Learners read one of the true stories and think about the questions. Explain that they will have to tell each other the stories without their books, so encourage them to take notes on a piece of paper. Finally, they choose a few adverbs to make their story more dramatic and interesting. Walk round and help with any problems while learners are preparing their stories.

4 👥 *Story telling.* Make sure learners close their books but understand that they can use their notes. Monitor while they are talking and take a note of any problems that impede communication.

5 *Round-up.* Talk as a class about the stories and how learners would feel (or did feel) in similar situations. Don't go into too much detail if learners have their own stories, because they will get a chance to talk about their own experiences in the Target activity.

4.3 Target activity

Goals: describe a dramatic experience ♻
explain how something happened ♻
say how you feel about an experience ♻

Core language:

TASK VOCABULARY	Common verbs in stories
4.1 VOCABULARY	Accidents and injuries
4.1 VOCABULARY	Saying how something happened
4.2 GRAMMAR	Narrative verb forms

Describe a dramatic experience

TASK LISTENING

1 a *Prediction.* Learners look at the pictures and guess what happened.

b *Listening for main idea.* Play recording **1.38** so learners can check their ideas. In pairs, learners answer the questions about the story. Going through the answers with the class will give you a good opportunity to check learners' use of the narrative tenses.

> 1 She was playing on the stairs with a friend. They were 'surfing' down the stairs.
> 2 Jane was in her study. She was working.
> 3 It went quiet because Megan had fallen and couldn't breathe properly. Her friend hadn't said anything because she was terrified.
> 4 Jane was scared because Megan couldn't speak or move. She was worried she'd hurt her back or neck.
> 5 Megan couldn't move because she was so frightened.

TASK VOCABULARY Common verbs in stories

2 *Listening for detail.* Play recording **1.38** again so learners can complete the sentences. Point out that learners may have to change the verb forms. In feedback, make sure learners notice the verb patterns (see language note below).

> 1 know 2 find out 3 realised 4 remember

Language note: Verb patterns

All these verbs are used to talk about understanding events and are often followed by *what* and verbs such as *happen*, *go on*, *do*. Both the past progressive and past perfect frequently follow these four verbs in the past simple and are interchangeable in sentences 1–3, e.g. *I didn't know what had happened. I went to find out what had happened. I immediately realised what was going on.* In sentence 4, the past progressive is also possible, e.g. *I can't really remember what was going on.*

TASK

3 👤 *Preparation.* Give learners plenty of time to think of an experience to describe and to prepare how to tell their story. Draw attention to the language prompts and remind learners that they can look back at relevant language sections to help. Walk round and help with ideas and language as necessary.

4 👥 *Story telling.* Get learners into groups of three or four and assign A, B, C (and D) roles. Learners take turns to tell their stories and ask for more information and detail. Monitor while they are talking and take a note of use of new language or any problems that made their stories unclear. You can focus on these examples in a feedback session now or later.

5 *Speaking.* Learners decide which story they liked best. Then form new groups of As, Bs, Cs (and Ds). They tell each other the stories they chose from their previous group.

Round-up. Ask the class to choose one or two stories which a lot of people found interesting.

4 Explore

Keyword: *over*

Goal: use common expressions with *over*

Core language:

Use of *over* as a preposition, adverb and adjective
Multi-word verbs with *over*

Meanings of *over*

1 *Listening for main idea.* Learners look at the picture and guess what the person was doing and what has happened. Learners read the question. Then play recording **1.39**. Go through the answers and draw attention to the following expressions:
– *sound-proof windows*
– *a pile of books*
– *burst out laughing*
– *went wrong*

> *They wanted to re-decorate their living room and put in sound-proof windows and a shelf over the door.*

2 Learners do the matching in pairs, or individually before comparing with a partner.

> 1 d 2 b 3 f 4 e 5 c 6 a

3 a 👥 Look at the example with the class (or do it on the board), then learners continue in pairs. Check as a class.

> 2 can't wait for today to be <u>over</u>.
> 3 takes <u>over</u> an hour to get to class.
> 4 has flown <u>over</u> a famous place in a plane.
> 5 goes <u>over</u> a river on the way to work.
> 6 has a picture <u>over</u> their bed.

b Look at the example for sentence 1, then quickly elicit the questions for sentences 2–6 from the class. Tell learners to walk round the class finding someone for each question. Remind them to find out more about each situation and to take a note of the person's name.

Round-up. Find out who said yes to the questions.

Multi-word verbs with *over*

4 a 👥 Focus learners on the picture and ask what has happened (*slip* and *fall over* are recycled from the first spread). Do the first one together, then learners continue in pairs.

> 2 e   3 a   4 f   5 b   6 g   7 c   8 d

b Do this as a class.

> accidents: 1, 2, 3, 8   car accident: 8

5 a 👥 Learners complete the questions. Check as a class and model the linking in the multi-word verbs, paying particular attention to *knocked over* /nɒktˈəʊvə/ and *go over* /ɡəʊwˈəʊvə/. This will help learners' fluency when they do **b**.

> 1 knocked over   2 go over   3 come over   4 get over
> 5 turn over

b *Asking and answering questions.* Learners discuss the questions together. Walk round and monitor use of the multi-word verbs.

Explore speaking

Goal: refer to an earlier topic or conversation

Core language:
Expressions with *say*, *mention*, *talk* for referring to an earlier topic or conversation

1 Learners read the questions to introduce the topic of mixing friends and work. Check understanding (and pronunciation) of *socialise* and *colleagues*. Learners discuss the questions in pairs. Ask a few learners for their ideas.

2 a *Listening for main idea.* Draw attention to the picture of António and see what learners can remember about him (he told the story about the eclipse on p32). Learners read the questions, then listen to recording **1.40**. Point out that *HR* is *human resources* and elicit or teach the meaning of this and *pretty (nervous)*. Sharp learners may have heard the gloss *quite nervous* later in the recording.

> Pam is Don's new girlfriend.
> She's the new head of HR (human resources) at António's company.
> She's feeling pretty nervous about the next day.

b *Listening for main idea.* Explain the context of the next recording, i.e. it's the next day and Pam is in her meeting, then play recording **1.41**. Talk about the question as a class.

> It didn't go very well. Her slide equipment didn't work, and she forgot what she was saying.

3 a 👥 Learners complete the sentences from the conversations. Point out that learners have to put the verbs in the correct form.

> 1 mentioned   2 mentioned   3 talking   4 talking
> 5 saying   6 saying   7 saying

b Learners check their own answers in the scripts on the right.

4 👤/👥 Learners read through the conversation first, and then complete the gaps with verbs from the expressions in **3a**. They compare with a partner, then practise the conversation.

> 1 were you saying
> 2 forgotten what we were talking about
> 3 saying
> 4 mentioned
> 5 was saying

5 a 👥👥 *Conversation.* Look at the topics with the class and check understanding of the activity. Give learners a few minutes to plan what they're going to say.

b Group learners in threes and assign A, B and C roles. Learners have their conversation. Monitor while they're talking for appropriate use of the new language. When learners finish, you could focus on any problems before they continue with **c**.

c Learners change roles and have another conversation.

4 Look again

Review

VOCABULARY Adverbs for telling stories

1 a Learners complete the adverbs in pairs. Check as a class.

> obviously, luckily, amazingly, suddenly, unfortunately

b Ask learners what they think is in the bowl (*noodles*). Then they complete the sentences with the adverbs. They could do this individually before comparing with a partner.

> 1 Amazingly   2 unfortunately   3 Obviously   4 Luckily
> 5 suddenly

c Demonstrate by changing the first sentence to make it true for you. Then learners continue individually before comparing with a partner.

GRAMMAR Narrative verb forms

2 a 👥 Learners read the story before completing it with the verbs. Check as a class.

> 1 rang
> 2 was having
> 3 got
> 4 drove
> 5 heard
> 6 hadn't seen

b 👥 Draw learners' attention to the examples. They then write a sentence (or more if they wish) to finish the story. Walk round and help as necessary. 👥👥 Then they compare stories with another pair. In feedback, ask a few learners to read out their endings and choose the best one with the class.

CAN YOU REMEMBER? – Unit 3 Facts and feelings

3 a Write the first sentence on the board and elicit lots of ideas from different learners. Then they continue completing the sentences individually. Walk round and help as necessary.

b 👥 *Speaking: Personalisation.* Learners talk about their sentences together, asking questions to find out more information. In feedback, ask different learners for their sentences and encourage the class to respond.

Extension

SPELLING AND SOUNDS /k/

4 a Point out the three spelling patterns for /k/. Then play recording **1.42** or say the words from Fran's story. Learners complete the words.

> 1 could   2 looked   3 like   4 canals   5 lucky   6 scary
> 7 because   8 quickly   9 actually   10 luckily
> 11 contact   12 back

b Learners read the spelling patterns to check their answers for **a**.

c *Spellcheck.* Play recording **1.43** or say the words for learners to write down. Let them check their own answers in a dictionary. Check if there are any problems before moving on and encourage learners to take a note of any words they find difficult in their vocabulary notebooks.

NOTICE Time expressions: past and present

5 a 👥 Learners read the sentences then, in pairs, categorise the expressions. Go through the expressions with the class.

> now: 4, 6
> the past: 1, 2, 3, 5

b *Writing.* Learners write a few sentences about themselves using the expressions. Walk round and help as necessary. Point out that they will talk about their sentences in a moment.

c *Speaking: Personalisation.* Learners talk together about their sentences. Encourage them to ask questions to find out more information.

Round-up. Ask a few learners about their partner's present or past activities.

Self-assessment

Go through the list of goals, eliciting language from the unit for each one. You may need to remind learners of the contexts for the goals and let them look back through the unit if necessary. Then they circle the appropriate number for each goal. Walk round while they are doing this and talk to learners about their progress. Remind learners about the extra practice opportunities under the box, and ask where they can find things.

Unit 4 Extra activities on the Teacher's DVD-ROM

Printable worksheets, activity instructions and answer keys are on your Teacher's DVD-ROM.

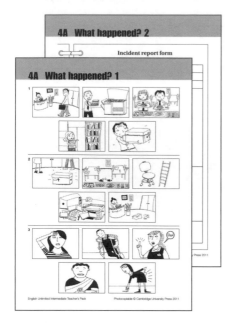

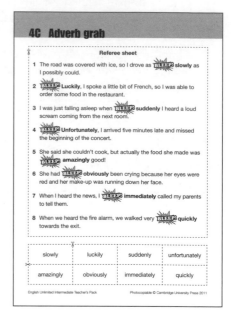

4A What happened?

Activity type: Speaking and vocabulary – Interview / Filling in a form – Pairs

Aim: To practise vocabulary for accidents and injuries and saying how something happened

Language: Accidents and injuries / Saying how something happened – Use at any point from 4.1.

Preparation: Make one copy of both worksheets for each learner. You may want to make more than one copy of Worksheet 2 if you want to repeat the activity.

Time: 30 minutes

4B Pompeii

Activity type: Reading and speaking – Ordering a narrative / Mingle – Groups

Aim: To practise using narrative verb forms

Language: Narrative verb forms – Use at any point from 4.2.

Preparation: Make one copy of the worksheet for every group of six learners and cut each worksheet into six sections. Also make one uncut copy of the worksheet for every learner.

Time: 30 minutes

4C Adverb grab

Activity type: Vocabulary and listening – Aural gap fill – Groups

Aim: To practise using adverbs for telling stories

Language: Adverbs for telling stories – Use at any point from 4.2.

Preparation: Make one copy of the Referee sheet and the Adverb cards for every three learners. Cut up the Adverb cards to make a set of eight cards.

Time: 15 minutes

Unit 4 Self-study Pack

In the Workbook

Unit 4 of the *English Unlimited Intermediate Workbook* offers additional ways to practise the vocabulary and grammar taught in the Coursebook. There are also activities which build reading and writing skills and a whole page of listening and speaking tasks to use with the Interview video, giving your learners the opportunity to hear and react to authentic spoken English.

- **Vocabulary:** Accidents and injuries; Saying how something happened; Natural events; Adverbs for telling stories; Knowledge and understanding
- **Grammar:** Narrative verb forms
- **Time out:** Jokes about accidents and injuries
- **Explore writing:** Web page: Sharing experiences
- **Interview:** A disastrous holiday – Matt

On the DVD-ROM

Unit 4 of the *English Unlimited Intermediate Self-study DVD-ROM* contains interactive games and activities for your learners to practise and improve their vocabulary, grammar and pronunciation, and also their speaking and listening, with the possibility for learners to record themselves, and a video of authentic spoken English to use with the Workbook.

- **Vocabulary and grammar:** Extra practice activities
- **Pronunciation:** Groups of words
- **Explore speaking:** Reacting to apologies
- **Explore listening:** A news broadcast
- **Video:** A disastrous holiday

5 A change of plan

5.1

Goals: discuss plans and arrangements
make offers and promises

Core language:

VOCABULARY	*be supposed to, be meant to*
GRAMMAR	Future forms
PRONUNCIATION	Common pairs of words 2

A helping hand

LISTENING

1 a 👥 / 👥 *Pre-listening discussion.* Focus learners on the list of situations and check understanding of *locked yourself out* and *broken down.* Learners discuss the situations in pairs or groups.

   b Ask one or two learners for their stories and a few others about what they would do in the situations.

2 *Listening for main idea.* Ask the class what they think has happened in the picture. Ask how he might get into his house and elicit *ladder* and *inside.* Allow learners to read the questions, then play recording **1.44**. Stop after each conversation, so learners can discuss the questions with a partner. Play the conversations again if necessary. Check all the answers. Draw attention to *runs out, goes dead* and *dying* for talking about mobiles.

> 1 *Rob's mum is visiting him.*
> 2 *He's locked himself out of the house, and his car keys and wallet are inside.*
> 3 *Jon's car is at the garage.*
> 4 *Amy offers to drive to the station to pick her up.*
> 5 *Rob's going to find a ladder so he can climb in an upstairs window.*
> 6 *Rob's mobile dies / the battery runs out.*

3 a *Listening for detail.* Learners read the sentences about Rob's situation and tick or correct them. Then play recording **1.44** again so they can check their answers.

> 1 ✓
> 2 ✓
> 3 *He hasn't lost his car keys, they're in the house.*
> 4 *Jon's car is in the garage, not Rob's.*
> 5 ✓
> 6 *Amy had arranged a bike ride, not Rob.*
> 7 *There is a window open upstairs.*
> 8 *Rob isn't supposed to be at work, but Jon is.*

   b *Prediction.* Get some ideas from the class about how Rob will get back into his house.

   c Play recording **1.45** so learners can check their ideas and round off the listening.

Optional extra: Prepositions

Write out these prepositional expressions from the first part of recording **1.44**, with the underlined prepositions gapped, and ask learners to fill the gaps:

locked myself <u>out</u>
<u>at</u> the train station
<u>in</u> the house
<u>on</u> her mobile
arriving <u>in</u> five minutes
go <u>to</u> the station
<u>at</u> home

Then play recording **1.44** again to check. Point out that *at* and *to* are pronounced as weak forms and help learners notice the schwa sounds and linking in the recording, e.g. *up at the train station* /pət/. Learners could say different parts of the script in pairs to practise the schwa sound and improve fluency.

VOCABULARY *be supposed to, be meant to*

4 Learners match beginnings and ends of sentences from the script. Draw attention to the use of *but* to explain why the plan didn't or isn't going to happen.

> *1c 2b 3a*

5 👤 Draw learners' attention to the example. Then learners continue individually and write two further sentences of their own.

 You could use photocopiable activity 5A on the Teacher's DVD-ROM at this point.

Sorting out arrangements

GRAMMAR Future forms

1 *Focus on meaning and form.* Learners read the three sentences from the conversations (1–3) and the three descriptions of use (a–c). Learners match them in pairs. Then check as a class and give learners a chance to say the sentences to practise the contraction *I'll*, and the weak form in *I'm going to* /tə/ *find.* Elicit the negative and question forms from the class.

> *1b 2c 3a*

2 a 👤 *Practice.* Learners read the conversation and circle the correct forms. Don't go through the answers, as this will pre-empt **b**.

> 1 *I'll make*   2 *I'm going to go*   3 *I'll come*   4 *I'll go*
> 5 *are we going to*   6 *we're going*   7 *we're going*
> 8 *are we going to*   9 *I'll look*

   b Learners discuss their answers together. Find out if there were any differences of opinion, then play recording **1.46** to check. Go through any problems with the class.

Note: Grammar practice

You could do the grammar practice on p138 at this point.

 You could use photocopiable activity 5B on the Teacher's DVD-ROM at this point.

PRONUNCIATION Common pairs of words 2

3 a *Books closed.* Learners write the six sentences they hear. Play recording **1.47** or say the sentences, giving learners time to write each one before playing the next one.

> 1 What are we going to see?
> 2 Do you want to do anything later?
> 3 I have to buy some food.
> 4 I need a few things at the shops.
> 5 We're going to the theatre.
> 6 I'll look for the theatre programme.

b 👥 Let learners compare their ideas with a partner before checking their sentences.

c Point out that there are pairs of words in each sentence that are often found together and are not always easy to distinguish because they are linked when we say them. Play recording **1.47** again or say each pair of words one at a time so learners can repeat them. Then learners practise saying them in the sentences.

SPEAKING

4 a 👥 *Preparation.* Explain to learners that they are going to have conversations about a problem in groups of three. They choose one of the situations together which they will prepare in **b** and perform in **5a**. Assign roles A, B and C to learners in each group.

b 👤 Focus learners on the flow chart of the conversation and give them a few minutes to prepare what they want to say. Remind them to use the vocabulary and grammar from the unit.

5 a 👥 *Role play.* Learners have their conversation. Monitor while learners are talking and check for any problems with the target language. You could go through any important problems with the class before learners do **b**.

b 👥 Learners change roles and choose a new problem. Then they have another conversation.

Round-up. Find out what sort of solutions learners found to their problems.

5.2

Goals: talk about something that went wrong
talk about changes of plan

Core language:

VOCABULARY	no chance, no way
GRAMMAR	Future in the past

Fate?

LISTENING

1 a *Listening for main idea.* Focus learners on the situations and talk about what they involve (fate and chance). This will set the context for the listening and provide a model for learners' discussions below. Learners read the summaries of the two people's views, then listen to recording **1.48** and circle the correct words.

> 1 happen   2 can   3 believes   4 like

---

b *Pre-reading discussion.* Learners discuss the question in pairs or groups. Get some feedback from the class.

> **Language note: Agreeing**
>
> In this authentic text, both Munizha and Pierre signal agreement in ways that are not often taught: *I'm exactly the same* and *Oh yes, absolutely.* You could ask learners to listen again and notice how they agree with each other. Give them an opportunity to practise saying the expressions, particularly focusing on the stress and intonation in *absolutely*.

READING

2 *Jigsaw reading.* Learners read the introduction. Ask what the stories are about. Then divide learners into As and Bs to read their story and answer the questions.

> **Hans's story**
> 1 He met Chin Mae when she came to Bonn in Germany about 30 years before.
> 2 Chin Mae had to go back to her home in Korea for family reasons and they lost touch.
> 3 He wrote a letter to her and sent it to her parents' address.
> 4 Hans was woken by the phone ringing. It was Chin Mae.
> 5 Her parents forgot to give it to her. It fell behind a bookcase and remained there for over 20 years.
> 6 They got married.
>
> **Maggie's story**
> 1 Maggie was planning to have a big party to celebrate her 25th birthday, with dinner and dancing.
> 2 There was a power cut.
> 3 There was a storm with rain and thunder.
> 4 He told her that the hall was struck by lightning which destroyed the roof.
> 5 She was upset because it ruined her party.
> 6 She found it funny.
> 7 She spent the evening talking to a man. They got on really well and he asked her out on a date. Later, they got married.

> **Alternative for weaker groups**
>
> Learners work in A/A and B/B pairs to answer the questions together and to prepare telling their story. In **3b**, they can join a B/B pair to tell their stories, but the previous support may make this unnecessary.

3 a 👤/👥 *Preparation.* Learners use the questions to prepare telling the story to a partner. Point out that the questions give learners the key points in each story. Let learners refer to the story if they need to check details. Walk round and help while they are preparing.

b 👥 *Round-up.* Working in A/B pairs, learners take turns to tell each other their stories. Monitor while they're talking and note any problems that impede communication. Get learners' opinions on the stories, and ask if there are any similarities between them.

VOCABULARY *no chance, no way*

4   🧍/👥 Learners match the expressions to the meanings. They can do this in pairs or individually before comparing with a partner. Check as a class.

> *1 b   2 b   3 c   4 a   5 d*

5   a   👥 *Writing sentences.* Learners choose two of these topics or their own idea. They talk about the topic and work out how they can use expressions from **4**. Walk round and help with ideas and language as necessary.

   b   👥 Learners swap partners and discuss the ideas they talked about in **a**.

   Round-up. Ask different learners for a sentence about each of the topics. Encourage the class to respond where possible.

What went wrong?

GRAMMAR Future in the past

1   a   *Focus on meaning.* Learners read the sentences from Maggie's story. Answer the questions as a class.

> *1 past plans*
> *2 were going to have; was supposed to be*

   b   *Focus on form.* Elicit the verb form that follows *were going to* and *was supposed to* (infinitive). Then learners check Hans's story for another example of each form which suggests an event didn't happen, *were going to* and *was supposed to*.

> *were going to: We were going to get married.*
> *was supposed to: She was only supposed to be in Germany for two weeks. / I'm so glad my letter ended up where it was supposed to be.*

Language note: Past progressive

These two uses of the past progressive reflect two common uses of the present progressive: **1** describing an activity (*she was helping her mother*) and **2** describing a plan (*We were going to get married*: future in the past).

2   a   👥 *Practice: Writing.* Ask who Maggie is and how she met her husband. Then focus learners on the story situation and pictures and ask them what her plans were by eliciting the end of the sentence in the prompt (e.g. *While he was at work I was going to … make him a cake.*). Walk round and help as necessary.

   b   Play recording **1.49** so learners can find out what went wrong. Ask if anyone came up with a different storyline.

3   *Writing.* Learners discuss possible endings for the story and write their versions. Walk round and help while they are writing. Then play recording **1.50**. Get learners' response to the ending.

Note: Grammar practice

You coud do the grammar practice on p139 at this point.

SPEAKING

4   a   🧍*Preparation.* Ask if anyone in the class has had a similar experience to Maggie's. Tell learners to think of their own stories about plans which have changed. Draw attention to the prompts, but make sure learners know they can choose their own ideas. Encourage learners to use the questions to help prepare their stories. Walk round and help with ideas or language while they're preparing.

   b   👥 *Storytelling.* Learners tell their stories in groups. If anyone couldn't think of a story, tell them to wait until the end to see if other learners' stories remind them of an experience of their own.

5.3 Target activity

Goals: discuss plans and arrangements ♻
               talk about changes of plan ♻
               catch up with old friends' news

Core language:

TASK VOCABULARY	Catching up
5.1 VOCABULARY	*be supposed to, be meant to*
5.1 GRAMMAR	Future forms
5.2 GRAMMAR	Future in the past

Attend a reunion

TASK LISTENING

1   *Pre-listening discussion.* Focus learners on the picture and see if they can guess what kind of party it is. Then learners read the introduction to the email. Find out if anyone in the class has been to a reunion party like this. Discuss the questions in pairs or as a class.

2   *Listening for main idea.* Check learners remember when Carolina and Iqbal were at university (ten years ago) and ask them to guess what they might talk about (e.g. work, families, memories about what they were going to do). Play recording **1.51**, then learners discuss the question in pairs.

> *Iqbal loves his life in Kuala Lumpur. Carolina is a bit bored at the moment.*

TASK VOCABULARY Catching up

3 a *Listening for detail.* Focus learners on the sentences from the conversation. Then play recording **1.51** again. Learners can write *C* or *I* after each sentence.

> 1 Iqbal 2 Carolina 3 Iqbal 4 Carolina 5 Carolina
> 6 Iqbal 7 Iqbal

Alternative

Learners predict the answers for **3a** before listening. Then play recording **1.51** to check.

b 👥 Do a few examples on the board. Then learners choose a word from each expression as a prompt. In groups, learners use their words to remember the expressions. Remind learners to record new words and expressions in their vocabulary notebooks.

TASK

4 a 👤 *Preparation: Ideas.* Talk through the situation with the class and point out the role cards. Assign roles, then learners complete their role cards.

b 👤 *Preparation: Language.* Give learners time to plan what they want to say. Walk round and help as necessary.

5 👥 Learners have their conversations in groups. Point out that they will have to remember what their partners told them for the next activity. Monitor while learners are talking and take a note of any useful language and common mistakes for a feedback session.

6 👥 Learners tell their new groups about the people they had conversations with in **5**.

5 Explore

Across cultures: Saying no

Goals: raise awareness of cultural similarities and differences
talk about how people say no politely in different cultures

Core language

VOCABULARY	Saying no politely

LISTENING

1 a *Listening for main idea.* Look at the pictures with the class and ask learners to predict what type of misunderstandings they might be about. Then play recording **1.52** so learners can answer the question.

> *Mark is talking about a work situation. Victor is talking about friends.*

b *Listening for detail.* Learners read through the questions. Then play recording **1.52** again. Stop after Mark's story, so learners can compare their ideas. Go through the questions or let learners check their ideas in the script on p151. Check understanding of *business deal* and *offended*.

> **Mark**
> 1 He was working in Paris, France.
> 2 He had to go to Japan to discuss a business deal.
> 3 He thought the Japanese had accepted the deal.
> 4 They sent an email the next day apologising for not accepting the deal.
>
> **Victor**
> 1 Victor is from Brazil, but he lives in Boston, USA.
> 2 Sarah is an American woman who married José Carlos, a friend of Victor's.
> 3 He told them he would love to come to their wedding, and Sarah thought that meant he would definitely come. So she was upset when, a couple of weeks before the wedding, he said he couldn't come.
> 4 He has learned to be more careful about saying no to Americans, to be more direct.

2 *Response.* Give learners a moment to discuss the reasons briefly, then talk as a class.

> *The misunderstandings arose from the different attitudes of the people involved towards saying no. According to the speakers, both the Japanese and the Brazilians in the stories were not comfortable saying no directly. Mark suggests this is not the case for the French and English, and Victor suggests the same about the Americans.*

Optional extra

Elicit more verb collocations with *business deal*, e.g. *discuss, sign, negotiate, agree on, accept, reject + a business deal*. You could also point out that another more colloquial (American) expression is *to shake on it* (to agree a deal by shaking hands). The fact that the men smiled and shook hands could have added to Mark's confusion.

VOCABULARY Saying no politely

3 a 👥 Learners categorise the extracts. Check understanding and pronunciation of *actually* /ˈæktʃəlɪ/ and *unfortunately* /ʌnˈfɔːtʃənətlɪ/ (learners should remember this from Unit 4). Ask which expressions are more formal (A and F) and why (they're written and in a work context). Model the expressions for the class, drawing learners' attention to the intonation.

> 1 F 2 D, E 3 A 4 B 5 C

b 👥 / 👥 Learners compare the ways of saying no with expressions in their own language(s). In feedback, find out about similar expressions in learners' language(s).

Language note: Softeners

All the expressions soften a rejection, written or spoken. It would be useful to compare this aspect with learners' languages, for instance, whether other languages use the polite convention (*Yes, but no*) as in English.

4 a 👤 Focus learners on the situations and check understanding of *acquaintance* and *suitable*. Do the first one together as an example, then learners continue on their own.

> 1 D, E
> 2 B, D
> 3 F
> 4 D, E
> 5 C
> 6 B, E, (D)

b 👥 Learners have conversations for the situations, taking turns to start each new conversation. Remind learners that the expressions are polite ('soft') ways of saying no.

c 👥/👥👥 Learners discuss what they would really do if these situations came up. Broaden this into a class discussion if learners have a lot to say.

SPEAKING

5 a *Preparation.* Give an example of your own to demonstrate the activity. Then give learners time to think of a situation and to prepare how to describe it. Walk round and help as necessary.

b 👥👥 *Discussion.* Learners discuss their situations in groups. Encourage them to respond to each other's stories, and to say whether they would do the same thing or something different.

Round-up. Ask a few learners to explain their situations to the class and find out what other learners would do and why.

Explore writing

Goals: make offers and promises in emails or letters
refer back in emails or letters

Core language:

Offers and promises to do something
Referring to previous topics of conversation

1 👥 Learners focus on the photo and context, then read the questions, before reading the emails between Maya and Kyoko, and the email from Melissa. They discuss the questions in pairs. If learners draw attention to the fact that the order of the emails would be reversed in real life, you can point out that authenticity has been suspended here in favour of clarity!

> 1 Maya promises to talk to a friend about schools and get back to Kyoko. She doesn't get back to Kyoko, but she does ask her friend to contact Kyoko directly with information.
> 2 Kyoko is going to stay with Maya in her spare room.
> 3 Kyoko offers to bring Maya something from Tokyo.
> 4 Melissa is a friend of Maya's who teaches at Addison's Language Centre in Dublin. She recommends a different school, Westbrook's, for Business English.

Language note: Register

The emails between the friends use an informal style in which words are dropped (e.g. *Great to hear ...*; *Haven't heard ...*), greetings are shortened (*Thanks, Maya*), words and names are abbreviated (*info, K*) and punctuation is relaxed (note the dashes). In contrast, Melissa's email is slightly more formal because she doesn't know Kyoko.

2 👥 *Focus on expressions.* Learners do the matching, then check as a class.

> | 1a 2c 3d 4b 5b 6d 7a 8b 9a |

3 a ✍ *Writing.* Tell learners to write 'real' requests for someone in the class. Walk round while learners are writing and help as necessary.

b ✍ Learners respond to the requests with language from **2**.

c 👥 Learners read the responses and discuss their exchanges together. In feedback, ask a few learners to read out some requests and responses in pairs.

4 a 👥 *Preparation.* Learners work together to generate ideas for their email exchanges. Walk round and help with ideas if necessary.

b 👥 Learners use their ideas to write an email to a new partner. Monitor while learners are writing and check their use of the new expressions. When they're ready, pairs exchange emails and read and reply to their partner's email. Pairs read and exchange again, giving explanations for what has or hasn't happened.

5 Learners exchange all their emails with another pair. They read the email 'chain' and answer the questions.

Round-up. Find out from a few learners what other pairs offered, if they did it, and if not, what excuses they gave.

 You could use photocopiable activity 5C on the Teacher's DVD-ROM at this point.

5 Look again

Review

VOCABULARY *be supposed to, be meant to*

1 a Do the first sentence together on the board as an example. Learners continue individually before comparing with a partner. Check as a class.

> *Possible answers*
> 1 I'm meant to be going to work now, but my car won't start.
> 2 I'm supposed to be doing my homework at the moment, but I'm too tired.
> 3 I'm supposed to be seeing a friend later on, but I'm not feeling well.
> 4 I'm meant to be having a meeting now, but my boss is late.
> 5 I'm supposed to be getting the bus home, but I have to work late.

b 👥/👥👥 Elicit a few alternative endings from the class. Learners brainstorm ideas in pairs.

GRAMMAR Future in the past

2 a Learners order the words to make sentences. Answer the question as a class. You could elicit some reasons why the party and holiday didn't happen.

> 1 I was going to have a big birthday party when I was 21.
> 2 I was supposed to be going on holiday last summer.
> 3 My friends were coming to visit me in Italy two years ago. / My friends in Italy were coming to visit me two years ago.
> (1 and 2 suggest something didn't happen.)

b ✍ *Preparation.* Give learners time to think of some ideas and to work out how to express their ideas. Walk round and help with language or ideas.

c 👥/👥👥 *Speaking: Personalisation.* Learners tell each other about their failed plans and how they felt about it.

Round-up. Find out about a few learners' experiences and how they felt.

CAN YOU REMEMBER? Unit 4 – Accidents and injuries

3 a Elicit possible collocations for *drop (something)* and point out that most of the verbs go with more than one option. Learners continue to match up the collocations in pairs.

> *drop something*
> *cut your finger / your head*
> *slip over, slip on something*
> *bang your head*
> *trip over, trip on something*
> *fall over*
> *break something / your finger*

b 👥 Elicit some examples from the class for the first one and write a sentence on the board, e.g. **If you're running for the bus, you might** *trip over something.* This sentence frame will help learners to discuss possible injuries while doing the activities in the list.

c 👥👥 Pairs work together to compare their ideas.

Round-up. Get some examples from different learners in the class.

Extension

SPELLING AND SOUNDS /r/

4 a Say the words or play recording **1.53**. Learners listen and underline the /r/ sounds.

> *wrong, wrote, wrap, promises, garage, ride, right, research, worry, borrow, arriving, correct*

b 👤 Learners should do this individually, then check with a partner.

> *1 promises, garage, ride, right, research*
> *2 wrong, wrote, wrap*
> *3 worry, borrow, arriving, correct*

c 👥 *Spellcheck.* Learners choose ten words from **a** and **b**, then dictate the words to a partner. They change roles, then check all the spellings together. Remind learners to write down any words they find difficult in their vocabulary notebooks.

NOTICE *this* in stories

5 a Look at the example sentences with the class and explain the use of *this* in informal stories. In feedback, encourage learners to practise saying the sentences with *this*. This will help them with **b**.

> 1 There was this incredible bolt of lightning.
> 2 My friends and I were preparing everything when suddenly we heard this huge crash.
> 3 I was walking down the road when I saw this man robbing a bank.
> 4 I've just bought this great new computer game.

> **Alternative**
>
> *Books closed.* Write the example sentences on the board and ask what *this* could be replaced by (*a/an*). Then dictate the sentences using *a* or *an*, e.g. *There was an incredible bolt of lightning.* In pairs, learners decide where to use *this* to replace the articles.

b *Preparation.* Give learners time to think of a story and to work out how to use *this* in their stories. Walk round and help as necessary.

c 👥 / 👥👥 *Storytelling.* Learners tell their stories in pairs or groups. Monitor for appropriate use of *this*.

Self-assessment

Go through the list of goals, eliciting language from the unit for each one. You may need to remind learners of the contexts for the goals and let them look back through the unit if necessary. Then they circle the appropriate number for each goal. Walk round while they are doing this and talk to learners about their progress. Remind learners about the extra practice opportunities under the box, and ask where they can find things.

Unit 5 Extra activities on the Teacher's DVD-ROM

Printable worksheets, activity instructions and answer keys are on your Teacher's DVD-ROM.

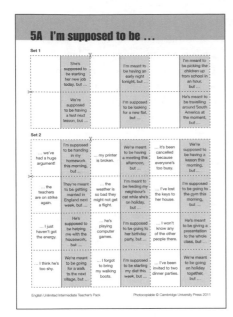

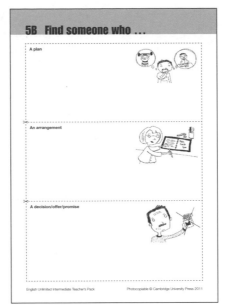

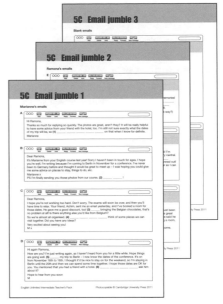

5A I'm supposed to be …

Activity type: Vocabulary – Dominoes – Pairs

Aim: To practise vocabulary used for changing plans

Language: *be supposed to, be meant to* – Use at any point from 5.1.

Preparation: Make one copy of the worksheet for every pair. Cut Set 2 to make a set of 12 dominoes. Do not cut up Set 1 until Stage 3 of the activity.

Time: 20 minutes

5B Find someone who …

Activity type: Grammar – Group mingle – Individuals/Groups

Aim: To practise future forms

Language: Future forms – Use at any point from 5.1.

Preparation: Make one copy of the worksheet for each learner.

Time: 30 minutes

5C Email jumble

Activity type: Reading, writing and vocabulary – Ordering activity – Pairs

Aim: To practise making offers and referring back in emails

Language: *I'll get back to you*; *As far as … is concerned, …*; *I'll ask … about it*; *… as promised*; *About …*; *You were going to …*; *Did you manage to …?*; *I'll remind …* – Use at any point from Explore writing.

Preparation: Make one copy of the three worksheets for every pair of learners.

Time: 30 minutes

Unit 5 Self-study Pack

In the Workbook

Unit 5 of the *English Unlimited Intermediate Workbook* offers additional ways to practise the vocabulary and grammar taught in the Coursebook. There are also activities which build reading and writing skills and a whole page of listening and speaking tasks to use with the Interview video, giving your learners the opportunity to hear and react to authentic spoken English.

- **Vocabulary:** *be supposed to, be meant to*; *no chance, no way*; Catching up; Saying no politely
- **Grammar:** Future forms; Future in the past
- **My English:** English words in other languages
- **Explore reading:** Web page: Planning a party
- **Interview:** Reunions – Fabiola and Leo

On the DVD-ROM

Unit 5 of the *English Unlimited Intermediate Self-study DVD-ROM* contains interactive games and activities for your learners to practise and improve their vocabulary, grammar and pronunciation, and also their speaking and listening, with the possibility for learners to record themselves, and a video of authentic spoken English to use with the Workbook.

- **Vocabulary and grammar:** Extra practice activities
- **Pronunciation:** Common pairs of words
- **Explore speaking:** *Oh*
- **Explore listening:** Rescheduling
- **Video:** Reunions

Let me explain

6.1

Goals: give advice
talk about how you manage money

Core language:

VOCABULARY   Linking expressions
Multi-word verbs: managing money

Saving money

VOCABULARY Linking expressions

Optional introduction

If you know your class well enough, ask them how much money they have in their pockets or bags today. Ask them if that's enough for the day. Compare the value of some of the amounts to a British pound. Then continue with **1**.

1   *Reading for main idea.* Draw attention to the headline of the article and the picture of Kath Kelly in the continuation of the article on p47. Check understanding of *a pound*. Then learners read the introduction to the article and answer the question. Discuss the relative value of a pound in learners' own currencies so they understand the context. Ask learners what they think of Kath's idea.

> In order to save money to buy a wedding present for her brother.

2 **a** Learners brainstorm ways of saving money. If you write their ideas onto the board, this will help learners when they write tips in **3b**.

b Focus learners on the tips and the pictures. Learners do the matching and compare their ideas with Kath's.

> A3 B5 C2 D1 E4 F6

c Discuss the tips with the class. Find out if anyone does or has done any of these things to save money.

Language note: Linking expressions

Learners should be familiar with *if, when* and *after,* but you'll need to check understanding of *instead of* (= in the place of somebody or something), *in case* (= because something might happen) and *whenever* (= at any time). You could give learners these extra tips and elicit the linking words from the class:
1 I recycle containers … I can. (*whenever*)
2 I read the news online … buying newspapers. (*instead of*)
3 Never hurry when you're shopping … you miss bargains. (*in case*)

3 **a** *Focus on form.* Draw attention to the patterns so learners can use the linking expressions productively.

> a if, when, whenever, in case
> b instead of
> c after

b *Practice.* Write *Cycle or hitchhike …* on the board and elicit different endings from the class. Learners then complete the advice with their own ideas and write three more tips. Remind them to use their ideas from **2a** and encourage them to be creative (but not necessarily too serious!). Walk round and help with ideas or language as necessary.

Alternative

Learners work in A/A and B/B pairs. Learner As complete tips 1–3, Learner Bs complete tips 4–6 with their own ideas on a piece of paper. Walk round and check learners' sentences while they're writing. Learners close their books and change to A/B pairs. A says their sentences to B, without saying the linking expressions. B guesses the linking expressions. Then change roles. A/B pairs write three new tips together. In **4**, you could focus only on learners' own tips.

4   Each pair chooses their top five tips from the lesson and tells the class. You could listen to all the tips, then vote as a class. Alternatively, with a big class, you could ask the class to choose the best one from each pair, put that tip on the board, then choose the top five at the end.

 You could use photocopiable activity 6A on the Teacher's DVD-ROM at this point.

Living cheaply

READING

1   *Reading for main idea.* Point out that this is the rest of the article about Kath Kelly. Learners read the questions before they start reading.

> 1 She made sandwiches and soup instead of going out to lunch. She bought fresh food at the end of the day when small shops were selling it cheaply. She picked fruit from bushes and trees and looked out for free buffets. She went to see her friends or left notes if they were out instead of phoning them. She used the library for free internet access. She picked up coins in the street.
> 2 yes
> 3 It changed her outlook on life. She used to enjoy spending money on treats, but after her year of saving, she didn't want expensive things and so didn't spend much money at all.

2   *Reading for detail.* Learners read the article again to find more detailed information. They can work individually before comparing ideas with a partner. Check as a class.

> 1 She used them to make soup.
> 2 She couldn't afford to take her friends out, so she took them to public events which were free.
> 3 It was her emergency fund, but she didn't need it.
> 4 She wanted to visit her brother in France.
> 5 She had to go to the dentist.
> 6 She moved in with Bruce Taylor, who she'd formed a relationship with.

3 *Discussion.* Learners discuss the question in groups, or talk about it with the class to round off the topic.

VOCABULARY Multi-word verbs: managing money

4 *Focus on multi-word verbs.* Tell learners to close their books and do the matching from memory. Then they read to check.

> 2 e   3 a   4 f   5 d   6 b

5 Learners complete the questions in pairs or individually before comparing with a partner.

> 1 saved up   2 keep to   3 look out for   4 given up
> 5 keep to / survive on

SPEAKING

6 *Speaking: Personalisation.* Learners ask and answer the questions in pairs or groups. Walk round and check use of the new language.

Round-up. Find out who is good with money in the class. Then go through any problems learners had with the language.

 You could use photocopiable activity 6B on the Teacher's DVD-ROM at this point.

6.2

Goals: give detailed instructions
give advice ♻

Core language:

VOCABULARY	Using equipment
PRONUNCIATION	Linking consonants and vowels
GRAMMAR	Verb + *-ing*

What do I do next?

READING

1 *Reading for main idea.* These two short true stories introduce the topic of following instructions. Although the texts are short, the vocabulary is quite challenging, but encourage learners to read them through and answer the question in pairs, before going through problems with the class. Make sure learners understand *building site, baggage chute* and *luggage belt* and model pronunciation of /ˈbægɪdʒ/, /ˈlʌgɪdʒ/ and /ʃuːt/. The stories may prompt learners' own stories of similar events in the news.

> **Optional extra**
>
> The stories include two lexical sets of words about driving and travelling by plane. Divide learners into As and Bs. Learner As underline all the words in the first story about driving (*motorist, satellite navigation system, drove, 4x4, crashed*). Learner Bs underline all the words about flying (*baggage chute, airport, check-in signs, boarding, international flight, departure lounge, suitcase, luggage belt*). They discuss the meaning of all the words, and divide up the unknown words to look up in dictionaries between them. Encourage them to record new words in their vocabulary notebooks.

2 a 👥 Check understanding of *assembling flat-pack furniture.* Learners discuss what their approaches would be to these problems. In feedback, find out what different learners would do.

b *Speaking: Personalisation.* Learners talk about their own experiences of not understanding instructions. Find out if different learners have had similar experiences.

LISTENING

3 a *Listening for main idea.* Look at the questions and ask learners to guess what is happening and who Vishal is talking to. Then play recording **2.1**. Learners answer the questions in pairs. Check as a class.

> 1 He can't get online.   2 no

> **Alternative for weaker classes**
>
> You may want to pre-teach some of the technical vocabulary from the conversation, e.g. *router, icon, screen, socket.*

b 👥 Learners try to put the stages in order from memory but also using their knowledge of computers. Point out that it is fine to guess at this stage. Don't go through the answers, as this will pre-empt **c**.

> e *suggests turning the computer off and on again.*
> d *gives Vishal some advice about his router.*
> a *tests the signal and says it's OK.*
> b *explains how Vishal can check his internet connection.*
> c *tells Vishal to test his equipment using a different socket.*

c Play recording **2.1** again so learners can check their ideas. Go through any problems with the class.

> **Alternative for weaker classes**
>
> If your group is put off by the technical topic or complexity of the listening, let them read the script while they listen and check the order.

VOCABULARY Using equipment

4 a *Focus on verbs for using equipment.* Read through the sentences with the class, then give learners a few minutes to try to complete them with the verbs. Draw attention to the example – *switching everything off* – and point out that the multi-word verbs are separated in the same way (which narrows down the options in the sentences). Don't go through the answers yet, as this will pre-empt **b**.

> 2 press   3 turned; off   4 check   5 Click on; open
> 6 plugged; in   7 shut; down   8 Unplug

b Play recording **2.2** to check the answers.

c *Focus on meaning.* Learners can discuss this in pairs. Then check as a class.

> 1 switch on – switch off; turn on – turn off; plug – unplug
> 2 switch on/off = turn on/off

d Talk about this with the class and encourage learners to use the new vocabulary if appropriate.

PRONUNCIATION Linking consonants and vowels

5 a *Focus on linking consonants and vowels.* Write *turn it on* on the board. Model it for the class and ask learners which sounds between words are linked. Elicit or teach the rule. Tell learners to say all the expressions to a partner and mark the links in pairs.

> 1 turn‿it‿on
> 2 switch‿it‿off
> 3 plug‿it‿in
> 4 shut‿it‿down
> 5 click‿on‿it

b Play recording **2.3** or say the expressions for learners to check. Stop after each one so learners can repeat the expressions.

SPEAKING

6 a *Listening for main idea.* Set the context for the class, then play recording **2.4**. Play it several times if necessary and let learners discuss their ideas with a partner before checking as a class.

> It's an MP3 player.

b 👥 Learners can use script **2.4** as a model for their own instructions. Walk round and help as necessary. Point out that learners should not say what the equipment is in their instructions.

c 👥 / 👥👥 Change pairs, or join pairs together, or ask pairs to read their instructions for the class to guess.

Have you thought about …?

GRAMMAR Verb + *-ing*

1 a 👥 Remind learners that they have heard all these sentences in Vishal's conversation to the helpline. Point out that the matching depends on context, not form, i.e. grammatically, there are a number of possibilities. Learners do the matching. Check as a class.

> 2 c   3 a   4 f   5 b   6 e

b *Focus on meaning.* Give learners a few moments to discuss this before going through it with the class.

> a: 1, 6   b: 2, 3, 4, 5

2 a *Practice.* Let learners try doing this individually before comparing with a partner. This gives you a chance to check that they have understood the expressions. Point out to learners that they need to put the verbs in the correct form. Don't check the answers at this stage.

> 1 can't face going   2 keeps asking   3 tried talking
> 4 avoid going   5 considered telling

b *Listening to check.* Play recording **2.5** so learners can check their answers. Give them an opportunity to repeat the gapped sentences to practise saying the verbs in context. Ask a few learners what they would do in Vishal's situation.

 You could use photocopiable activity 6C on the Teacher's DVD-ROM at this point.

SPEAKING

3 👤 *Preparation.* Give learners time to think of some things they aren't happy about and to work out how to talk about them. Walk round and help with ideas or language.

4 👥 / 👥👥 *Speaking: Personalisation.* Either refer learners to Vishal and Nicky's conversation or demonstrate by talking to a confident learner yourself. Then learners discuss their problems in pairs or groups and give each other advice. Monitor while they are talking and check for any problems that impede communication.

6.3 Target activity

Goals: give advice ♻
talk about how you manage money ♻
give reasons for advice

Core language:

TASK VOCABULARY	Giving reasons
6.1 VOCABULARY	Linking expressions
6.1 VOCABULARY	Multi-word verbs: managing money
6.2 GRAMMAR	Verb + -ing

Give expert advice

TASK LISTENING

1 *Pre-listening discussion.* Learners look at the pictures and the question. They talk in pairs or discuss the question as a class. This will set the context for the listening.

> **Intercultural note**
>
> In multilingual/multicultural classrooms, there are likely to be very different attitudes towards money and how it should be handled in a couple. The advice in the listening is typical of a Western European viewpoint, but not all learners will agree with Jörg. Encourage the class to be open to different opinions and try to help people to feel comfortable expressing their ideas.

2 **a** *Listening for main idea.* Focus learners on the context and ask what kind of radio show it is and if they listen to this kind of show. Then play recording **2.6**. Learners put the advice in the correct order.

> d, a, c, b

b *Listening for detail.* Give learners a minute to think about this with a partner before playing recording **2.6** again. Discuss whether it's good advice with the class (see *Intercultural note* on the previous page).

> *4 Because money is a source of conflict, and often relationships fail because couples don't communicate about money.*
> *1 Because couples often share the payment for lots of things, e.g. household expenses.*
> *2 So you can pay your bills but also have enough for holidays and emergencies.*
> *3 So you can buy nice things occasionally.*

TASK VOCABULARY Giving reasons

3 **a** Learners read the sentence beginnings from the recording and complete Jörg's advice with a partner. Play recording **2.6** again for them to check or allow them to check their ideas in the script on p152.

> *1 the consequences can be very serious.*
> *2 a big issue ...*
> *3 online.*
> *4 financial issues.*
> *5 resentment about money.*
> *6 negotiate these payments every month ...*
> *7 buy yourself something from time to time.*

b Draw attention to the pairs or groups of sentences, pointing out that each group has a similar meaning or function, apart from 6 and 7. Focus learners on the form, then give them time to answer the questions in pairs before going through it with the class.

> *1 nouns: because of, due to; subject + verb: because, since, as, so, so that*
> *2 In sentence 7, you can use 'so' and 'so that'.*

> **Language note: so and so that**
>
> *So* has two different functions in the two sentences: in 6, it gives a result and in 7, it explains purpose. *That* is optional, but if you **can't** include *that* (as in 6), the function is giving a result. If learners don't understand this point, focus on the first part of the sentence and ask *Why?* If the second part answers the question, the function is purpose, not result.

4 **a** *Writing sentences.* Learners think of their own advice about managing money and write four sentences using the prompts. Walk round while they're writing and help as necessary.

b *Discussion.* Learners discuss their ideas in groups. Find out if there are different opinions in the class.

TASK

5 **a** *Preparation: Ideas.* Focus learners on the list of options, but point out that they can give advice about any topic they know about. Learners choose their topic. Walk round and help with ideas if any learners are having trouble thinking what to talk about.

b *Preparation: Language.* Give learners time to think about what they want to say and how to say it, looking back through the unit for ideas and language. Help as necessary.

6 **a** *Giving advice.* Learners take turns to explain how to do something to the group. Remind learners to ask questions to find out more information or clarify things. Point out that they will have to explain what they have found out to a new group in the next stage. Monitor while groups are talking and take a note of good and incorrect language for a feedback session. You could focus on learners' language before **b** or at the end of the task.

b *Speaking.* In new groups, learners explain what they found out from people in their first group.

Round-up. Ask if anyone found out something completely new or unexpected from someone in the class.

6 Explore

Keyword: *mean*

Goal: raise awareness and practise different uses of *mean*

Core language:

I mean: to add or correct information; to give yourself time to think
Patterns with *mean*
Softening expressions with *mean*

I mean

1 a *Listening for main idea.* This section focuses on three frequent uses of the expression *I mean*: to add information to something you've said, to correct or clarify information, and to give yourself time to think. Focus learners on the picture and ask them to guess information about Felipe and Sabrina, e.g. *What's their relationship? What are they looking at?* Then play recording **2.7**. Learners discuss the questions in pairs before checking as a class.

> They were students together.
> Felipe is in Italy for work.

b Learners look through the script for *I mean* and underline the four examples. Point out the uses and look at the examples with the class.

Language note: *I mean*

The different uses of *I mean* are rather similar and can be difficult for the listener to categorise. However, by looking carefully at the script, it is possible to narrow down the meaning of each expression. For instance:
- I wish I was a student here again! I mean, it's too bad I've got to work! (adding/clarifying)
- I'm at the Arezzo Palace, no, sorry, I mean the Arezzo Hotel. (correcting)
- It's OK. It's a bit quiet. I mean, there's nobody else staying there! (adding/clarifying)
- Erm, well, we've got the whole afternoon … I mean … we could just walk around. (thinking time)

Patterns with *mean*

2 a This section focuses on three different patterns with *mean* (*mean* + infinitive with *to*; *mean* + *-ing*; *mean* + *a lot, everything, nothing* + *to* somebody) and their functions. Learners do the matching.

> 1 a   2 c   3 b

b 👥 Learners complete the questions in pairs, or individually before comparing with a partner. They then discuss the questions. Walk round and help if learners are having problems with the language.

> 1 changing   2 a lot   3 to do

Softeners with *mean*

3 a *Listening for main idea.* Look at the picture and ask the class to predict possible problems with Felipe's passport and Burger World. Then play recording **2.8**. Learners answer the questions in pairs, before checking as a class. Check understanding of *falling apart*.

> a Felipe's passport is not in good condition (i.e. it is falling apart).
> b Felipe would rather eat somewhere Italian.

b Look at the expressions with the class and point out the use of *mean* in expressions to 'soften' opinions, questions or facts. Learners do the matching. Check as a class, focusing on the intonation and pointing out how this differs according to meaning. Give learners an opportunity to practise saying the sentences focusing on the intonation.

> 1 d   2 a   3 c   4 b

c Talk about this with the class.

> intention

d 👥 Learners work together to complete the sentences.

> 1 I don't mean to worry you, but I can smell gas.
> 2 I've been meaning to ask you, are you driving to Emily's party on Saturday?
> 3 I don't mean to sound rude, but I really don't like your dress.
> 4 I'm sorry I shouted. I didn't mean to upset you.

Optional extra

Tell learners to write sentences or endings like the ones in **3d**, e.g. *Have you got the five euros I lent you the other day?* They swap and complete or add expressions to soften the sentences, e.g. *I've been meaning to ask you, have you got …?*

4 a 👤 Give learners a few minutes to think of some ideas for each category.

b 👥 Learners work in pairs and do the role play. Monitor and help as necessary, ensuring that learners are using the language from **3b** appropriately.

Preparation for Explore speaking

If you're planning to do the Explore speaking section in the next class, tell learners to think of a board game, card game or sport they know well, in advance of the lesson. The lesson will work best if learners can physically look at the games that are being explained, but what is possible will depend on learners' circumstances. Here are some possibilities:
- Learners bring a suitable game into class.
- Learners don't have the game, but can access the rules and pictures of the game on the Internet. Tell them to find the rules and pictures on a website and print them out if possible.
- Bring in a popular board game yourself, which you can explain to the class. Also bring in several packs of cards, if possible, for any learners who haven't got anything to bring in or are short of ideas.

Explore speaking

Goals: say you don't understand
ask for help
explain something

Core language:
Expressions for talking about understanding
Expressions for asking for clarification or clarifying

1 Learners talk about different games in groups or as a class. Find out what games are common in learners' countries, and which they play or used to play. Learners could explain one of these games in greater detail later in the lesson.

2 👥 Learners look at the photos of people playing Mahjong (a Chinese game). Find out if any learners know the game. If they do, you can make use of them during the class. It's worth pointing out that Mahjong is similar to many card games, but using tiles rather than cards.

> 1 B 2 C 3 D 4 A

3 a *Listening for main idea.* Look at the questions with the class, then play recording **2.9**. Let learners discuss the questions in pairs. Check understanding of: *shuffling* (= mixing up), *face down, score, get rid of* (= throw away). These words will help learners describe their own games later.

> 1 No. Jen doesn't know how to play.
> 2 You win by having the highest score when the game ends.

b Learners read the script under the photos to check their ideas. Go through any problems with the class.

4 a 👥 Learners look at the highlighted expressions in the script. In pairs, they categorise the expressions. Don't go through the answers at this stage.

> 1 say you don't understand: 1, 5
> 2 say you partly understand: 7
> 3 explain something: 2, 3, 4, 6

b Play recording **2.10** so learners can check their ideas. Stop after each expression so learners can practise saying the expressions.

5 a 👥 *Practice.* Learners read the continuation of the conversation and choose suitable expressions to complete it. Check as a class.

> 1 I'm lost. / I don't get it.
> 2 I get that bit.
> 3 The idea is to
> 4 It's like

b 👥 *Vocabulary expansion.* Learners substitute their answers in the conversation with the new expressions. Go through it with the class, dealing with any problems that come up.

> 1 I don't know what you mean.
> 2 I think I've got that.
> 3 You're supposed to …
> 4 It's similar to …

Optional extra

Learners practise the extract using the new expressions.

6 a 👤 *Preparation.* This activity will work best if learners have the game or pictures of the game and a copy of the rules in class (see preparation above). This replicates the way we normally explain a game to other people. Give learners time to plan how to explain the rules of a game or sport. Walk round and help with ideas and language as necessary.

b 👥 *Explaining rules.* It would be good to demonstrate this by explaining a game you know well. Keep the explanations as simple as possible and use the props you have with you to illustrate what you mean. Then put learners in groups to do the same thing. Walk round and keep an eye on how the groups are coping. If they are having problems, identify whether the problems are due to language or to complex rules, and help if necessary.

7 *Round-up.* Get learners' opinions on the different games they have talked about and find out which games they'd like to try playing.

Optional extra

If you have time and have access to enough of the games, groups can choose a game to play, either in the current or in a future (designated) class. This would be a good way to practise the language in a real-life context and would be a satisfying outcome to the lesson.

6 Look again

Review

GRAMMAR verb + -ing

1 a Learners match the beginnings and endings in pairs, or individually before comparing with a partner.

> 1 e 2 c 3 b 4 d 5 a

b Write the underlined sentence beginning on the board and elicit different endings from the class. Learners continue individually or in pairs.

c 👥 Learners work with a new partner or in groups to compare their ideas.

VOCABULARY Multi-word verbs: managing money

2 a Learners read through the email. Ask a few comprehension questions to check understanding, e.g. *What did the person's son want to do? Could he afford it? What did he do? Did he have enough money? What didn't he do?* Then they complete the sentences individually or in pairs

> 1 240,000 pesos.
> 2 going to the fitness centre.
> 3 1,500 pesos a day.
> 4 on one or two days.

b 👥 / 👥 Give learners a moment to think of a story and to work out how to use the multi-word verbs to talk about it. Then they talk together. Check their use of language.

3 a *Preparation.* Give learners a time limit to write their diaries and cancel a few arrangements.

b *Making arrangements.* Point out that the day learners are talking is Wednesday. Remind learners how to talk about failed plans and arrangements (*I was meant to be -ing, but .../ I was supposed to be -ing, but ...*). Learners have their conversations.

Round-up. Find out what learners have arranged.

Extension

SPELLING AND SOUNDS /ɔː/

4 a Play recording **2.11** for learners to underline the /ɔː/ sounds. Check as a class.

> orchestra, m<u>or</u>ning, d<u>oor</u>, <u>or</u>dinary, aw<u>ard</u>, res<u>our</u>ce, w<u>ar</u>drobe, sc<u>ore</u>, f<u>or</u>ty, l<u>aw</u>, f<u>our</u>, dr<u>aw</u>ing, w<u>ar</u>m, bef<u>ore</u>, p<u>oor</u>

b Learners complete the four spelling patterns.

> 1 or   2 ar   3 or, our, aw   4 or, ore, aw, oor

c *Vocabulary expansion.* Elicit more words from the class.

d *Spellcheck.* Play recording **2.12** or say the words. Learners write them down, then check their own spelling in a dictionary. Remind them to make a note of any difficult words in their notebooks.

NOTICE Collocations

5 a Focus learners on the table and ask what a *collocation* is (words that often go together). Point out to learners that they have seen all these collocations in the article about Kath Kelly, but not to check in the article until they've done the exercise.

> N + N: wedding present, internet access
> Adj + N: mobile phone, free events
> Vb + N: pick fruit, see friends
> Vb + Adv: change dramatically, live together

b Elicit a question from the class for *wedding present*. They can ask you the question or someone else in the class. Then learners write questions in pairs or individually. Walk round and help as necessary.

c Learners ask and answer each other's questions.

Round-up. Ask what one or two learners found out about someone in their group.

Self-assessment

Go through the list of goals, eliciting language from the unit for each one. You may need to remind learners of the contexts for the goals and let them look back through the unit if necessary. Then they circle the appropriate number for each goal. Walk round while they are doing this and talk to learners about their progress. Remind learners about the extra practice opportunities under the box, and ask where they can find things.

Unit 6 Extra activities on the Teacher's DVD-ROM

Printable worksheets, activity instructions and answer keys are on your Teacher's DVD-ROM.

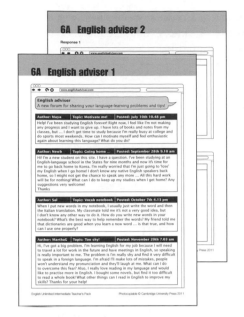

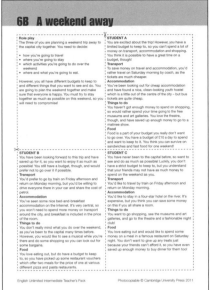

6A English adviser

Activity type: Reading, writing and vocabulary – Giving tips/advice – Pairs

Aim: To practise using linking expressions to give tips

Language: Linking expressions – Use at any point from 6.1.

Preparation: Make one copy of both worksheets for every pair of learners.

Time: 45 minutes

6B A weekend away

Activity type: Speaking, reading and vocabulary – Role play – Groups

Aim: To practise using multi-word verbs for managing money

Language: Multi-word verbs: managing money – Use at any point from 6.1.

Preparation: Make one copy of the worksheet for every three learners. Cut up each worksheet to make one Role-play card and one Role card each for Students A, B and C.

Time: 20 minutes

6C Tell us about …

Activity type: Speaking – Board game – Groups

Aim: To practise using verb + -ing

Language: Verb + -ing – Use at any point from 6.2.

Preparation: Make one copy of the board game (enlarge to A3 size if possible) for every three or four learners. You will also need a die for every group and a counter for every learner.

Time: 30 minutes

Unit 6 Self-study Pack

In the Workbook

Unit 6 of the *English Unlimited Intermediate Workbook* offers additional ways to practise the vocabulary and grammar taught in the Coursebook. There are also activities which build reading and writing skills and two whole pages of listening and speaking tasks to use with the Documentary video, giving your learners the opportunity to hear and react to authentic spoken English.

- **Vocabulary:** Linking expressions; Multi-word verbs: saving money; Using equipment; Giving reasons
- **Grammar:** Verb + -ing
- **Time out:** 'Satnav' stories
- **Explore writing:** Leaving a note
- **Documentary:** The chef manager

On the DVD-ROM

Unit 6 of the *English Unlimited Intermediate Self-study DVD-ROM* contains interactive games and activities for your learners to practise and improve their vocabulary, grammar and pronunciation, and also their speaking and listening, with the possibility for learners to record themselves, and a video of authentic spoken English to use with the Workbook.

- **Vocabulary and grammar:** Extra practice activities
- **Pronunciation:** Linking consonants and vowels
- **Explore speaking:** Adding, correctly
- **Explore listening:** Calling the bank
- **Video:** Documentary – The chef manager

7 Personal qualities

7.1

Goal: describe qualities you need for different activities

Core language:

VOCABULARY   Personal qualities
                          Matching people to jobs and activities

A high achiever

READING

1   *Reading for main idea.* Focus learners on the picture
and ask what they know or can guess about Carlos
Acosta (e.g. age, what he does, how successful he
is). Find out if learners have similar short, written
interviews with interesting or famous people in
newspapers in their countries. Learners read the
interview and discuss the question in pairs. Feed
back as a class. Check understanding of *principal*,
numerous, *talent*; learners will probably ask about *in a
nutshell* (= briefly).

> **Possible answers**
> *interested in learning, talented, ambitious, successful,
> not arrogant*

2 **a** *Reading for detail.* Remind learners that they can find
lots of information about Carlos in the introduction
to the interview. They read it again to find the facts
and opinions. Let them compare with a partner before
checking as a class.

> **Possible answers**
> Facts:
> * *He is from Cuba.*
> * *He has travelled all over the world.*
> * *He has danced for ballet companies in Cuba (as
>   principal) and England.*
> * *He has won lots of international prizes.*
> * *His father went to jail.*
> * *He wanted to be a footballer as a child.*
> Opinions:
> * *He thinks art is important and should get more
>   support from the government and the public.*
> * *He thinks people should do what makes them happy,
>   because life is special.*
> * *He thinks he isn't good at art.*
> * *He thinks he's good at music and sport.*

  b *Books closed.* Learners compare their ideas with a
partner.

WRITING AND SPEAKING

3   *Preparation.* Tell learners to imagine they are a
well-known person and have been asked to complete
the interview questions. Give them plenty of time to
complete the sentences with their own ideas. Walk
round and help as necessary.

4 **a** *Speaking: Personalisation.* Learners go through
the questions, taking turns to say their sentences and
to respond, e.g. by asking questions to find out more
information. Monitor and feed back to individual
learners on any errors that impede communication.

  b *Round-up.* Let every learner say one surprising thing
about their partner. If time, encourage the class to
respond and find out more.

> **Alternative: Milling**
>
> After learners have prepared their interviews, divide the
> interview questions up between the class. Tell learners to walk
> round and speak to as many people as they can within the
> time limit you set (five or six minutes should be plenty). Tell
> them that they will tell the class about the most interesting
> or surprising answers at the end, so they may need to take
> notes. When the time is up, learners take turns to tell the class
> what they discovered about people in the class.

It's the kind of job that ...

VOCABULARY Personal qualities

1 **a** 👥 *Focus on expressions.* Learners quickly look at the
quotes about success and try to work out what they
mean from the surrounding context. Go through them
with the class and check pronunciation of *discipline*
/ˈdɪsəplɪn/ and *initiative* /ɪˈnɪʃətɪv/. Then learners
discuss their opinions, giving reasons for their ideas.
Feed back as a class.

> **Optional extra: Language of agreeing and disagreeing**
>
> Remind learners of the language for expressing opinions
> covered in Unit 2 (e.g. *I'd say ...; I reckon ...; Some people
> say ...; There's no point / harm in ...*). Also remind them of
> the pattern: *It's* + adjective + *to* to express an opinion (see
> Unit 5). In addition, it would be a good moment to revise the
> language of agreement and disagreement, e.g. *I (completely/
> totally) agree/disagree with that. I think that's true / I don't
> think that's true at all.*

  b *Preparation.* Ask the class what personal qualities you
need in the army (e.g. you need to have discipline and
initiative (to make important decisions when things
go wrong) and you probably need to have confidence
in your abilities). When learners offer ideas, ask
them why and encourage them to give reasons.
Learners then continue in pairs, or individually before
comparing with a partner.

  c 👥 *Discussion.* Learners talk in groups about their
ideas, or you could do this as a class discussion.

 You could use photocopiable activity 7A on the
Teacher's DVD-ROM at this point.

LISTENING

2   *Listening for main idea.* Focus learners on the picture
of Anne and ask the class what they can guess about
her from the picture (in contrast to Carlos). Then play
recording **2.13**. Learners put the topics in order. Feed
back as a class.

> *motivation, body shape, competition, disappointment*

3   *Listening for detail.* Learners read through the list of
points. Check understanding of *be pushed* (= made to
do something (that you don't necessarily want to do))

and *be skinny* (= be thin). Play recording **2.13** again. Learners tick the things Anne says are important. They compare with a partner before checking as a class.

| *1, 3, 5, 6, 7*

Alternative

Learners discuss the answers before listening again. They may have grasped enough of the listening to do this from memory, or they can predict on the basis of world knowledge and opinion.

4   👥 Learners could talk about these two points from Anne's interview in groups or as a class.

Speaking note: 'Quiet' learners (see Unit 1, p23)

By this stage in the course, learners who were reticent or under-confident in expressing their opinions in front of others will hopefully have gained enough confidence to participate in class discussions. Encourage quieter learners to contribute, but don't push learners to speak in front of the class if they're clearly uncomfortable.

VOCABULARY Matching people to jobs and activities

5   👥 Look at the first sentence with the class and elicit some ideas, e.g. a novelist or actor. Learners continue in groups, making a list for each sentence. Feed back as a class.

6   ℹ *Preparation.* If some of your learners don't work, tell them to write about the job of someone they know well, a job they've done or a job they'd like to do one day. Remind learners to use language from both vocabulary sections. Walk round and help as necessary while learners are writing.

SPEAKING

7 **a** 👥 / 👥 *Describing.* Learners take turns to describe the job they've written about. They listen to each job in turn and discuss who would be best suited to it in their group. Monitor and note learners' use of the new language.

  b *Round-up.* Each group feeds back to the class on the person they chose and why.

Goals: describe personality
            make comparisons

Core language:

VOCABULARY	Personality
GRAMMAR	Comparing
PRONUNCIATION	Contrastive stress

A great character

READING

1   👥 / 👥 *Pre-reading discussion.* The discussion questions introduce the topic of keeping pets. Learners may have strong (contrasting) opinions about this, so this could make for a lively class discussion.

2 **a** 👥 Focus learners on the picture and get learners' responses to the pet and its owner, e.g. *Do they look alike? Can you guess what the owner is like from the picture? What about the pet?* Learners read the statements and decide whether they're true or false. Don't check the answers, as this will pre-empt **b**.

  b *Reading for main idea.* Learners read the article and check their ideas in **a**. They compare in pairs. Then check as a class.

| *1 true 2 false 3 true*

3   👥 / 👥 *Speaking.* Learners talk in pairs or groups. Make sure pet owners are divided among the groups. Ask one or two learners for their examples.

LISTENING

4   👥 Learners match the pictures with the animals. Check as a class. Ask learners if they can guess what kind of personality any of the animals might have. Find out if anyone has one of these animals and what they're like. This will set the context for the listening.

| *A a hamster B a goldfish C a lizard*
| *D a dog E a parrot*

5 **a** *Listening for main idea.* Set the context, then play recording **2.14**. Learners match the owners with the pets. They compare with a partner, then check the answers.

| *1 B 2 C 3 E 4 D 5 A*

Alternative for weaker groups

Pre-teach the personality words and expressions (see **5c** for a list). Then play recording **2.14** and continue as in **5b**.

  b *Listening for detail.* Play recording **2.14** again, stopping after each monologue so learners can discuss the personalities in pairs. Don't go through the answers, as learners will check their own in **c**.

> 1 It's not clear if the woman is like her goldfish. She says she's happier because of him, though.
> 2 Tim is unusual, like his lizard. He's calm, so his lizard tends to be calm too.
> 3 The woman who owns the parrots says she's eccentric and unusual, like her parrots. She shares different qualities with her parrots, e.g. a sense of humour, a love of people and a tendency to show off.
> 4 The dog owner says they're both quite grumpy, not very tolerant and love their food.
> 5 The hamster owner says they're both nice!

c Learners check their ideas in the script. In feedback, check understanding of the personality words and expressions. Draw up two lists on the board, discuss meaning and check pronunciation.

Adjectives: *unusual, calm, eccentric, grumpy, fussy, tolerant, nice, strange*

Expressions: *a little bit of a show-off, an absolute lunatic, have a great sense of humour*

Optional extra: Vocabulary expansion

These scripts are very rich in descriptive language, and although some of it is quite specific, learners may ask for clarification. Go through these expressions fairly quickly, explaining them or asking learners in the class to explain what they know to each other: *swirl around, aquarium, reptile, sits on his knee, feathered friends, bob my head, traits, like our own bit of space, wagging his tail*.

An alternative approach is to ask each learner to choose five words or expressions they don't know from the scripts. Tell them to underline the key word if it's an expression, e.g. *swirl, feathered* or *bob*, and to look them up. Walk round and help if learners are having trouble working out the meaning. Then learners explain their words and expressions in groups. This shouldn't take too long, as they will almost certainly have chosen some of the same words.

VOCABULARY Personality

6 a Look at the three sets of expressions describing personality with the class and point out that they are all possible and frequently go together. Check understanding of *difficult*, *miserable*, *bright* and *charming* and draw attention to the use of *guy* in informal speech. Pairs then try to remember which adjective is used with the nouns 1–3 in the listening. They check their ideas in the script.

> 1 a great character   2 a calm person   3 a nice guy

b Learners discuss the possibilities and complete the sentences in pairs.

> Possible answers
> 1 My boss is a difficult character.
> 2 She's a very interesting person.
> 3 My new assistant is a bright guy.
> 4 That teacher is such a miserable character.
> 5 The new managing director is a strange person.
> 6 He's such a charming guy.

SPEAKING

7 a *Preparation.* Give learners time to come up with some ideas and to make notes if they want to. Walk round and prompt learners if they need ideas.

b Learners talk about people they know in groups. Encourage them to ask follow-up questions. Monitor and check use of the new language.

Round-up. Ask a few learners to tell the class about someone interesting they or someone in their group know.

Similarity and difference

GRAMMAR Comparing

1 a Learners will be very familiar with the scripts by now and they should also be familiar with a lot of the words in the grey boxes, so they should be able to have a go at completing the sentences individually. Walk round and see how they're doing. Then let them compare with a partner before checking their answers in the script. You can deal with any problems in **b**.

> 2 a little   3 far   4 slightly   5 not quite   6 just

b Give learners a moment to do the matching individually or in pairs before doing this with the class. Check understanding of *far*, *slightly* and *marginally*. Model the pronunciation of the sentences, reminding learners of the weak forms in *than* and *as ... as*.

> 1 B, C   2 A   3 D

Note: Grammar practice

You could do the grammar practice on p139 at this point.

 You could use photocopiable activity 7B on the Teacher's DVD-ROM at this point.

PRONUNCIATION Contrastive stress

2 a Play recording **2.15** or say the sentence, emphasising the two contrasting words and showing how this makes the meaning clear. Learners repeat the sentence after you or the recording.

b Learners say the sentences to each other to work out which words express contrasting ideas. Point out that 1 and 3 contrast two words, as in the example, but that in sentence 2, there are two sets of contrasting words (so four in total). Walk round and monitor progress, but don't check the answers yet.

c Play recording **2.16** (or say the sentences) one by one so learners can check and repeat.

> 1 <u>Tim</u>'s generally a calm person, so <u>she</u> tends to be calm now too.
> 2 I enjoy <u>my</u> food just as much as <u>he</u> enjoys <u>his</u>.
> 3 If their <u>owner</u> gets stressed, then <u>they</u> get stressed too.

3 *Writing: A descriptive paragraph.* Demonstrate the idea here by telling learners about someone you know well. Give learners plenty of time to choose someone they're close to and to write a short paragraph about them. Walk round and help as necessary.

SPEAKING

4 a 👥 *Speaking.* Learners take turns to describe their person and to respond by asking questions. Monitor and take a note of good and incorrect language use for a feedback session later.

b 👥 Learners talk in groups or as a class.

Round-up. Ask a few people who they'd most like to meet and why.

7.3 Target activity

Goals: describe personality ♻
     say how a person has influenced you

Core language:

TASK VOCABULARY	Describing someone's influence
7.1 VOCABULARY	Personal qualities
7.1 VOCABULARY	Matching people to jobs and activities
7.2 VOCABULARY	Personality
7.2 GRAMMAR	Comparing

Talk about people who have influenced you

TASK LISTENING

1 👥 / 👥👥 Check learners understand *role model* and *be influenced by someone.* Then learners discuss the questions about role models together. In feedback, ask several learners to tell the class about their role models and get different opinions about role models in learners' countries and who they think role models should be (which may be the same or not).

2 a Focus learners on the picture of Tara, then play recording **2.17**. Learners compare ideas, then check as a class.

> *Her physics teacher and her best friend at high school*

Alternative

While learners are comparing ideas about **2a**, they recap any details they can remember of how the two people influenced Tara. This will help when they listen again in **2b**.

---

b Play recording **2.17** again for learners to make notes of the way both people influenced Tara. Direct them to the script to check their ideas.

TASK VOCABULARY Describing someone's influence

3 a Learners read the sentences and discuss who Tara is talking about: her teacher or her friend. Feed back as a class, and check understanding and pronunciation of all the expressions, giving learners an opportunity to practise saying them.

> *1 friend   2 teacher   3 friend   4 friend   5 teacher*
> *6 teacher   7 teacher*

b *Focus on form.* Give learners a moment to look at the patterns with a partner, then check as a class. If possible, project the sentences onto a board or screen and highlight the verbs, nouns or comparative adjectives (or ask a learner to come up and highlight the verbs first and then the nouns).

> *+ verb: 3, 5, 7*
> *+ noun: 1, 2, 6*
> *+ comparative adjective: 4*

TASK

4 a 📖 *Preparation: Ideas.* Look at the list of possible role models and the diagram, and encourage learners to think about role models at different times of their lives, including the present.

b 📖 *Preparation: Language.* Give learners time to prepare what they want to say about the different people. Walk round and help as necessary and encourage learners to use language from previous lessons in the unit to express their ideas.

5 a 👥👥 *Speaking.* Monitor while learners are talking and take a note of any problems for a feedback session later. Remind them to respond to each other to show they are listening and to ask follow-up questions to find out more about each other's role models.

b 👥👥 *Round-up.* Learners discuss the biggest influences on their lives together. In feedback, ask learners from different groups to tell the class about the role models in their peers' lives.

7 Explore

Across cultures: Roles in life

Goal: raise awareness of different cultural viewpoints on roles and responsibilities

Core language:

VOCABULARY	Roles and opinions

LISTENING

1 a *Listening for main idea.* Focus on the pictures and elicit the different roles from the class. Look through the list of roles with the class, then play recording **2.18**. Learners compare their ideas with a partner. Then check as a class. Check understanding of *retire(d)* and *retirement, struggled (to do something), family ties* and *to support somebody* or *be supported by somebody.* Hayes uses the colloquial expression *(not such) a big thing (for me)* twice. Point out that this is a colloquial way to refer to something that is important for you.

> *A: friend, father, son, colleague*
> *H: businesswoman*

b *Listening for detail.* Learners read through the questions. Give them a few minutes to think about the answers before they listen again. Then play recording **2.18** again. Check as a class.

1 'Hi, I'm Hayes, website designer'; to start a
  conversation
2 He doesn't know what to do with himself.
3 They're expected to look after their parents when
  they're old.
4 Because he doesn't have a job.

c 👥 / 👥👥 Learners compare their attitudes to those
of Hayes and Alex. In feedback, find out who most
learners identified with and why.

2 👥 / 👥👥 If you can, project the first three questions
onto the board so learners can talk about them in
pairs or groups. Get some feedback about learners'
discussions, then project the questions on family roles
onto the board and do the same. This will break up the
discussion and give it more focus.

Alternative: Multicultural groups

Divide the class into As and Bs and tell As to discuss work
roles (in pairs or groups) and Bs to discuss family roles (in
pairs or groups). When they're ready, rearrange learners
into A/B pairs (or groups) to explain how people in their first
group answered the questions and to find out if the situation
is the same or different in their new partners' countries. Get
feedback from several learners at the end.

VOCABULARY Roles and opinions

3 *Focus on expressions.* Check that learners understand
the two categories that they are being asked to
differentiate, then do the activity with the class,
checking any problems as you go along.

1, 3, 4, 5 are about roles.
2, 6, 7 are about opinions.

SPEAKING

4 a *Preparation.* Give learners a moment to think about
how they see themselves and their different roles.
Point out that their roles may have changed and that
they can talk about this, too.

b 👥👥 *Discussion.* Learners discuss their respective roles
in groups. Monitor and see whether learners make use
of the new language in their discussions. In feedback,
find out if learners shared similar or very different
roles and why.

5 👥👥 *Discussion.* Focus learners on the list of roles
and check understanding of *househusband*. Learners
discuss their ideas.

Round-up. Ask several learners to report back on
what people in their groups talked about. Get some
opinions on each role from different people in the
class and ask what learners know about perceptions of
these roles in different parts of the world.

Explore writing

Goals: compare and contrast two alternatives
organise ideas 1

Core language:
Linking expressions for organising ideas in writing

1 Introduce the topic with the discussion questions.
Find out what learners think are important features in
hotels and why.

2 👥 Focus learners on the picture of the hotel at the
bottom of the page and ask them if they would
like to stay there. Ensure learners understand the
context outlined in the rubric, then draw attention
to Katherine's list of pros and cons for each hotel.
Learners read Mauro's email and complete the list
in pairs.

Possible venues	Pros	Cons
The Excelsior	more facilities, bigger, shopping arcade, lots of places to eat, café with Wi-Fi access, good discounts	a bit impersonal
The Hotel Arts	good food, large conference room, beautiful to look at, cheaper	smaller, business centre not so well equipped, fewer places to eat

3 *Focus on linking expressions.* Focus learners on the
expressions, then let them categorise the expressions
and underline relevant information in pairs. Check as
a class.

a on top of that, there are plenty of places to eat
  as well as a more formal dining room and a café with
  Wi-Fi access
b however, although (x2), whereas
  They're lovely and would both be fine. However, there
  are some differences
  Although we'll probably be working too hard to use
  the swimming pools and tennis courts, some people
  might appreciate the shopping arcade.
  The business centre isn't quite as well-equipped,
  though I think it would be sufficient for our needs.
  it might feel rather impersonal, whereas the Arts feels
  a bit more special.
c on balance

4 Learners read through the email first, then use the
linking expressions to complete the sentences. Check
as a class.

1 On balance   2 as well as   3 although / though
4 whereas   5 However

5 a 👥👥 *Preparation.* Focus on the context with the class
and find out if anyone has experience of doing this sort
of work. Draw attention to the information at the back
of the book. Learners prepare their ideas in groups.

b 🧍 *Writing.* Learners write their emails using Mauro's
email as a model. Walk round and help as necessary.

6   *Round-up.* Learners exchange emails and read other people's. Find out which hotel most learners preferred and why.

7 Look again

Review

VOCABULARY Personality

1 a Write *m__s__r__bl__* on the board and elicit the missing vowels from the class. Learners continue alone before comparing with a partner.

> 1 miserable   2 charming   3 calm   4 great
> 5 bright   6 difficult   7 interesting   8 strange

   b Play the first description or tell the class one of your own and ask learners to say someone the descriptions might describe. Then play recording **2.19**. Stop after each one so learners can think and write down names.

   c *Speaking.* Learners talk together about the people they wrote down.

GRAMMAR Comparing

2 a Quickly answer the questions with the class to remind learners of these expressions.

> 1 much, far, a lot, not nearly
> 2 a little, slightly, a bit, marginally, not quite, almost
> 3 just

   b *Writing sentences.* Give learners a moment to compare two people who are famous in their countries or around the world. Then they write sentences comparing them. Walk round and help as necessary.

   c *Speaking.* Learners discuss their sentences.

CAN YOU REMEMBER? Unit 6 – Multi-word verbs

3 a Learners try to complete the sentences individually, before comparing with a partner. Check as a class, or tell learners to go back to the previous unit and check their own answers.

> 1 go over   2 saved up   3 keep to   4 shut down
> 5 plugged in   6 switched off

   b *Personalisation.* Learners rewrite the sentences to make them true for them.

   Speaking. They then compare their answers and decide who is more careful. Find out who is careful in the class and ask for examples.

Extension

SPELLING AND SOUNDS /iː/

4 a Write /iː/ on the board and elicit the sound from the class. Then play recording **2.20** or say the words while learners underline the /iː/ sound.

> cr*ea*ture, m*ee*t, r*ea*son, *ea*sy, compl*e*te, bel*ie*ve, *ea*ch, betw*ee*n, kn*ee*, th*e*se, t*ea*cher, coll*ea*gue, employ*ee*, s*ee*n, agr*ee*, f*ie*ld, rec*ei*ve

   b Focus learners on the spelling patterns. In pairs, they match the patterns to the words in **a**.

> 1 complete, these
> 2 creature, reason, easy, each, teacher, colleague
> 3 meet, between, knee, employee, seen, agree
> 4 believe, field, receive

   c *Spellcheck.* Learners choose ten words and take turns to say their words to a partner and test each other.

NOTICE Comparing with *like*, *alike*

5 a Learners complete the sentences in pairs or individually before comparing with a partner.

> 1 like   2 like   3 like   4 alike

   b Learners read to check.

   c Learners do the matching in pairs.

> a 3   b 2   c 4   d 1

   d *Speaking.* Learners discuss the questions. Get feedback from several learners.

 You could use photocopiable activity 7C on the Teacher's DVD-ROM at this point.

Self-assessment

Go through the list of goals, eliciting language from the unit for each one. You may need to remind learners of the contexts for the goals and let them look back through the unit if necessary. Then they circle the appropriate number for each goal. Walk round while they are doing this and talk to learners about their progress. Remind learners about the extra practice opportunities under the box, and ask where they can find things.

Unit 7 Extra activities on the Teacher's DVD-ROM

Printable worksheets, activity instructions and answer keys are on your Teacher's DVD-ROM.

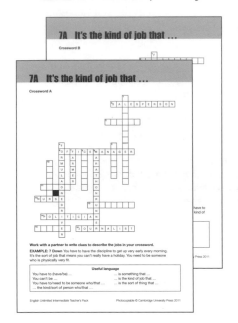

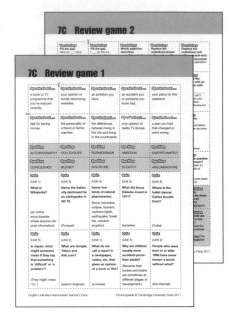

7A It's the kind of job that ...

Activity type: Vocabulary and speaking – Half a crossword – Pairs/Groups

Aim: To practise describing personal qualities and identifying people and things

Language: Personal qualities / Identifying qualities for different activities – Use at any point from 7.1.

Preparation: Make enough copies of Crosswords A and B so that half the learners get a copy of Crossword A and half get a copy of Crossword B.

Time: 45 minutes

7B Either ... or ...

Activity type: Grammar and speaking – Discussion activity – Groups

Aim: To practise comparing things

Language: Comparing – Use at any point from 7.2.

Preparation: Make one copy of the worksheet for every four learners. Cut up each worksheet to make a set of 12 Picture cards.

Time: 30 minutes

7C Review game

Activity type: Vocabulary, speaking, grammar, spelling and pronunciation – Dice game – Groups

Aim: To review language from Units 1–7

Language: Various language taken from across Units 1–7 – Use after Unit 7.

Preparation: Make one copy of both worksheets for every four or five learners and cut them up to make a set of 60 cards. Separate the cards into the six categories. You will also need a die for each group.

Time: 40 minutes

Unit 7 Self-study Pack

In the Workbook

Unit 7 of the *English Unlimited Intermediate Workbook* offers additional ways to practise the vocabulary and grammar taught in the Coursebook. There are also activities which build reading and writing skills and a whole page of listening and speaking tasks to use with the Interview video, giving your learners the opportunity to hear and react to authentic spoken English.

- **Vocabulary:** Personal qualities; Identifying qualities for different activities; Personality; Describing someone's influence; Roles and opinions
- **Grammar:** Comparing
- **My English:** Speaking in a foreign language
- **Explore reading:** Personality and behaviour
- **Interview:** Have you got what it takes? – Raquel and Valerie

On the DVD-ROM

Unit 7 of the *English Unlimited Intermediate Self-study DVD-ROM* contains interactive games and activities for your learners to practise and improve their vocabulary, grammar and pronunciation, and also their speaking and listening, with the possibility for learners to record themselves, and a video of authentic spoken English to use with the Workbook.

- **Vocabulary and grammar:** Extra practice activities
- **Pronunciation:** Contrastive stress
- **Explore speaking:** *must, must have*
- **Explore listening:** A job interview
- **Video:** Have you got what it takes?

8 Lost and found

8.1

Goals: talk about attitudes to possessions
describe objects

Core language:

VOCABULARY   Multi-word verbs: tidying and cleaning
Describing products

Clutter, rubbish, stuff

READING

1 a Focus the class on the heading of the article and the picture of Michelle Passoff and ask learners to predict what it might be about. Learners then read the introduction to the article and talk about the questions together. Check the three words and get some feedback from the class. Finally, ask learners what they think *declutter* means and explain that it is a 'creative' play on the word *clutter*, making it negative.

> a rubbish   b clutter   c stuff

b Give learners time to read through the rest of the article and the comments in the tint panel below it, then discuss the potential benefits of decluttering as a whole class.

Language note: *clutter, rubbish, stuff*

The three words have a similar meaning in this context, but very different uses beyond the text. *Stuff* is extremely high frequency (195 in the CIC frequency list) because, like *thing*, it is a general noun (uncountable) which is used to refer to everything from physical objects to ideas, events or states. It is commonly used in vague expressions, e.g. *and stuff like that*, *that kind of stuff*. See further examples in the comments at the end of the article. *Rubbish* refers both to physical things and to ideas of no value (e.g. *That's absolute rubbish!*), while *clutter* refers only to physical objects.

---

2 *Reading for detail.* Learners scan the article to find who says the things in sentences 1–5. Learners check their ideas in pairs. Then feed back as a class.

> 1 Manuel (in comments)   2 Michelle Passoff   3 Roger (in comments)   4 Don Aslett   5 Ana (in comments)

3 Learners discuss the opinions in pairs or groups. In feedback, find out what learners feel about the topic.

VOCABULARY Multi-word verbs: tidying and cleaning

4 *Focus on multi-word verbs.* Make sure learners cover the article and then complete the sentences in pairs. They can check their own answers in the article when they're ready.

> 1 throw away   2 tidy up   3 clean up   4 put away
> 5 get rid of   6 give away

Language note: Separable multi-word verbs

Most of the multi-word verbs in **4** are separable, i.e. the object pronoun goes between the verb and the particle: *throw (it) away*, *tidy (it) up*, *clean (it) up*, *put (it) away*, *give (it) away*. However, you can only say *get rid of it* (**not** *get rid it of*). When the object is stated (not a pronoun), it follows the multi-word verb, e.g. *clean up **the kitchen***. Remind learners to record new words and expressions in their vocabulary notebooks and to write sentences to illustrate meaning and use.

 You could use photocopiable activity 8A on the Teacher's DVD-ROM at this point.

SPEAKING

5 / Learners discuss the questions in pairs or groups. In feedback, ask one or two learners for their answers to the third question. This will lead into the next activity.

Freecycle

VOCABULARY Describing products

1 Learners read about the website, Freecycle. Check any global problems together before learners discuss the questions in pairs.

2 a *Focus on expressions.* Do the first expression with the class, then learners continue in pairs.

> *Good points: instructions are included; in good working order; comes with; in quite good condition; ideal for*
> *Bad points: play up; could do with*

b Learners cover the previous offers and complete the microwave text. They can do this in pairs, or individually before checking with a partner.

> 1 order   2 play   3 included   4 with   5 for

 You could use photocopiable activity 8B on the Teacher's DVD-ROM at this point.

WRITING AND SPEAKING

3 Give learners a few moments to think of something to describe. Walk round and help with ideas if necessary. Monitor while learners are writing their descriptions and help as necessary.

4 Learners exchange descriptions with three or four people. This should enable them to find something they need and to find a new home for their unwanted products. Encourage learners to find out more about each other's products.

Alternative: Milling

In **4**, learners can walk round the class reading each other's descriptions and asking questions. Set an appropriate time limit, e.g. three or four minutes. Then learners get into groups of three or four and talk together.

8.2

Goals: talk about unexpected travel situations
discuss options and decide what to do
make deductions

Core language:

VOCABULARY	Travel situations
GRAMMAR	Modals of deduction and speculation
PRONUNCIATION	Emphatic stress

A nightmare journey

LISTENING

1 *Pre-listening discussion.* Focus learners on the pictures and elicit some ideas about what Alice and Javier might be talking about. Direct attention to the question and discuss it as a class or in pairs.

2 *Listening for main idea.* Explain that Alice and Javier (pictured next to this activity) are on a journey and that a number of things go wrong. Point out that A–F relate to conversations at the different times shown. Learners read the first two questions, then listen to recording **2.21**A. Learners discuss their ideas in pairs. Play the conversation again if necessary before checking as a class. Continue as above for each conversation, B–F.

> A 1 They're going to Sue's birthday party (a barbecue).
> 2 They get on the wrong train (to Newmont, not Beauville where they want to go).
> B 3 They need to go (direct) to Newmont, get a train back to where they started, then get a train to Beauville.
> C 4 All the trains to Beauville are cancelled, so they have to get a bus instead.
> 5 Learners' own ideas
> D 6 The bus breaks down.
> 7 Learners' own ideas (e.g. hitchhike)
> E 8 They should wait for the next bus.
> 9 Alice thinks they should start walking and try to get a lift with someone.
> F 10 No. They miss the party.

VOCABULARY Travel situations

3 *Focus on expressions.* Learners read through Alice's description of her journey. Remind them to think about the form of the verbs. Do the first one together, then learners continue in pairs.

> 1 got on 2 get off 3 were cancelled 4 broke down
> 5 got a lift 6 got stuck 7 got lost 8 gave us a lift

SPEAKING

4 **a** Focus learners on the situations and give them a few minutes to remember travel problems they've had and think about what to say. Tell learners not to worry if they don't have a story for all the situations; when they talk together in **b**, other learners' stories may remind them of similar things that have happened to them.

b Walk round while learners are talking and take a note of uses of the target language for a feedback session at the end of the activity.

> **Optional extra**
>
> In a multicultural class, encourage learners to compare the efficiency of transport systems in their countries. In a monocultural class, focus on transport that is available in the learners' country, e.g. if there are no trains, talk about buses and how reliable they are.

Lost

GRAMMAR Modals of deduction and speculation

1 **a** Read the example sentences, stressing the modal verbs for emphasis. This will help learners with the meaning and also with the pronunciation work on emphatic stress which follows.

> 1 The train must go from here.
> 2 There might be a local bus that goes past. There could be one further along.
> 3 This can't be our train!

b Direct learners to p154 to find another example of each modal verb in the scripts. Remind them that they should only look for modal verbs with the meanings in **a**.

> C That can't be the only way, surely!
> D There must be a problem with the engine. Well, it could be an hour before it gets here.
> E We might be able to hitchhike.

2 **a** Learners complete the conversation with modal verbs.

b Play recording **2.22** so learners can check their own answers. Point out that *could* is also possible in gap 3.

> 1 can't 2 must 3 might 4 must 5 can't

> **Note: Grammar practice**
>
> You could do the grammar practice on p140 at this point.

PRONUNCIATION Emphatic stress

3 **a** Play recording **2.23** or say the sentences yourself and ask learners in which sentences the stress makes the speaker sound more or less certain.

> 1, a more certain, 2, b less certain

b Learners practise saying the sentences, emphasising the modal verbs in each one.

SPEAKING

4 **a** Focus learners on the picture and give them time to read the situation. Explain that the activity is a sort of puzzle and that they need to discuss and choose the best option in each case as a pair or group. Remind them that they should discuss the options using modals of deduction as appropriate, and decide what to do at each stage. Discuss the first four options as a class, putting learners' ideas on the board if they're different from the examples. This will serve as a reminder to learners to try to use the target language in their discussions. Then learners continue in pairs, following their chosen paths through the different scenarios at the back of the book. Monitor while

learners are talking and help if there are any problems moving forward. Take a note of how learners use the modals for a feedback session.

b *Round-up.* Find out who got home first and last and feedback on learners' use of language.

8.3 Target activity

Goals: describe objects ♻
make deductions ♻

Core language:

TASK VOCABULARY	Describing objects
8.1 VOCABULARY	Describing products
8.2 GRAMMAR	Modals of deduction and speculation

Find something at lost property

TASK LISTENING

1 *Pre-listening discussion.* Focus learners on the pictures of the objects and ask learners where they might find them all in one place (to elicit *lost property office*). Discuss the questions as a class or in pairs. This will set the context for the listening.

2 Explain the situation and give learners time to read the questions, then play recording **2.24**. Learners match the pictures with the conversations.

> 1 1E 2D 3F
> 2 It has the mobile phone, but not the black leather wallet or the sports bag.

TASK VOCABULARY Describing objects

3 a Learners match sentences 1–7 with the pictures.

> 1E 2F 3E 4D 5D 6D 7F

b Learners work through a–c in pairs, before checking as a class.

> a size – colour – material
> b Learners' own answers
>   Possible answers: colour: red, blue, gold, purple, yellow, etc.; material (adjectives): plastic, metal, canvas, glass, wooden, etc.; size: tiny, large, huge, medium-sized
> c on the top; on the back

4 a *Writing.* Give learners time to think of a possession and to write a description of it. Remind them not to say what the possession is. Walk round and help as necessary.

b 👥👥 Learners listen to each other's descriptions and guess what the possessions are. Monitor and be prepared to help out if there are problems that impede communication.

TASK

5 👤 *Preparation.* Set up the role play and walk round while learners are preparing and help as necessary.

> **Alternative for weaker groups**
>
> Learners prepare for the role play in A/A and B/B pairs.

6 a *Role play.* Learners have their conversations. In feedback, find out if the lost property office has their possession (it does).

b Learners change roles and have another conversation using different information. Monitor while learners are talking. You may want to feed back to learners on useful and incorrect language from their conversations before they continue with further role plays.

c Learners do two further role plays.

d *Round-up.* Find out if learners found all the things they lost.

8 Explore

Keyword: *have*

Goal: use *have* in a range of different uses

Core language

have in present and past perfect
have to for obligation
Causative *have*
have + noun
Expressions with *have* + noun

Uses of *have*

1 a Focus learners on the questions, then play recording **2.25**. Feed back as a class.

> 1 her coat
> 2 at the bus stop

b 👥👥 Learners read the sentences from the conversation (1–4) and match them to a–d. Check as a class.

> 1c 2d 3b 4a

c 👥👥 Learners read the email and do questions 1 and 2 together.

> 1 An old man found it at the bus stop outside her office.
> 2 Guess what! I've found my coat. It took most of the day to find it. I couldn't get through to lost property on the phone so I had to go there, but nobody had handed it in. I thought it might be at the office so I had to go all the way into town to check but it wasn't there either. I had some lunch with Lorna, and I then saw an old man wearing my coat! I asked him about it and he said he had found it at the bus stop outside the office. I said he could keep it, as I had just bought a new one. Have you found your phone yet?
> Anyway, I have to go now. See you later.
> Mx

Causative *have*

2 a Focus learners on the short conversation and answer the questions as a class. Write the pattern on the board so learners can refer to it when they write their questions in **b**. Point out that *get* and *have* are interchangeable in this structure and add *get* to the pattern on the board.

> 1 Someone else did it (the dry cleaners).
> 2 have + noun + past participle

b *Writing questions.* Do the first one with the class and write it on the board as an example. Point out that learners can also ask for information such as *where* (do you have your hair cut?) or *how often*, etc.

> Possible questions
> Do you have your car fixed or do you do it yourself?
> Do you have your windows cleaned or do you do them yourself?
> Where do you have your hair cut?
> How often do you have your nails manicured?
> Do you have to have your accounts done by someone?
> How often do you have your home cleaned?

c 👥 / 👥👥 *Asking and answering.* Learners talk in pairs or groups. Encourage them to ask for more details, e.g. *how often*, *where*, etc., and decide who is the most self-sufficient.

> **Alternative: Survey**
>
> You could do this as a class survey, with each learner taking one action and writing two or three questions for it (as suggested above). Learners then mill around the class asking their questions. Give them a time limit, e.g. three or four minutes. Depending on the size of the class, learners then get into groups to share what they found out or report their information to the class.

Common expressions with *have* + noun

3 a Draw attention to the highlighted expressions in a–g. Learners do the matching in pairs or individually before comparing with a partner.

> 1 e   2 a   3 g   4 d   5 c   6 b   7 f

b 👤 *Find someone who.* Elicit a question for the first item from the class and write it on the board. Then give learners a moment to prepare the rest of the questions to ask a partner.

> 2 Do you always have a word with your boss when you have a problem?
> 3 Do you have a go at fixing things in the home? / Have you ever had a go at fixing things in the home?
> 4 Have you had a chance to do your homework?
> 5 Do you have something boring to do at the weekend, but don't have a choice (about this)?
> 6 Do you have a feeling that something exciting will happen today?

c 👥👥 *Asking and answering.* Learners talk together. Encourage them to find out more information by asking questions. Monitor while they are talking and feed back as necessary.

 You could use photocopiable activity 8C on the Teacher's DVD-ROM at this point.

Goals: describe objects you don't know the name of
use vague language to describe things

Core language:
Vague language

1 Focus learners on the pictures and talk about what the objects might be used for with the class.

2 *Listening for main idea.* Play recording **2.26** and get learners to match the conversations to the objects in the pictures. Then they discuss the three questions in pairs before checking as a class.

> 1 B   2 A   3 C
> 1 the mbira (conversation 3)
> 2 the tallboy (conversation 1)
> 3 the bilum (conversation 2)

3 a *Listening for detail.* Play recording **2.26** again, stopping after each conversation so pairs can discuss the similarities and differences. Don't go through the answers at this stage.

b Learners check their ideas in the conversations on the page.

> Possible answers
> 1 It's not nearly as big and it's made of wood with metal keys.
> 2 It's much taller.
> 3 It's like rope, but more delicate than rope.

4 The distinctions between the three categories are quite subtle, so do this with the class and don't spend too much time on the differences between the three sets of expressions.

> 1 c   2 a   3 b

5 a 👤 *Preparation.* Give learners time to choose something to describe and to prepare what they want to say. Walk round and help with ideas and vocabulary as necessary while they're working.

b 👥👥 *Speaking and listening.* Learners take turns to describe and listen to each other's descriptions and guess what they're describing (and perhaps draw the object). Encourage them to find out more information about the objects by asking further questions. Monitor while they're talking and take a note of good and incorrect language use for a feedback session at the end.

8 Look again

Review

GRAMMAR Modals of deduction and speculation

1 a Look at the first sentence and examples with the class and elicit more ideas from learners. Write the ideas on the board to demonstrate the activity, then learners continue in pairs.

b Walk round while learners are writing more situations and help as necessary. Put pairs into groups to guess what is happening. Feed back as a class by asking learners to present and guess situations in open pairs.

VOCABULARY Travel situations

2 a Learners do the matching individually before checking with a partner.

> get stuck, get on/off, get a lift, get lost, (get down)
> give somebody a lift
> break down
> be stuck, be cancelled, be lost

b 👥 Learners read the situations and complete the sentences by inserting expressions at the points indicated. Remind them that they may have to change the forms of the verbs.

> 1 get stuck   2 broken down   3 is cancelled   4 get on

c 👥 Give learners a few minutes to think about the situations and to come up with ideas. Then they can take turns to tell each other what they did. Ask different learners to give an idea for each situation.

CAN YOU REMEMBER? Unit 7 – Matching people to jobs and activities

3 a 👥 Learners complete the sentences. Check as a class.

> 1 someone   2 person   3 something   4 thing

b 👤 *Writing sentences.* Walk round while learners are writing and help as necessary.

c 👥 *Speaking.* Learners discuss the activities. In feedback, find out if they agreed with each other.

Extension

SPELLING AND SOUNDS /ɑː/

4 a Say the /ɑː/ sound for the class so learners know what to listen for, then play recording **2.27** or say the words yourself. Learners underline the letters (one or two letters) which make the /ɑː/ sound, then check with a partner. In feedback, check learners are aware of the silent *l* in *calm*, *half* and *halve* (/ɑː/).

> <u>ar</u>gument, d<u>a</u>nce, d<u>ar</u>k, <u>ar</u>ticle, b<u>ar</u>, c<u>a</u>lm, al<u>ar</u>m, h<u>a</u>lf,
> c<u>a</u>stle, st<u>ar</u>, ex<u>a</u>mple, h<u>a</u>lve, <u>ar</u>m, l<u>ar</u>ge, f<u>ar</u>

Language note: Variation in pronunciation

For many speakers, *ar* is pronounced /ɑːr/, depending on where the speaker comes from (e.g. USA, Scotland, Ireland). *A* in the middle of words is pronounced /æ/ by many speakers, e.g. in the North of England and in the USA.

---

b 👥 Learners match the spelling patterns to the words in **a**. Remind learners to say the words out loud to each other.

> 1 argument, dark, article, bar, alarm, star, arm, large, far
> 2 calm, half, halve
> 3 dance, castle, example

c *Spellcheck with books closed.* Play recording **2.28** or say the words for learners to write them down. They can check their own spelling at the end.

NOTICE Using synonyms

5 This activity draws attention to the use of synonyms in written English. If learners are struggling, let them look back at the article to find the words.

> 1 rubbish, stuff, things, possessions
> 2 Learners' own answers
> 3 throw away, have a clear out, get rid of, give away

Self-assessment

Go through the list of goals, eliciting language from the unit for each one. You may need to remind learners of the contexts for the goals and let them look back through the unit if necessary. Then they circle the appropriate number for each goal. Walk round while they are doing this and talk to learners about their progress. Remind learners about the extra practice opportunities under the box, and ask where they can find things.

Unit 8 Extra activities on the Teacher's DVD-ROM

Printable worksheets, activity instructions and answer keys are on your Teacher's DVD-ROM.

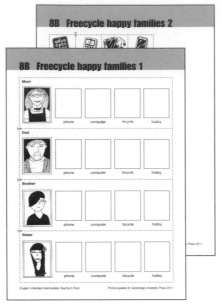

8A Clearing out

Activity type: Speaking and writing – Reconstruct note from visual cues and a 'word cloud' – Individuals/Pairs

Aim: To practise using multi-word verbs for cleaning and tidying

Language: Multi-word verbs: tidying and cleaning – Use at any point from 8.1.

Preparation: Make one copy of the worksheet for each learner (and one copy of the original note for each learner if desired).

Time: 20–30 minutes

8B Freecycle happy families

Activity type: Speaking – Card game – Groups

Aim: To practise describing products and asking for things politely

Language: Describing products – Use at any point from 8.1.

Preparation: Make one copy each of Worksheets 1 and 2 for each group. Cut up Worksheet 1 to make a set of four Character cards. Cut up Worksheet 2 to make a set of 16 Object cards. Shuffle the Object cards.

Time: 15–20 minutes

8C Story generator

Activity type: Speaking and writing – Collaborative story-building/rehearsal/retelling – Groups

Aim: To practise uses of *have*

Language: Keyword *have* – Use at any point from Keyword *have*, p67.

Preparation: Make one copy of the worksheet for each group of learners. Cut up each worksheet to make one Introduction slip and one set of 20 Story slips.

Time: 20–30 minutes (plus further writing time if required)

Unit 8 Self-study Pack

In the Workbook

Unit 8 of the *English Unlimited Intermediate Workbook* offers additional ways to practise the vocabulary and grammar taught in the Coursebook. There are also activities which build reading and writing skills and a whole page of listening and speaking tasks to use with the Interview video, giving your learners the opportunity to hear and react to authentic spoken English.

- **Vocabulary:** Multi-word verbs: tidying and cleaning; Describing products; Travel situations; Describing objects
- **Grammar:** Modals of deduction
- **Time out:** Quiz: Are you organised or disorganised?
- **Explore writing:** Selling things online
- **Interview:** Nightmare journeys – Clare and Andrés

On the DVD-ROM

Unit 8 of the *English Unlimited Intermediate Self-study DVD-ROM* contains interactive games and activities for your learners to practise and improve their vocabulary, grammar and pronunciation, and also their speaking and listening, with the possibility for learners to record themselves, and a video of authentic spoken English to use with the Workbook.

- **Vocabulary and grammar:** Extra practice activities
- **Pronunciation:** Emphatic stress
- **Explore speaking:** *What a ... !*
- **Explore listening:** A lost item
- **Video:** Nightmare journeys

9 Make up your mind

9.1

Goals: describe problems in the home
discuss solutions

Core language:

VOCABULARY   Problems in the home
Discussing problems and solutions

Power cut

READING

1 a Focus on the two pictures and ask learners to talk
about them in pairs. In feedback, listen for learners'
knowledge of vocabulary describing the situations,
such as *power cut, flooded*, etc.

  b *Reading for main idea.* Learners read the
stories to check their ideas. Find out how many
learners predicted the situations correctly. Check
understanding of *midwife, torch, candles, storm,
blown off, blown down*. If learners ask about the target
language, you can elicit from the class or explain that
you will deal with this in the next section.

2 a Tell learners to cover the stories and to see what they
can remember about the four things listed for each story.

> **Kurt's story**
> 1 his son: He was born at home. His name's Kurt, too.
> 2 the heating: It went off in the house during the birth.
> 3 candles: Kurt (father) lit candles around the room so
> they could see.
> 4 the lights: They came back on just after his son was
> born.
> **Phillip's story**
> 1 a storm: There was a big storm in the middle of the
> night.
> 2 roof: It blew off. In the morning, there was a big hole
> in it.
> 3 water: Some pipes burst and there was water
> everywhere in the house.
> 4 outside the house: A tree blew down in the garden. It
> was a complete mess.

Alternative: Conversational strategies

It will be useful to listen to learners' coping strategies
while they are doing this task. Listen to see if they ask
for clarification, clarify things they've said or check
understanding while they are trying to remember the details
of the text and if they paraphrase unknown vocabulary (for
instance, using some of the expressions from the previous
Explore speaking on p68). If you think they need extra help
with these conversational strategies, write useful exponents
on the board when learners have finished and check they
record them in their vocabulary notebooks. For example,
*What exactly do you mean by …?, I meant to say …, Do you
mean …?, It's a sort of …, It's sort of like a …*.

---

  b *Reading for detail.* Learners read the stories again to
check their ideas. Get learners' responses to the stories
as a class, finding out how they think both people felt
after the events.

VOCABULARY Problems in the home

3 a Focus learners on the pictures of problems in the
home. They match the pictures with the descriptions
of the problems. Remind them to check their ideas by
looking back at the items that are contextualised in the
stories above.

> 1 D 2 F 3 G 4 H 5 B 6 C 7 E 8 A

  b Learners work through the sentences together.
Point out that in some sentences, it can be both.
Model the sentences with the contractions and give
learners the opportunity to repeat them until they feel
confident saying them.

> 's = <u>has</u> in sentences 2 and 3
> 's = <u>is</u> in sentences 1, 4, 6 and 8.
> It could be either in sentence 7.

  c Learners talk about this in pairs or you could have a
class discussion. Learners may be keen to tell their
own anecdotes, but ask them to wait until **4** when they
will have a chance to listen to each other's stories.

  d Learners can use the pictures and expressions to
jog their memories.

> *Kurt's story: There was a power cut*
> *Phillip's story: There was a power cut; some pipes burst
> and the upstairs was flooded.*

  e Give learners time to talk about the situations and
complete the sentences together. They may come up
with different answers, which is fine.

> *Possible answers*
> 2 We had to use candles all evening because there was
> a power cut.
> 3 We'll have to call a plumber because the pipe's burst.
> 4 Don't go in the kitchen because it's flooded.
> 5 We can't get out of the front room because the door's
> stuck.
> 6 You won't be able to open that window because the
> handle's come off.
> 7 That torch won't work because the batteries are flat.
> 8 There's no hot water because there's a power cut.

You could use photocopiable activity 9A on the
Teacher's DVD-ROM at this point.

SPEAKING

4 Learners discuss the questions. In feedback,
find out who is good at solving problems like these.
Ask one or two confident learners to tell their own
stories to the class if they'd like to.

What shall we do?

LISTENING

1 a *Listening for main idea.* Draw attention to the picture
and ask the class to predict what problems Lidia and
Ben might have. Then play recording **2.29** so learners
can check their predictions and answer the question.

> The room with the washing machine has flooded, and Ben doesn't have a clean shirt. Lidia's parents are arriving soon.

b *Listening for detail.* Give learners time to read the questions and talk about them with a partner before playing recording **2.29** again. Learners check in pairs before checking as a class.

> **a** *They might go out for lunch.*
> **b** *They turn the water off at the mains and decide to call a plumber.*
> **c** *Lidia suggests Ben buys another shirt.*

VOCABULARY Discussing problems and solutions

2 Focus learners on the highlighted expressions from Lidia and Ben's conversation. Learners categorise the expressions in pairs. Model the sentences, focusing on the linking in *What are we going to do about … ?*, *give it a try* and *have a go*. Give learners an opportunity to repeat all the sentences, and to practise the contractions in *I'll/We'll (have to)*. This will help with fluency in the next activity.

> **1** c **2** a **3** b

SPEAKING

3 a Give learners time to think about the situations and prepare what they are going to say. Walk round and help as necessary.

> **Alternative for weaker groups**
>
> Let learners plan in A/A and B/B pairs before changing partners and having their conversations.

b Learners choose a situation and talk about it together using the expressions in **2**. Monitor learners' conversations and take a note of any problems that impede communication. Feed back on these before learners have their next conversation.

c Learners choose another situation and have a second conversation. Let them change partners if they wish.

4 *Round-up.* Put pairs together to compare their solutions, before getting some feedback from the class. Ask different learners what they did in the three situations. You could ask the class to decide who thought of the best solutions to each problem.

> ## 9.2
>
> **Goals:** talk about decision-making
> discuss solutions
> discuss the consequences of decisions
>
> **Core language:**
>
> | | |
> |---|---|
> | VOCABULARY | Decision-making |
> | GRAMMAR | Real and unreal conditionals |
> | PRONUNCIATION | Groups of words 2 |

Decision-making

READING

1 a Ask learners to think about how easy or difficult they find it to make decisions in relation to the different contexts listed. Tell them to think of some examples of decisions they've had to make, and why the decisions were easy or difficult.

b Learners can compare their ideas in pairs or small groups before you discuss this with the class. Find out what kind of decisions learners find hardest to make.

2 Focus learners on the two questions before they read the introduction to the article. They can answer the question in pairs. Check as a class.

> The technique helps people make better decisions by changing how they think. It also shows people how to solve problems by thinking in a number of different ways.

3 *Reading for main idea.* Draw learners' attention to the six hats and the summaries a–f. Learners read the descriptions and do the matching. They can compare answers with a partner before you check with the class.

> **a** yellow hat **b** black hat **c** green hat **d** red hat
> **e** blue hat **f** white hat

> **Alternative for weaker groups**
>
> Some learners may find the topic of the article rather abstract and subsequently difficult to understand. One way to make the topic simpler for learners is to ask them to predict the matching of a–f with the six hats. Which colour hat is likely to represent someone who thinks positively, negatively, creatively, etc.? This will probably reflect learners' different cultural attitudes, but whatever answers they come up with, the prediction will give them time to interact with the topic and text and thoroughly process the task before they read the text in detail to check their ideas.

4 Learners discuss the ideas in the article in pairs or groups. Ask a few learners which hat best represents the way they make decisions and why. In feedback, find out how many learners think they use one hat most of the time, or different hats for different kinds of decisions. You could also ask if they would like to 'try on' a hat which represents a thinking approach they wouldn't normally use.

VOCABULARY Decision-making

5 *Focus on collocations.* Learners cover the article and think about which verbs go with the nouns and noun phrases in 1–9. When they're ready, let them check their own ideas and point out that the items are in the same order they appear in the introduction and in the main body of the article.

> **1** make decisions **2** solve problems **3** trust your intuition
> **4** listen to your heart **5** look at the facts
> **6** come up with a new plan **7** brainstorm ideas
> **8** develop solutions **9** hold a meeting

SPEAKING

6 a Look through the stages of the activity with the class. Demonstrate it by explaining a situation of your own to the class. Assign roles to a few learners and talk about your decision with them. Tell them what you have decided to do at the end. Then tell learners to do the same in groups, first giving learners time to think about a decision they have to make. Walk round and help with ideas as necessary. Groups can vary in size, as learners can take on more than one 'Thinking Hat' role. Alternatively, not all Thinking Hats have to be covered in a group discussion. Monitor learners while they are talking and take a note of any errors that impede communication.

b Have a class discussion about how effective the Thinking Hats technique was.

Problems and solutions

LISTENING

1 *Listening for main idea.* Focus learners on the picture and ask them to predict answers to the questions. Then play recording **2.30**. Let learners compare ideas with a partner before you check with the class.

> Their business is a café. They're discussing its success and how to cover and manage all the business they're getting.

2 a *Listening for detail.* Give learners time to read the questions and think about the answers with a partner before you play recording **2.30** again. Then go through the answers with the class.

> 1 Simon   2 Yelena   3 Lidia   4 Yelena   5 Simon   6 Lidia

b You could discuss this with the whole class. Encourage learners to give reasons for their ideas.

GRAMMAR Real and unreal conditionals

3 a *Focus on meaning.* Focus learners on the five extracts from the conversation. In pairs, they match the extracts with the two categories. Check as a class, talking through any problems learners have with the meanings.

> 1 a, e   2 b, c, d

b *Focus on form.* Learners complete the patterns in pairs first before you elicit and write the form for both structures on the board.

> 1 if + *present simple*, will/won't + *infinitive*
> 2 if + *past simple*, would/wouldn't + *infinitive*

c *Focus on use.* Make sure learners understand *consequence* (= the result of a particular action). They discuss the two sentences in pairs.

> Sentence d is a suggestion (unreal conditional, because Yelena doesn't think the suggestion is practicable). Sentence e is a negative consequence (real conditional, setting out what would happen).

Note: Grammar practice

You could do the grammar practice on p140 at this point.

You could use photocopiable activity 9B on the Teacher's DVD-ROM at this point.

PRONUNCIATION Groups of words 2

4 a Write the example sentence on the board with the // and ask for a confident volunteer to say the sentence or play recording **2.31**. Ask learners what the double lines show, and why we use groups of words when we speak.

b Tell learners to say the sentences out loud to each other and to decide together where the sentences divide into groups. Point out that there is not one correct answer (i.e. that speakers make choices about how they speak depending on what they want to express), but that some divisions are certainly more likely than others. Walk round and help any learners who are struggling by saying the sentences for them. Then play recording **2.32** so they can check their answers. Give learners time to practise saying the sentences after you or the recording, or on their own if they are confident.

> b But it's too expensive. // And if we did that, // it would take a lot longer to serve people outside.
> c Hm, // that's a problem for me. // I mean, // if I didn't have three children, // I'd do it, // no problem.
> d This is just an idea, // but if we employed another person, // we wouldn't have to do so many hours.
> e That's not a bad idea. // But if we employ another person, // we'll take home less money.
> There may be additional groups in the final parts of the sentences, e.g. it would take a lot longer // to serve people outside.

SPEAKING

5 a *Preparation.* Look at the table of ideas with the class and brainstorm some more positive and negative consequences of having your own business. Then elicit some conditional sentences from different learners.

Point out that what is realistic and possible for one person may be impossible for another, so try to get a range of examples from the class to illustrate the possibilities. Learners then continue preparing their ideas individually. Walk round and help as necessary.

Alternative for weaker groups

Learners prepare in A/A and B/B pairs so they have more support in the planning stage. They then swap pairs for the next stage of the activity (**5b**). If you think your class needs help with the suggestions, brainstorm more ideas with the class and write them on the board.

b 👥 / 👥👥 *Discussion.* Monitor while learners talk about their suggestions and the consequences together. Take a note of good and incorrect language for a feedback session later. In feedback, find out if learners agreed about the possible consequences of their decisions.

9.3 Target activity

Goals: describe problems in the home ♻
discuss solutions ♻
discuss the consequences of decisions ♻
negotiate

Core language:

TASK VOCABULARY	Negotiating
9.1 VOCABULARY	Discussing problems and solutions
9.2 VOCABULARY	Decision-making
9.2 GRAMMAR	Real and unreal conditionals

Reach a compromise

TASK LISTENING

1 Focus learners on the dictionary entry and check understanding and pronunciation of *compromise* /ˈkɒmprəmaɪz/. Give an example of situations where you (personally) have to compromise, then talk about learners' situations.

2 👥 *Pre-listening discussion.* Use the questions to introduce the topic of friends living together (in house or flat shares). Learners discuss possible disagreements in pairs. In feedback, find out how many learners have experience of flat shares or if anyone shares a flat or house at the moment and if they have to compromise in any of these areas.

3 a *Listening for main idea.* Focus on the picture and ask the class for ideas about what is happening in it. Play recording **2.33** and ask learners to label the picture with the correct names. Learners check in pairs before you go through the answers as a class.

> Luis is in the kitchen. Nasser is on the sofa listening to the radio. Brad is in the armchair trying to read.

b *Listening for detail.* Learners discuss the three questions in pairs. Then play recording **2.33** again so they can check their answers. In feedback, find out how different learners would feel about living with Luis, Nasser or Brad (or, if this is culturally inappropriate, with people similar to them).

> 1 They discuss the washing-up, the shower and noise.
> 2 They agree to do their own washing-up. Brad agrees to use the bathroom later when the others have left the house. Nasser agrees to listen to the radio quietly only in the kitchen with the door shut.
> 3 Learners' own answers

TASK VOCABULARY Negotiating

4 a *Focus on expressions.* Look at the three pairs of sentences with the class. Do the first sentence with the class (they're talking about making a rota for the washing-up). Then learners continue in pairs. Don't check the answers, as this will pre-empt **b**.

b *Listening to check.* Play recording **2.33** again so learners can listen to check. Draw learners' attention to the intonation and the word groups which tend to be particularly pronounced when we're negotiating, e.g. *But if I agree to do that // could you please do something for me?*

> 1/2 making a rota for the washing-up
> 3 listening to the radio
> 4 the washing-up and using the bathroom
> 5 using the bathroom
> 6 the washing-up

c *Focus on meaning.* Learners categorise the expressions in pairs, then check as the class.

> 1 C   2 A   3 B

5 👥 *Practice.* Learners work in pairs to complete the sentences with suitable expressions.

> 1 That way   2 How about if   3 Or we could just
> 4 but if I   5 that would mean

TASK

6 a 🧍 *Preparation.* Direct learners to the role cards and walk round and help while they're preparing their roles. Remind them that they can check language, e.g. conditionals, in previous pages in the unit.

b 👥👥 *Role play.* Monitor while learners are having their conversations and take a note of their use of conditionals and other negotiating language. When they've finished their conversations, feed back on the language.

Round-up. Find out if different groups reached different compromises. You could decide as a class on the best solutions to the problems.

 You could use photocopiable activity 9C on the Teacher's DVD-ROM at this point.

9 Explore

Across cultures: Dealing with conflict

Goals: raise awareness of cultural differences in dealing with conflict
talk about different attitudes to conflict

Core language:
VOCABULARY   Dealing with conflict

SPEAKING

1   Focus on the pictures at the bottom of the page and ask learners what they think is going on. This may elicit responses such as *They're arguing / having an argument / having a fight*. Find out if they think the people are very angry and know each other or not, and where they think they might be from. This may give you an insight into learners' opinions on dealing with conflict at the outset of the lesson. Learners then discuss the questions in pairs or groups. Get feedback from several different learners. If you are not from the same country as your learners, be prepared to talk about how you deal with conflict where you are from, particularly if you are teaching a monocultural class.

LISTENING

2 a *Listening for main idea.* Draw attention to the picture and information about Çigdem (pronounced /'tʃɪːdem/). Let learners read the topic summaries, then play recording **2.34**. They compare with a partner, then go through the answers as a class.

> 1 c   2 b   3 a   4 d

b *Listening for detail.* Learners look at the options for questions 1–4 and decide which they think is correct in each case. Then play recording **2.34** again, while learners listen to check their ideas. Let them discuss answers briefly together again before checking as a class.

> 1 a   2 b   3 b   4 a

c Give learners a moment to discuss their ideas in pairs before talking about this with the class. If learners start discussing their own situations, ask them to wait, as they will have an opportunity to talk more about their own cultures later in the lesson. If you have learners from Turkey, however, it is important to ask them if they agree or disagree with Çigdem's opinions and why.

> She says that in England, people do a lot of talking behind the scenes. They are embarrassed if you ask them about a problem directly. In Turkey, they are less inhibited and have more arguments, because everything is out in the open, in both work and family situations.

VOCABULARY Dealing with conflict

3 a *Focus on verb + noun collocations.* Do the first one with the class, then learners continue in pairs.

> 1 English families   2 her father   3 Turkish people
> 4 her father   5 English families
> 6 Çigdem and her mother   7 Çigdem and her clients

b Learners practise remembering the collocations. See *Games to improve fluency* on p83 for alternative ways to practise collocations.

SPEAKING

4   *Discussion.* Walk round while learners discuss the questions in groups. Take a note of interesting ideas learners express in their discussions and at the end, ask them to explain their ideas to the class. Encourage other learners to respond and find out if most people share similar views and if their cultures have broadly similar or different attitudes to dealing with conflict.

Explore writing

Goals: write a web posting explaining an argument
organise ideas 2

Core language:
Expressions for linking ideas and for contrasting ideas

1   *Introducing the topic.* Find out what learners think happens mostly in their countries and get their views on the advantages and disadvantages of buying or renting homes.

2   *Reading for main idea.* Focus learners on the picture and the text type before they read and answer the questions in pairs. Check as a class.

> 1 His rent will be doubled and he can't afford to pay it, so he will have to move out.
> 2 Ian doesn't sympathise because Tomas has had a low rent and one home for 20 years. Amie does sympathise because Tomas has been a good tenant and looked after landlord's flat.

3   Discuss the different positions held by the three people and find out who learners agree with and why.

4 a Learners can try to complete the expressions with a partner before checking against the text.

> 1 also   2 but also   3 nor   4 and   5 but that   6 or
> 7 but at the same time

> **Alternative for weaker groups**
>
> Learners can search through the postings and complete the expressions. Although they are copying from the text, they will still be noticing and processing the language.

b *Practice.* Walk round and help while learners complete the sentences with their own ideas. Then they compare with a partner.

5   *Preparation.* Direct learners to the posting at the end of the book. They discuss their opinions with a group, then plan their own response individually before writing a comment. Walk round and help with language while learners are writing.

6 a *Responding.* Learners exchange comments. They should read three or four and choose one to respond to.

b 👥 Learners give their replies to the writer of the
original comment they chose. If possible, both writers
should have time to talk about their comments together.

Round-up. Find out if any learners strongly disagreed
with each other's opinions and why.

9 Look again

Review

GRAMMAR Real and unreal conditionals

1 a 👥 Do the first one with the class, then learners
continue in pairs.

> 1 If I had enough money ...
> 2 If there's a good film on tonight, ...
> 3 If there was a good pool nearby, ...
> 4 If I really needed to learn a language, ...
> 5 If I have some time later, ...
> 6 If I could have any car I wanted ...

b ✎ *Writing sentences.* Walk round while learners
complete the sentences and check to see if anyone
is still having problems forming real and unreal
conditional sentences. Give learners a chance to
compare their ideas and in feedback, find out if there
were any unusual ideas in the class.

VOCABULARY Problems in the home

2 a 👥 Learners replace the underlined expressions with
the expressions in the box.

> 2 flat   3 flooded   4 not working   5 has burst
> 6 come off   7 is stuck

b *Speaking.* Learners discuss what to do in situations
1–7. Monitor while learners are having their
conversations, and check to see how and if learners
are using the target language.

CAN YOU REMEMBER? Unit 8 – Modals of deduction and speculation

3 a 👥 Learners complete the conversations in pairs.
Check as a class.

> 1 might/could   2 must   3 can't   4 must

b 👤 Draw learners' attention to the three underlined
expressions in **a** and the example. Then learners
continue individually. Walk round and help with ideas
as necessary.

c 👥 *Speaking.* Learners work in pairs using their
sentences from **b**. Go round the class and ask different
pairs to 'perform' their mini-conversations for the class.

Extension

SPELLING AND SOUNDS /ɜː/

4 a Model *world* for the class and write the IPA symbol
on the board. Then continue saying the other words
while learners underline the letters, or play recording
2.35. Give learners time to practise saying the words
to themselves.

> w*or*ld, b*ur*st, b*ir*th, w*or*king, em*er*gency, d*ir*ty, l*ear*n,
> alt*er*native, *ear*n, f*ir*st, *ur*gent

b Learners can do this individually before comparing
with a partner.

> 1 burst, birth, emergency, dirty, alternative, first, world,
>   working
> 2 learn, earn, urgent

c *Spellcheck.* Learners do this individually before
comparing with a partner, then checking their answers.

> 1 furniture   2 thirteen   3 heard   4 earth   5 purpose
> 6 rehearse   7 confirm   8 determined   9 urban

NOTICE on, off

5 a Remind learners that they have seen these sentences
earlier in the unit. They complete the sentences in pairs.

> 1 off   2 on   3 off   4 off   5 on   6 on

b Learners check their own answers in the texts and
scripts on the pages shown.

c Learners complete the sentences individually using
verbs from **a** before comparing with a partner.

> 1 try   2 come   3 come   4 went   5 having

Self-assessment

Go through the list of goals, eliciting language from the
unit for each one. You may need to remind learners of the
contexts for the goals and let them look back through the
unit if necessary. Then they circle the appropriate number
for each goal. Walk round while they are doing this and talk
to learners about their progress. Remind learners about the
extra practice opportunities under the box, and ask where
they can find things.

Unit 9 Extra activities on the Teacher's DVD-ROM

Printable worksheets, activity instructions and answer keys are on your Teacher's DVD-ROM.

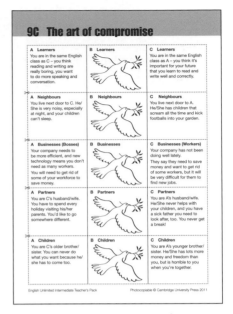

9A In every dream home ...

Activity type: Speaking, writing and reading – Writing an email – Pairs

Aim: To practise describing problems around the house and suggesting solutions

Language: Problems in the home – Use at any point from 9.1.

Preparation: Make one copy of the worksheet for each pair.

Time: 20 minutes

9B But what if ...?

Activity type: Speaking – Pyramid discussion or group intensive discussion – Pairs / Whole class

Aim: To discuss problems and solutions in a variety of contexts

Language: Real and unreal conditionals – Use at any point from 9.2.

Preparation: Make one copy of the worksheet for each pair. Cut up each worksheet to make a set of ten Challenge cards.

Time: 20–30 minutes

9C The art of compromise

Activity type: Speaking – Small-group role play – Groups

Aim: To practise negotiation and compromise language

Language: Negotiating and discussing solutions – Use at any point from 9.3 (Target activity).

Preparation: Make one copy of the worksheet for every three learners. Cut up each worksheet to make a set of five cards.

Time: 20–30 minutes

Unit 9 Self-study Pack

In the Workbook

Unit 9 of the *English Unlimited Intermediate Workbook* offers additional ways to practise the vocabulary and grammar taught in the Coursebook. There are also activities which build reading and writing skills and two whole pages of listening and speaking tasks to use with the Documentary video, giving your learners the opportunity to hear and react to authentic spoken English.

- **Vocabulary:** Problems in the home; Discussing problems and solutions; Decision-making; Negotiating; Dealing with conflict
- **Grammar:** Real and unreal conditionals
- **My English:** Reiner from Germany
- **Explore reading:** Lateral thinking
- **Documentary:** The hairdressing entrepreneurs

On the DVD-ROM

Unit 9 of the *English Unlimited Intermediate Self-study DVD-ROM* contains interactive games and activities for your learners to practise and improve their vocabulary, grammar and pronunciation, and also their speaking and listening, with the possibility for learners to record themselves, and a video of authentic spoken English to use with the Workbook.

- **Vocabulary and grammar:** Extra practice activities
- **Pronunciation:** Groups of words
- **Explore speaking:** *I suppose ...*
- **Explore listening:** An angry caller
- **Video:** Documentary – The hairdressing entrepreneurs

10 Impressions

10.1

Goals: talk about memory
talk about what you remember

Core language:

VOCABULARY	Remembering an event
GRAMMAR	Verb patterns

Witness

LISTENING

1 Focus learners on the question and the list of ideas. They can discuss this in pairs or you could talk about it as a class. In feedback, find out if learners have any special techniques for remembering different types of information.

2 **a** Make sure learners understand *witness* (= someone who sees a crime being committed, or evidence of a crime, and later gives a report of what they saw to the police). Find out if anyone thinks they would be a good witness (and why). If anyone wants to tell a story of a crime they have witnessed, tell them they will have a chance to do this later in the lesson. Check understanding of *CCTV*, then focus attention on the CCTV image of a crime. 🔒 Learners study the image in silence for 30 seconds and try to remember as much important information as they can. 👥 After time is up, learners close their books, listen to recording **2.36** and take notes.

Optional extra: Live listening

To give the remembering activity more focus, tell learners to close their books and read out the following list of questions. Learners listen and take notes, then do **2b**. Afterwards, find out if anyone could answer all the questions (or none of them!).

1   What was the crime?
    A teenager broke into someone's home and stole some things.
2   Where was the crime?
    It was in a street of flats.
3   What was the criminal wearing?
    A top with a hood over his head and a number '3' on the back. He was tall, thin and young.
4   Were there any witnesses?
    There were two witnesses. A man getting into his car and a woman walking past on the street.
5   What did the witness or witnesses look like?
    The man was quite old and was wearing a dark jacket. The woman on the street was young; she was wearing a hat and carrying a shoulder bag.

---

b 👥 Learners check their ideas against the image and discuss what they did and didn't remember. In feedback, find out who thinks they remembered all (or none) of the important information. The question previews the vocabulary item *notice*. Listen to see if learners understand it, but it's not necessary to explain the word at this stage unless learners cannot answer the question.

3 **a** *Listening for main idea.* Play recording **2.37**, then discuss whether Hiromi's recollection was accurate or not.

> Not very good, as she missed some things and got some details wrong.

b *Listening for detail.* Focus learners on the image again and tell them to listen carefully to Hiromi's account once more to spot the four details she got wrong. Play recording **2.37** again if necessary. Learners compare ideas in pairs. Then go through the answers with the class.

> She got the following details wrong:
> The boy's shirt had a number '3' on it, not a number '1'.
> The boy was wearing a top with a hood, not a baseball cap.
> It was a young woman who was passing, not a man.
> She said there was nobody else around, but there was also a man getting into a car.

4 *Discussion.* Talk about this with the class. If you have a story, tell it to the class first, which may prompt their memories of similar incidents. Encourage learners to ask questions to find out more information.

VOCABULARY Remembering an event

5 **a** *Focus on expressions.* Learners match the beginnings and ends of the sentences from Hiromi's account. They can do this in pairs, or individually before comparing with a partner. Learners look at the script on p156 to check their answers.

> 2 d   3 c   4 e   5 g   6 b   7 a

Language note: Expressions for remembering an event

The vocabulary section focuses on high-frequency expressions for remembering events. Learners will focus on the grammar and how to generate new sentences with the various verbs later. Encourage learners to practise saying the expressions and focus on the stress in *I can't remember … but I can remember …*, pointing out that *can* is pronounced /kæn/ in this context (rather than the more common use of the weak form) because it is contrasted with what Hiromi can't remember.

---

b 👥 / 👥👥 *Practice.* Give learners a minute to think about their answers and how they can express them using the target language, before they talk together. In feedback, ask different learners the questions and focus on how the expressions from **a** are used in their responses.

 You could use photocopiable activity 10A on the Teacher's DVD-ROM at this point.

False memories

READING

1 Talk about the first question with the class to check understanding of the four words and pronunciation of: *judge* /dʒʌdʒ/, *jury* /ˈdʒʊəri/ and *lawyer* /ˈlɔːjəʳ/. Then learners can continue in pairs or groups. In feedback, find out what different learners think are the most difficult things they have to do and why.

> 1 The judge has to decide what sentence to give for crimes committed.
> The jury has to listen to all the evidence and make a decision about whether they think the person is guilty or not.
> A lawyer has to present the facts for or against the defendant (the person accused of the crime) to the judge and jury.
> A witness has to explain what they saw of the crime as accurately as they can.

Alternative

Books closed. Bring in or project a picture of a courtroom onto the board (you can find a selection in Google images). Elicit who is who in the picture, then learners discuss their roles in pairs or groups and discuss question 2.

2 *Reading for main idea.* Focus learners on the gist question before they read the article. Encourage them to read quickly at this stage. (It's helpful to give a time limit, say two minutes.) Let them know they will have time to read in more detail in a minute.

> The problem with using witnesses in court is that it is difficult to be sure that their evidence is accurate.

3 *Reading for detail.* Check understanding of *rely on* in the question and see if learners know *reliable*. Give learners plenty of time to read the article in detail to find three reasons. Learners compare ideas with a partner first, then check as a class.

> 1 People often forget details of things that have happened.
> 2 People remember things that didn't happen at all, e.g. if they hear false information, it can change their memories of something.
> 3 Once we tell a story or give an account of something (which may include incorrect details or leave out facts), that account replaces the original event in our minds.

4 👥 / 👥👥 *Discussion.* Learners discuss their opinions about witnesses and the problems of using witnesses in response to the article. In feedback, find out if they came up with any possible solutions to the problems.

Note: Building confidence in discussions

This topic is rather abstract and so more difficult for intermediate learners to discuss. Give learners the opportunity to talk first in pairs or small groups before talking together as a class, so they have time to collect and express their thoughts to a few peers before talking in front of the whole group. Encourage learners to try to express what they mean, without focusing on the language they use. If necessary, reformulate their ideas or ask questions to help them express what they want to say.

GRAMMAR Verb patterns

5 a Tell learners to cover the article and focus them on the four sentences with *remember* in the box. If they can, they complete the sentences from memory, first individually, then with a partner. They check their own answers against the article and script.

> 1 what   2 that   3 to   4 wondering

b *Focus on form.* Learners match the four patterns to the example sentences.

> a 4   b 3   c 1   d 2

6 a Focus learners on the dictionary entry for *forget*. All good learner dictionaries highlight the patterns which follow verbs, although different dictionaries may present the same information in different ways. Depending on how familiar your learners are with monolingual dictionaries, give them enough time to look through the entry and check the patterns against the previous exercise.

> It has all four patterns in 5b: *-ing*, to *infinitive*, *question word* and *that*.

Language note: Patterns and meaning

Some verbs change their meaning depending on whether they are followed by *-ing* or *to* infinitive.

This is the case with *remember* and *forget*. It's a good idea to point out the difference in meaning to your learners. One way to do this is to write on the board:
1 *remember/forget* + *-ing* refers forward / back in time. (back)
2 *remember/forget* + *to* infinitive refers forward / back in time. (forward)

Ask the class to look at the example sentences with *-ing* and *to* infinitive in the grammar box and to decide which pattern refers forward and which one refers back in time. You can also refer learners to the Grammar reference, which gives more information on this point.

b *Vocabulary expansion.* Point out that many verbs in English are followed by these and similar patterns and that it is important to get in the habit of checking the patterns when learning and recording new verbs. Tell learners to look up the list of verbs on p130 and to record the patterns in their vocabulary notebooks, using example sentences to show the meanings.

> *remind:* to + *infinitive*, *question word*, + *object* + of
> *know: question word*, *that*
> *understand: that*, *question word*
> *find out: question word*, *that*

Note: Grammar practice

You could do the grammar practice on p141 at this point.

SPEAKING

7 a 🧍 *Writing.* Ask the class to complete the first question together and write various possibilities on the board to demonstrate the activity. Learners continue individually or in pairs. Walk round and help as necessary.

b *Personalisation.* Learners talk in pairs. Monitor while they are talking and take a note of good and incorrect language use for a feedback session later.

10.2

Goals: talk about complaining
complain about goods or services
ask for a refund or replacement and explain why

Core language:

VOCABULARY	Problems with things you've bought
PRONUNCIATION	Intonation in questions
GRAMMAR	Present perfect simple and progressive

It's scratched

LISTENING

1 *Pre-listening discussion.* Look through the questions with the class. Check understanding of *annoys* and *queue* /kjuː/ and elicit a few examples of rule-breaking on public transport, e.g. putting feet on seats or smoking in non-smoking areas. Learners talk about them in pairs or groups. In feedback, ask a few learners what they do and if they think their behaviour is typical of people in their countries.

2 *Listening for main idea.* Focus on the question, then play recording **2.38**. Learners discuss the answer in pairs. Learners read the script to check their answers. In feedback, focus on the sentence: *They might sigh and moan about it to someone they're with, but often they won't actually say anything directly to the person, even though they're angry about it.* Check understanding of *sigh* and *moan (about something)* and use this to spark learners' responses to the text, i.e. would they say something directly to someone or not?

> *Tariq says that in Paris, people will express their anger directly to someone if they break the rules on public transport or go to the front of a queue, whereas he's not sure that people would say something in the UK. He mentions that people do complain when it comes to poor service or business transactions, either by phone or in writing.*

VOCABULARY Problems with things you've bought

3 a Focus learners on the pictures. They do the matching in pairs. In feedback, go round the class checking the answers, but ask learners to say what the object is (rather than saying 1C, for example).

> 1 C The T-shirt's the wrong size.
> 2 E The colour's faded.
> 3 A The mug's chipped.
> 4 G The MP3 player doesn't work.
> 5 H The car's dented.
> 6 D The paper's torn.
> 7 B The mug's cracked.
> 8 F The screen's scratched.

b Learners cover the expressions and test each other on the expressions using the pictures. Focus on the pronunciation of the *-ed* endings by putting three columns on the board (see below). Tell learners to put the five adjectives ending in *-ed* into the correct column according to the pronunciation of the ending. Make sure they say the words out loud to themselves and a partner.

(*-ed*) /t/	(*-ed*) /d/	(*-ed*) /ɪd/
cracked, chipped	scratched	faded, dented

c *Extension.* You could brainstorm this with the class, or give learners a few moments in groups to think of more examples, before going through their ideas together.

4 *Personalisation.* Give learners a minute to think about problems and how to explain what they did. They can then talk about their experiences in pairs or small groups. Ask one or two learners to explain their problems to the class.

> You could use photocopiable activity 10B on the Teacher's DVD-ROM at this point.

Making a complaint

LISTENING

1 *Pre-listening.* Focus learners on the picture of Mariah and her email of complaint. Talk through the complaints with the class.

> **The book she bought was damaged. The company hasn't replied to her earlier email.**

2 a Ask learners to predict what will happen in Mariah's phone call. Accept all sensible suggestions offered by the class, but don't comment on their ideas at this stage.

b Play recording **2.39** so learners can check to see if their predictions were correct.

3 *Listening for detail.* Learners read the questions, then play recording **2.39** again. They compare ideas with a partner before checking as a class.

> 1 Mariah's cross that no one has been in touch with her about the problem.
> 2 The customer services person puts Mariah on hold while he speaks to his supervisor, and he orders Mariah another copy of the book.

PRONUNCIATION Intonation in questions

4 a Introduce this by giving a few simple example questions that demonstrate the intonation patterns. For example, *What's your father's name?* (falling intonation) *Is this your book?* (pointing to book: rising intonation). Then play recording **2.40** or say the questions yourself (though you have to be careful if you do this).

> ↘ intonation: B
> ↗ intonation: A

b Learners complete the rules about intonation in questions.

> yes/no *questions* = rising ↗ intonation
> wh- *questions* = falling ↘ intonation

c Learners practise saying the questions with the appropriate intonation patterns. It is common for learners to transfer intonation patterns from their L1s, so it's worth comparing L1 and L2 to either confirm that they're the same or notice the differences if they're not. So ask learners to translate the questions and think of short responses in their own language, and to find out if the rising and falling patterns are the same in L1 and English.

Language note: Rising and falling intonation patterns

There is evidence that these patterns are similar in many languages: in research, 14 languages (including English) were found to use a falling intonation for *wh-* questions, and three to use a rising intonation. For *yes/no* questions, 37 languages used a rising intonation, against four using a falling intonation. (Cruttenden, A. 'Falls and Rises: Meanings and Universals' *Journal of Linguistics* 17, 1981)

---

5 a *Writing.* Look at the items and ask the class which ones are checking information (the order number and date). Point out that learners can write the first three items either as genuine or checking questions, e.g. *What's your name?* or *Is your name Wendy Barham?*, but remind them to make sure they have a mix of *wh-* and *yes/no* questions so they can practise the rising and falling intonation patterns.

b *Asking and answering.* Monitor while learners are talking in pairs and help out if any learners are having problems.

GRAMMAR Present perfect simple and progressive

6 Focus on the example sentences and discuss the questions with the class. This will allow you to draw attention to relevant information in the sentences and so direct learners more efficiently to the correct answers.

---

1 • *how long something takes = B (the present perfect progressive)*
• *the result of a finished activity = A (the present perfect simple)*
2 *The present perfect simple (A)*

---

7 a Walk round while learners complete the email individually and find out if anyone is having problems. Refer learners back to the rules above to help with their decisions.

Alternative for weaker groups

Learners can complete the email in pairs, talking through the reasons for their choices. They then swap partners and compare their ideas.

---

b Learners compare their answers and give reasons for their choices. Go through the answers with the class.

---

1 've written   2 haven't had   3 've been phoning
4 haven't got   5 has provided   6 've had
7 've been buying   8 've arrived   9 haven't complained

Note: Grammar practice

You could do the grammar practice on p141 at this point.

 You could use photocopiable activity 10C on the Teacher's DVD-ROM at this point.

SPEAKING

8 a *Preparation.* Explain the scenario for the role play and direct learners to the correct pages to complete their role cards. Learners fill in the gaps with their own ideas. Walk round and help if necessary. Give them a few moments to plan what they need to say.

b 👥 *Role play.* Monitor while learners are talking and take a note of the target language and of any language that impedes communication. You may want to feed back on this before learners do the second role play.

c 👥 Learners prepare for the second role play in the same way, then have another conversation.

d 👥 *Round-up.* Learners work in groups of four and repeat one of their conversations while the other pair listen. They discuss their responses in groups, then get some feedback from the different groups. Find out how easy learners found it to follow each other's conversations and answer the two questions. Also raise awareness of register, by asking for reactions to the customer services people, i.e. were they polite? helpful? how easily or skilfully did they deal with the customer's complaint(s)?

10.3 Target activity

Goal: make a complaint politely

Core language:

TASK VOCABULARY	Softeners
10.1 GRAMMAR	Verb patterns
10.2 GRAMMAR	Present perfect simple and progressive

Resolve a dispute

TASK LISTENING

1 a Focus learners on the picture and brainstorm a list of possible problems between neighbours.

b 👥 / 👥 *Pre-listening discussion.* Learners discuss the questions. Feed back as a class, finding out what differences in attitude exist among learners.

Note: Multicultural groups

In mixed-nationality classes, there are likely to be substantial differences in attitude for dealing with disputes and dealing with neighbours (note Across cultures, p75). Remind learners of the language they covered for dealing with conflict and encourage them to think about cultural similarities and differences in talking about this topic.

---

2 *Listening for main idea.* Play recording **2.41** and ask learners what the problem is between the two neighbours.

The neighbour's son keeps kicking his ball into next door's garden, and it's ruining the plants and flowers as well as often going near the window.

TASK VOCABULARY Softeners

3 a *Focus on expressions.* Learners match the sentence beginnings and ends from the conversation. Play recording **2.41** again to check. Ask learners what the person complaining is using the highlighted expressions for. Find out if learners' L1s have similar expressions or not.

> 1 f 2 c 3 e 4 a 5 b 6 d

b Refer learners to the script on p157 to find two sentences with similar meanings to 1 and 6. Check as a class.

> same as 1: I've been wanting to speak to you for some time about this.
> same as 6: If you could ask him to try not to kick the ball into our garden, I'd really appreciate it.

c 👥 Learners discuss which expressions best complete the complaints. Check as a class.

> 1 to be honest 2 it's just that 3 I'd be grateful
> 4 a bit 5 I've been meaning to talk to you.

TASK

4 a *Preparation.* Explain the scenario for the role play and direct learners to the appropriate role cards. Walk round and help with ideas and vocabulary as necessary.

> **Alternative for weaker groups**
> Learners can prepare their roles in A/A and B/B pairs, then swap partners for the role play.

b 👥 Learners change roles and prepare for a second role play. Monitor and take a note of learners' use of softeners for a feedback session.

5 👥👥 *Round-up.* Put learners into different groups to report back on their conversations. In feedback, find out if everyone resolved their disputes, and if not, why not.

10 Explore

Keyword: *of*

Goals: use *of* in two common patterns
use *of* in a variety of expressions

Core language:
Adjectives with *of*
Verbs with *of*

Adjectives with *of*

1 Learners look at the picture of two neighbours. Ask them what they can remember about Hiromi (she recently moved into a flat opposite a house that was burgled by a teenager). Read the question, then play recording **2.42**.

> They seem to have made a good impression on each other because they compliment each other quite a lot.

2 a *Focus on adjectives with* of you. Learners match the sentences with the responses from the neighbours' conversation. They can work in pairs, or individually before comparing with a partner.

> 1 b 2 c 3 a

b Learners can continue to work in pairs, or you could do this quickly with the class. Brainstorm more adjectives in this pattern together, which give compliments or thank someone, e.g. *clever*, *sweet*, *helpful*.

> 1 a 2 b, c

c Play the first sentence of recording **2.43** and ask the class to agree on a response with a partner to demonstrate the activity. Play the rest of the recording, stopping after each one so learners can respond in pairs initially before checking as a class.

> **Possible answers**
> That's/How:
> 1 kind of you / nice of you / thoughtful of you.
> 2 nice of you
> 3 kind of you / thoughtful of you.
> 4 kind of you / helpful of you.
> 5 brave of you.

3 a Learners complete the gaps with the adjectives. Check as a class and brainstorm more adjectives that go with *of* (e.g. *tired of, full of, aware of*).

> 1 afraid 2 capable 3 fond 4 proud 5 sick

b 👥 *Personalisation.* Give learners time to think of sentences about themselves before they talk together. Encourage them to respond (as in the example) or to ask questions to find out more information about each other.

> **Alternative for weaker groups**
> Learners write their sentences. When they talk together, tell them to cover their sentences and discuss their ideas in pairs.

Verbs with *of*

4 Direct learners' attention to the headline and ask what they think a *first impression* is. Give learners a few minutes to read the article to find four things you can do to give a good first impression.

> 1 Be open and confident. Be positive and use confident body language.
> 2 Avoid nervous habits.
> 3 Give the person your attention and remember to switch your phone off.
> 4 Prepare by thinking of some questions to ask the other person.

5 a *Focus on verbs with* of. Learners cover the article and try to complete the sentences in pairs. Don't go through the answers, as this will pre-empt **b**.

b Learners check their own answers in the article. Afterwards, ask learners to think of more verbs which go with *of*, e.g. *talk of, accuse (sb) of, rob (sb) of*.

> Everybody's heard of the power of positive thinking.
> Get rid of any negative thoughts.
> Remind yourself of any nervous habits you have.
> Think of some interesting questions.

6 👥 / 👥👥 *Speaking.* Learners talk together. Feed back as a class.

Explore speaking

Goal: add comments to say how you feel
Core language:
which comment clauses

1 👥👥 *Pre-listening discussion.* Talk about this with the class.

2 *Listening for main idea.* Learners look at the picture of Mariah and Pat. Ask the class what they can remember about Mariah. (She ordered a book and complained about its condition: see p80.) Then learners read the questions. Play recording **2.44**, stopping after each conversation so learners can discuss the answer with a partner, before checking with the class.

> **Conversation 1:** *They decide to take Friday off so they can have a long weekend together because Mariah's essay will be finished.*
> **Conversation 2:** *They only get Saturday free. (They're seeing Pat's parents on Sunday.)*

3 a *Listening for detail.* Learners read the statements before listening to recording **2.44** again. Don't go through the answers, as this will pre-empt **b**.

> **Alternative for stronger groups**
> Learners read the statements and discuss whether they're true or false with a partner before listening again to check.

   b Learners read the scripts to check their own answers.

> *1 false   2 false   3 true   4 true   5 false   6 true*

4 *Focus on meaning.* Learners discuss what the comments refer to and whether each one is a positive or negative comment.

> *1 1 Mariah's essay*
> *2 how she feels about finishing her essay by Wednesday evening*
> *3 taking a day off on Friday (rather than earlier in the week)*
> *4 driving to university*
> *5 being stressed while driving*
> *6 not doing much on his day off*
> *7 having the rest of the weekend free*
> *2 positive feelings: 3, 6, 7*
>   *negative feelings: 1, 2, 4, 5*

> **Language note: Comment clauses**
> Comment clauses are the most frequent relative clauses in spoken language. In addition to *which is/was* + adjective or noun phrase, we often use a range of words and expressions embedded in the clause to emphasise our attitude. For instance, note the use of the following in the clauses in the script: *I think, a bit, probably, actually.*

5 a Ask learners to read the conversation and tell you who is talking and what about (two friends talking about the weekend). Then learners choose which expressions to use to complete the conversation. Point out that there are no 'right' answers, but some are more likely than others.

   b Learners talk about their choices with a partner. Feed back as a class.

> *Possible answers*
> *1 which was great / nice*
> *2 which was unfortunate / a shame*
> *3 which was great / excellent / nice*
> *4 which was tricky / unfortunate / a shame*
> *5 which was understandable / unfortunate*

   c Give learners time to think of a suitable ending to the conversation, helping them to fit in two more *which* expressions as necessary.

   d Learners work in groups of four to listen to each other's conversations. Ask several pairs to report back to the class on their favourite ending.

> **Alternative for stronger groups**
> Point out the speakers' use of these extra words and expressions to emphasise attitude in the scripts: *I think, a bit, probably, actually.* (See language note above.) In **5b**, tell learners to add some of these words and expressions to the *which* clauses in the conversation to add attitude to the conversation and make it more interesting, e.g. *Erin wasn't very well, which was a bit unfortunate; they got in a mess, which actually was understandable, but …*

6 *Speaking.* Draw attention to the two underlined questions at the beginning of both conversations. Give learners a moment to think of some ideas to answer the questions using comment clauses. Monitor while learners are talking and take a note of good and inappropriate uses of comment clauses in learners' conversations. Incorporate this into a feedback session later.

10 Look again

Review

GRAMMAR Present perfect simple and progressive

1 a Learners read through the conversation before filling in the gaps. Quickly elicit the uses and forms of the present perfect simple and progressive, and refer learners back to the relevant page if they can't remember. Learners can complete the conversation alone, before comparing with a partner.

> *1 've been missing   2 've had   3 've been having*
> *4 has been going on   5 've had   6 've been doing*

   b Play recording **2.45** so learners can check their ideas. Only go over the answers if there are problems. Ask the class what advice they would give to the couple.

   c *Preparation.* Give learners a moment to think about their answers to the questions and remind them to think about what language to use in expressing their ideas. Walk round and help as necessary.

   d *Speaking.* Monitor while learners talk about their week and take a note of their use of both verb forms, to inform you as to what further work needs to be done, at either an individual or class level. In feedback, find out what advice several learners gave to their partners.

VOCABULARY Problems with things you've bought

2 a Give learners a moment to complete the words alone, before comparing with a partner.

> *1 size   2 faded   3 chipped   4 work   5 dented   6 torn*
> *7 cracked   8 scratched*

   b *Speaking.* Draw attention to the list of products. Learners talk together about problems they've had with any of the products in the list. In feedback, ask several learners to tell the class about one of the problems.

CAN YOU REMEMBER? Unit 9 – Decision-making

3 a Learners match the verb–noun collocations. Check as a class.

> hold a meeting, solve a problem, brainstorm ideas, look at the facts, trust your intuition, make a decision, come up with a new plan

---

Alternative for stronger groups

Do the matching activity as a class. Tell learners you're going to call out a noun and they have to think of an appropriate verb to make a collocation about decision-making. Learners can work in pairs or small groups, and you can give a point to the first group to raise their hand. To raise the level of challenge, you could also give an extra point to the first group if they can say the complete collocation correctly (with appropriate pronunciation and linking).

---

b *Writing.* Learners write sentences about things they've done, using the collocations. Walk round and help while they're writing.

c *Speaking.* Learners talk together. In feedback, ask which collocations they think are most useful for them and make sure they have recorded these in their vocabulary notebooks.

Extension

SPELLING AND SOUNDS /uː/

4 a Model *balloon* for the class and ask which letters make the /uː/ sound. Then play recording **2.46** or say the rest of the words yourself. Learners underline the correct letters, then compare with a partner.

> ball<u>oo</u>n, aftern<u>oo</u>n, J<u>u</u>ne, r<u>ou</u>te, thr<u>ew</u>, ch<u>oo</u>se, m<u>oo</u>n, incl<u>u</u>de, r<u>u</u>le, s<u>u</u>per, gr<u>ou</u>p, fl<u>ew</u>

b Remind learners to say the words out loud while they're working together. Feed back as a class, checking that learners use the same sound to say all the spelling patterns in these words.

> 1 balloon, afternoon, choose, moon
> 2 route, group
> 3 threw, flew
> 4 June, include, rule, super

c *Vocabulary expansion.* Brainstorm more words for each pattern with the class. Write the words on the board, or ask different learners to come up and write the words on the board.

d *Spellcheck with books closed.* Play recording **2.47** or say the words yourself, stopping after each one and giving learners plenty of time to think and write down each word. Learners check their own answers in a dictionary.

NOTICE Noun phrases with *of*

5 a Focus learners on the two sentences with *of* from the unit. You could ask learners how they say the highlighted expressions in their L1 (i.e. does it translate or do they use a different preposition?).

b Learners complete the questions either in pairs or alone before comparing with a partner. In feedback, point out that in two of these expressions the article is fixed: *the front of*, *a couple of*, but in the remaining expressions it can be *a/an* or *the*, depending on the context. Draw attention to the linking in the expressions and encourage learners to practise saying the expressions before they move on to the questions.

> 1 part 2 impression 3 copy 4 picture 5 front
> 6 couple

c *Asking and answering.* Learners talk about the questions together.

Round-up. Ask a few learners to tell the class their partner's most interesting answer.

Self-assessment

Go through the list of goals, eliciting language from the unit for each one. You may need to remind learners of the contexts for the goals and let them look back through the unit if necessary. Then they circle the appropriate number for each goal. Walk round while they are doing this and talk to learners about their progress. Remind learners about the extra practice opportunities under the box, and ask where they can find things.

Unit 10 Extra activities on the Teacher's DVD-ROM

Printable worksheets, activity instructions and answer keys are on your Teacher's DVD-ROM.

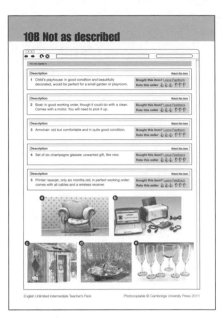

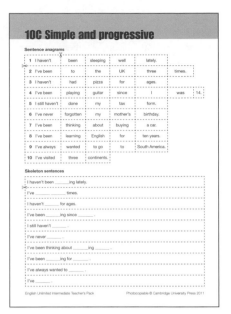

10A CSI memory

Activity type: Speaking – Memory game – Pairs/Groups

Aim: To practise memory language

Language: Remembering an event – Use at any point from 10.1.

Preparation: Make one copy of the worksheet for each pair. Cut up each worksheet to make two pictures.

Time: 15–20 minutes

10B Not as described

Activity type: Writing – Writing in response to cues – Individuals/Pairs

Aim: To practise complaining and explaining problems with things you've got

Language: Problems with things you've bought – Use at any point from 10.2.

Preparation: Make one copy of the worksheet for each learner/pair.

Time: 10–15 minutes

10C Simple and progressive

Activity type: Speaking – Sentence anagrams and personalisation – Pairs/Groups

Aim: To practise common uses of present perfect simple and progressive

Language: Present perfect simple and progressive – Use at any point from 10.2.

Preparation: Make one copy of the worksheet for every pair or group. Cut up each worksheet to make one set of ten Sentence anagrams and one set of ten Skeleton sentences.

Time: 20–30 minutes

Unit 10 Self-study Pack

In the Workbook

Unit 10 of the *English Unlimited Intermediate Workbook* offers additional ways to practise the vocabulary and grammar taught in the Coursebook. There are also activities which build reading and writing skills and a whole page of listening and speaking tasks to use with the Interview video, giving your learners the opportunity to hear and react to authentic spoken English.

- **Vocabulary:** Remembering an event; Problems with things you've bought; Softeners
- **Grammar:** Verb patterns; Present perfect simple and progressive
- **Time out:** Crossword: Problems in the home
- **Explore writing:** Review on a travel website
- **Interview:** Witnessing a crime – Carlos and Aurora

On the DVD-ROM

Unit 10 of the *English Unlimited Intermediate Self-study DVD-ROM* contains interactive games and activities for your learners to practise and improve their vocabulary, grammar and pronunciation, and also their speaking and listening, with the possibility for learners to record themselves, and a video of authentic spoken English to use with the Workbook.

- **Vocabulary and grammar:** Extra practice activities
- **Pronunciation:** Intonation in questions
- **Explore speaking:** A softener with *of*
- **Explore listening:** Returning an item
- **Video:** Witnessing a crime

Truth and lies

11.1

Goal: relate a conversation

Core language:

VOCABULARY	Verbs of communication
	Relating a conversation
PRONUNCIATION	Quoting

Gossip

VOCABULARY Verbs of communication

1 a Introduce the topic by telling the class who you've talked to that day and what the conversations were about (briefly). Then learners talk in pairs. This will set the context for the listening.

b *Listening for main idea.* Play recording **3.1**. Learners listen and match each conversation with one of the topics in the list. Check as a class.

> *A politics   B friends   C something that frightened or shocked you   D your plans today   E the weather F a problem   G work*

2 a *Listening for detail.* Focus learners on the verbs and the questions. Then play recording **3.1** again. Learners match the conversations to the functions or manner (e.g. was the conversation shouted, screamed or whispered?), then they compare with a partner. In feedback, check understanding and pronunciation of the new words.

> *1 E   2 G   3 A   4 B   5 D   6 C   7 F*

b 👥/👥👥 Learners talk together, or you can discuss this with the class. To give more focus, you could add: Think about conversations:
- at home
- with friends
- at work
- when you're travelling.

 You could use photocopiable activity 11A on the Teacher's DVD-ROM at this point.

READING

3 a 👥 *Prediction.* Learners read the statements and decide whether they're true or false. Don't go through the answers, as learners will read to check.

b Learners read the factfile, then discuss their answers with the same partner. Check understanding of: *develop and maintain a sense of community*, *relieve stress* and *is devoted to criticism and negative evaluation of others*.

> *1 true   2 true   3 false   4 true   5 false*

4 👥/👥👥 *Discussion.* Learners talk in pairs or groups, or as a class. Ask if learners have changed their ideas about what gossip is.

A secret

LISTENING

1 *Listening for main idea.* Focus learners on the pictures of the family members and ask what they think the relationship might be between Suresh and Meninda (*they are cousins*). Learners read the questions, then play recording **3.2**. Learners compare with a partner, then check as a class.

> *1 Suresh has a secret which he is keeping from his parents.*

2 Ask who the next conversation is between (*Meninda and Indra*). Then play recording **3.3**. Find out if anyone guessed what the secret was about.

3 a 👥 Learners talk through the questions. Don't check the answers, but play recording **3.3** again when they're ready, so learners can listen to check. Check understanding as a class, and let learners look at the script if they want to.

> *1 his parents   2 Suresh   3 Meninda   4 Suresh 5 his parents   6 Indra and Meninda*

b 👥👥 *Discussion.* Talk about this with the class, encouraging learners to engage with the text and respond naturally to the topic.

VOCABULARY Relating a conversation

> **Language note:** *go, be like* to report speech
>
> The use of *go* and *be like* to dramatise direct speech is considered by many people to be non-standard and ungrammatical. You may not wish your learners to use these expressions in their own speech, as they are highly idiomatic and may, to some ears, make the speaker sound careless or uneducated. However, we feel that it is good for learners to be able to recognise these very informal ways of reporting speech, as corpus research shows that they occur very frequently in spoken English.

4 👥 Learners read through the sentences from the script and discuss the questions with a partner. Go through it with the class, explaining any problems as you go along. Although the focus is on speech, it is worth pointing out the punctuation used in direct speech. Ask the class: *What punctuation comes just after the highlighted expressions?* (a comma); *What punctuation comes after that?* (opening speech marks); *What punctuation comes after that?* (closing speech marks). This will be useful for the writing in **6b**.

> *1 the exact words people say 2 both statements and questions 3 to make a story more dramatic*

> **Language note:** *says/said*
>
> *Said me* is such a common error that it's worth drawing attention to. Ask learners this question:
> *Which of these forms are correct?*
> a He says/said, '…'   b He says/said me, '…'
> c He says/said to me, '…'
> (a and c are both correct.)

PRONUNCIATION Quoting

5 a Check understanding of *quoting* using the extract from the script. Read the explanation, then play recording **3.4** several times, checking learners can hear the rise in pitch.

b Play recording **3.4** again. Learners repeat the sentences either one by one after the recording, or at the end of the recording.

SPEAKING AND WRITING

6 a 👥 *Discussion.* Learners predict what will happen in the conversation between Suresh and his father. Feed back as a class to help any learners who haven't got many ideas, as they will need to think of something for the next stage.

b 👥 Encourage learners to have a bit of fun with this conversation and remind them to use the direct speech punctuation referred to earlier. Walk round and help as necessary while learners are writing.

c 👥 Learners change partners and relate their conversations to their new partner. This will give learners a reason to listen. Remind learners to raise their voice pitch when quoting and encourage them to exaggerate but keep the activity light and fun. In feedback, ask several confident pairs to relate their conversations to the class.

7 *Round-up.* Play recording **3.5** so learners can find out the end of the story and compare the actual ending with their ideas. Find out if anyone predicted the conversation more or less accurately.

11.2

Goals: talk about truth and lies
summarise what people say

Core language:

GRAMMAR   Reporting speech

The lie detector

READING

1 *Discussion.* Introduce the topic by focusing learners on the picture. Ask what is happening in it and elicit or teach *lie detector test*. Learners discuss the questions together, or you could talk as a class.

2 a *Listening for main ideas.* Play recording **3.6** and get learners' reactions to the speakers' opinions.

b Focus on the expressions Jamie and Emma use and play the recording again if necessary so learners can hear them in context. Check understanding of *charcoal* and remind learners about the *white lies* in **1** to give them a clue. By *black lie*, Emma means a lie which is morally wrong to tell. James uses the expressions *grey lie* and *charcoal lie* to talk about a middle ground between *white* and *black lies*.

3 *Reading for main idea.* Focus learners on the headline and ask learners what they think an *email liar* is. Read the question together, then learners read the article. They discuss their ideas with a partner. Get some responses from different learners and ask them to give reasons for their ideas.

4 *Reading for detail.* Learners read the questions, then read the article again carefully. They can discuss their ideas with a partner. Feed back as a class.

> 1 They built up a database of information by asking people to come in and write emails telling lies and other emails telling the truth.
> 2 Hancock has discovered that the following points are common in lying emails:
> 1 longer messages; 2 the overuse of sense words such as 'see', 'feel', 'touch'; 3 the use of pronouns like 'he', 'we' and 'they' rather than 'I' to distance themselves from the lie; 4 the use of negative emotional words, e.g. 'sad', 'angry', 'unhappy' and 'stressed'.
> 3 Peter Collett doesn't believe computers will be able to 'see' if someone is lying from their words alone; he believes body language and other clues when people talk are more reliable.

5 a Learners read the two emails, then talk together about who is lying and telling the truth. Make sure learners say why in feedback (i.e. they should relate their answers back to the article).

> *Hi Kyoko,* ❶ *Sorry but won't be able to come to work today. We* ❷ *had chicken last night and I think it was bad.* ❶ *Woke up at three this morning and felt awful* ❸*.* ❶ *Was sick for four hours.* ❶ *Saw* ❹ *the doctor but he* ❷ *wasn't any help.* ❶ *Am exhausted.* ❶ *Feel stressed out* ❸ *because I'm not at work. Anyway,* ❶ *really sorry. I should be back at work tomorrow. Best wishes, Maya*
>
> *The writer of this email is lying, or feels guilty about something. It's too long, and there's too much detail. Examples:* ❶ *The writer doesn't say 'I' or 'I am'. She tries to distance herself from her story.* ❷ *Instead, she uses 'we', 'he' and 'they'.* ❸ *She uses negative language like 'horrible' and 'awful'.* ❹ *She uses 'saw', a sensory term which makes the story seem more real.*
>
> *Hi Kyoko, I'm really sorry but I can't come to work today. I've been sick all night. Anyway, I'm really sorry. I should be back at work tomorrow. Best wishes, Simon*
>
> *This email is short and direct, without unnecessary detail. The writer uses 'I' frequently and he is not trying to distance himself from the message.*
>
> *[Adapted from The Sunday Times, 25 February 2007, p7. Source: Jeff Hancock, Cornell University, New York]*

b 👥 Learners work in groups to compare their ideas.

SPEAKING

6 *Discussion.* Learners talk initially in pairs or small groups. Ask some learners for their partner's response to the questions in feedback.

But he said …

LISTENING

1 *Listening for main ideas.* Focus learners on the picture and read the two questions. See if learners can predict one of the lies from the picture. Then play recording **3.7**. Learners compare ideas with a partner first, then feed back as a class.

> *Kyoko mentions that Simon, her production assistant, said he was sick (but he wasn't really). Learners should find this surprising because they will have concluded from his email in 5a that he was telling the truth. Naomi says her son lied about eating chocolate.*

GRAMMAR Reporting speech

2 a *Focus on meaning.* Learners look through the sentences from the conversations then complete them in pairs. Don't go through the answers yet, as this will pre-empt **b**.

b Play recording **3.7** again so learners can check their answers.

> A said; told   B told; explained   C asked; told
> D promised; agreed

3 a *Focus on verb patterns.* Do this with the class. Point out that other patterns are also possible, for instance *ask* + question word, e.g. *He asked me where I was going.*

> 1 tell, explain (B)   2 ask, tell, promise, agree (C, D)
> 3 say (A)

b Check understanding of *object pronoun* (= *me*, *him*, *her*, etc.). Then ask the class to scan the sentences again to find the two examples.

> *'Ask' and 'tell' are followed by a person (object pronoun) before patterns 1–3.*

Note: Grammar practice

You could do the grammar practice on p142 at this point.

 You could use photocopiable activity 11B on the Teacher's DVD-ROM at this point.

SPEAKING

4 a ▲ *Writing.* Demonstrate the activity by giving an example of your own for the first one. Learners continue working on their own. Walk round and help as necessary.

b ▲▲ *Speaking.* Walk round while learners talk about their sentences together. Take a note of good and incorrect uses of the verb patterns for a feedback session after the activity.

Optional extra: Story telling

Tell the class to think of an occasion when someone told a lie. It could be you, someone you know or someone you read about.
1   What was the lie about?
2   How did you or other people find out it was a lie?
3   What happened in the end?
Give learners time to think of a story and to plan how to tell the story using language from the lesson. Walk round and help as necessary. Then they listen to each other's stories in groups. In feedback, find out which story each group thought was the most interesting and ask learners to tell it to the class, if you have time.

 You could use photocopiable activity 11C on the Teacher's DVD-ROM at this point.

11.3 Target activity

Goals: relate a conversation ♻
summarise what people say ♻
find out news about people you know

Core language:

TASK VOCABULARY	Exchanging news
11.1 VOCABULARY	Verbs of communication
11.1 VOCABULARY	Relating a conversation
11.2 GRAMMAR	Reporting speech

Chat about friends

TASK LISTENING

1 Focus learners on the picture and ask what they think the relationship between the people is (*they're friends*). Then learners discuss the questions in pairs, or as a class.

2 *Listening for main idea.* Learners read the questions. Then play recording **3.8**. They compare ideas with a partner, then feed back as a class.

> 1 Hussein had problems with a flight to Buenos Aires where he was supposed to be meeting his wife.
> 2 He arrived a day late.

TASK VOCABULARY Exchanging news

3 a ▲▲ *Focus on expressions.* Learners complete the expressions in pairs. Do not go through the answers yet, as learners will check them in **b**.

b Play recording **3.8** again so learners can check their answers.

> 1 hear   2 heard   3 told   4 said   5 spoken   6 heard
> 7 heard   8 said

4 a ▲▲ Explain that the sentences are the start of three different conversations. Demonstrate by writing the first question on the board and complete it with a name. Pairs choose names (preferably of people they know) to complete the conversation beginnings. Then they choose a conversation to work on.

b ▲▲ *Writing.* Learners take turns to write sentences to continue the conversation, using the expressions from **3a**. Walk round and help as necessary.

c ▲▲▲ *Speaking.* Put pairs together, so they can perform their conversations for each other.

TASK

5 ▲ *Preparation.* Make sure learners understand the scenario by asking what Frank's friends are doing (*meeting in a café to talk about Frank's problem at work*). Direct learners to the appropriate pages for their role cards and walk round while they're reading and planning and help as necessary.

6 ▲▲▲ *Role play.* Monitor while learners are having their conversations. In feedback, find out what they think Frank should do.

7   *Round-up.* Direct learners to Frank's email at the end of the book and get learners' reactions to his situation.

11 Explore

Across cultures: Attitudes to family

Goals: raise awareness of cultural similarities and differences
    talk about family attitudes in different cultures

Core language:
VOCABULARY   Upbringing

LISTENING

1   *Listening for main idea.* Direct learners' attention to the questions, then play recording **3.9**. Learners compare ideas, then check as a class.

> *a Quang   b Çigdem   c Patty*

2   *Listening for detail.* Focus learners on the first two questions. Then play the first monologue of recording **3.9** again. Learners compare ideas in pairs, then check as a class. Deal with any problems as they come up and get learners' reactions to the content. Do the same for the other two monologues. In Quang's monologue, check understanding of *frustrated by something* (= *annoyed or upset that you can't achieve what you want to do*).

> 1 *Children are expected to take part in family activities and are more protected by their families than children in Britain.*
> 2 *Children can do what they want more and tend to have more independence.*
> 3 *Quang says people tend to continue to live with their elderly parents or very close to them.*
> 4 *His friend couldn't afford to marry his girlfriend because he was supporting his parents.*
> 5 *Usually when they get married.*
> 6 *They still do what they're told by their parents and take part in their parents' social life.*

VOCABULARY Upbringing

3 **a** be + *adjective / past participle* + to *infinitive*. Look at the first sentence together and ask the class which country the person is talking about. If they can't remember, ask who says the sentence (*Patty*) and which countries she talks about (*Italy and Britain*). Learners can continue in pairs, but don't check answers at this stage. Check understanding and pronunciation of the expressions and give learners time to try saying them. This will help when they talk in **c**.

> *2 Italy   3 Britain   4 Vietnam   5 Turkey   6 Britain*
> *7 Turkey*

   b Direct learners to the script so they can check their own answers.

   c *Discussion.* Learners discuss the questions in pairs. Monitor to see how they cope with the new language.

SPEAKING

4 **a** *Preparation and speaking.* Focus learners on the questions and give them time to think about their answers. Then put them in small groups, with learners from other cultures if possible, to discuss the questions. In feedback, find out if learners share similar attitudes to family and what differences there are amongst them.

   b *Round-up.* Ask the class what they know about attitudes in other countries. If you come from a different culture from your learners, tell them about attitudes in your country.

Explore writing

Goal: write a factual report

Core language:
Expressions for talking about tables and figures in a report

1 **a** Focus learners on the pictures, on the list of activities and the questions. Talk about this with the class.

   b Direct learners' attention to the table and ask some questions about it to check understanding, e.g. *What country are the figures about? (Japan) How much sleep do men get every day? (7½ hours) What about women? (7¼ hours) Who spends more time commuting? (men)*. Learners can then discuss the questions in pairs. In feedback, find out if learners think the information would be very different in their countries and if you have any learners from Japan, ask them for their opinions.

2   *Reading for main ideas.* Read the summaries of the four paragraphs, then learners read the report and do the matching. Let them compare with a partner, before checking answers with the class.

> *a2 b1 c4 d3*

3 **a** Learners can work together to find the expressions in the report. Make sure they record the expressions in their notebooks or on a piece of paper. They will need to refer to this when they do **b**. Walk round and help as necessary.

refer to the table: Figure 1 shows, According to the, As the ... shows
refer to topics: when it comes to ..., As far as ... is concerned
approximate figures: just under, around, only around, about, just over
compare and contrast: twice as much ... as, compared to, about the same amount of, in contrast to

---

Alternative for weaker groups

Pair stronger learners with weaker ones and divide the load between them, with the stronger learner finding more expressions, then directing their partner to the relevant parts of the report.

---

b Make sure learners cover the report. Walk round while learners are talking about the information in the table and help with any problems.

4 a 👥👥👥 *Preparation.* Explain that learners are going to do a class survey, then write a report on the results. Look at the three topics and example questions, but tell learners they can choose any topic to ask about and brainstorm some more ideas with the class. Walk round while learners are writing their questions and help as necessary.

b 👥👥👥 *Survey.* Learners mill around the class asking their questions. With a small class, learners can divide the questions between them and ask everyone in the class. With a large class, divide the class into groups, and learners ask the people in their group all the questions. Remind them to take notes, as they will need this information for their reports.

c 👥👥👥 *Planning.* Learners work with their original groups and report back on what they found out from other people in the class. Tell them to choose a scribe to write the information into a table. They discuss how to organise the results and think about how to use the language from the lesson in their reports.

5 👥👥👥 *Collaborative writing.* Divide up the paragraphs of the report among learners in the group. Each learner (or pair) writes a draft of their paragraph. Make sure they check each other's work and agree on the final content. Then one learner can write out the final report, or it can be typed up on a computer if available.

Alternative: Homework

If **5** will take too long, get learners to revise their paragraphs at home on a computer and communicate by email to put the final report together. They can bring them into the next class and respond to them as in **6**.

---

6 *Round-up.* Learners exchange reports (or you can put them on the classroom walls). Ask what information in each other's reports they found surprising and why.

11 Look again

Review

VOCABULARY Verbs of communication

1 a Learners can do this individually before checking with a partner. You can add challenge by doing it as a race in pairs.

whisper, complain, scream, boast, argue, gossip, shout

b 👥👥 *Writing.* Walk round while learners write short conversations with a verb of their choice. Help as necessary.

c 👥👥👥 Put two pairs together to perform their conversations. Each pair has to guess which verb the other pair's conversation is illustrating. In feedback, find out how easy it was for learners to guess and ask one or two pairs to perform their conversations for the class.

GRAMMAR Reporting speech

2 a Learners can work in pairs or alone before checking with a partner.

1 My mum always used to explain why we couldn't do something.
2 I promised to do a favour for a friend but I forgot.
3 My boss always tells me what to do.
4 I don't like asking friends to do favours for me.
5 I always say what I'm thinking when I'm with a friend.

b 👤 Learners change the sentences if necessary to make them true for them.

c 👥👥 / 👥👥👥 *Speaking.* Learners discuss their sentences together. In feedback, find out if their ideas were similar or different.

CAN YOU REMEMBER? Unit 10 – Remembering an event

3 a Learners complete the questions in pairs or individually before comparing with a partner. Remind them that they may have to change the form of the verb.

2 forgotten   3 reminds   4 recognise   5 notice   6 remind   7 forget

b 👥👥 / 👥👥👥 *Asking and answering.* Walk round while learners are talking and check to see how they are dealing with the verbs. Feed back at the end.

Extension

SPELLING AND SOUNDS /juː/

4 a Model *human* for the class and ask what sound they can hear after the *h*. Write /juː/ on the board and isolate the sound for them. Then play recording **3.10** or say the words yourself, while learners underline the letters which make the /juː/ sound. Check as a class.

> h<u>u</u>man, <u>u</u>niversity, arg<u>ue</u>, comp<u>u</u>ter, n<u>ew</u>, f<u>u</u>ture, d<u>ue</u>, comm<u>u</u>nication, kn<u>ew</u>, f<u>ew</u>, barbec<u>ue</u>, <u>u</u>sually

b 👥 Learners match the words to the patterns in pairs. Remind learners to say the words out loud while they're working and check pronunciation in feedback.

> 1 *university, usually*
> 2 *human, computer, future, communication*
> 3 *argue, due, barbecue; new, knew, few*

c Learners complete the words in pairs, or individually before comparing with a partner. They check their own answers in a dictionary.

> 1 *useful*   2 *continue*   3 *renew*   4 *community*   5 *huge*
> 6 *nephew*   7 *rescue*   8 *altitude*   9 *value*

d 👥 *Spellcheck with books closed.* Learners test each other, then check together at the end. Remind learners to record any words they find difficult to remember.

NOTICE Science and research

5 a Learners look back at the article on email liars on p88, alone or with a partner, to find the nouns.

> 1 *software*
> 2 *labs (abbreviation for 'laboratories' /ləˈbɒrətriz/)*
> 3 *a database*
> 4 *data*
> 5 *research*

b 👥 Learners complete the questions, then talk about them together. Ask a few learners for their answers in feedback and develop any promising questions into a class discussion to round up the unit.

> 1 *software*   2 *labs/laboratories*   3 *database; data*
> 4 *research*

Self-assessment

Go through the list of goals, eliciting language from the unit for each one. You may need to remind learners of the contexts for the goals and let them look back through the unit if necessary. Then they circle the appropriate number for each goal. Walk round while they are doing this and talk to learners about their progress. Remind learners about the extra practice opportunities under the box, and ask where they can find things.

Unit 11 Extra activities on the Teacher's DVD-ROM

Printable worksheets, activity instructions and answer keys are on your Teacher's DVD-ROM.

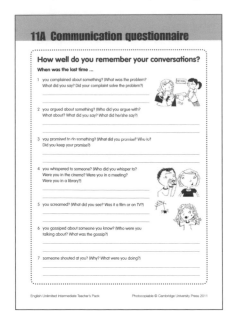

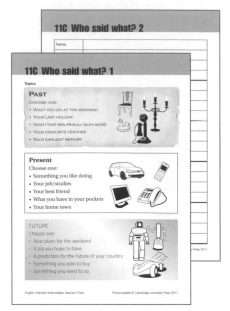

11A Communication questionnaire

Activity type: Speaking and writing – Questionnaire / Group discussion – Individuals/Pairs/Groups

Aim: To practise verbs of communication and reporting speech

Language: Verbs of communication / Reporting speech – Use at any point from 11.1.

Preparation: Make one copy of the worksheet for every learner.

Time: 15–20 minutes

11B Would I lie to you?

Activity type: Speaking – Milling activity – Pairs / Groups / Whole class

Aim: To relate conversations

Language: Reporting speech – Use at any point from 11.2.

Preparation: Make one copy of the worksheet for the class. Cut up the worksheet to make a set of 12 strips. If the class is very large, it may be necessary to split the class into two or more groups with one set of strips per group, in which case you'd need to make more copies of the worksheet.

Time: 15–20 minutes

11C Who said what?

Activity type: Speaking and writing – Group milling discussion – Individuals/Groups

Aim: To practise reporting/summarising speech

Language: Reporting speech / Relating a conversation – Use at any point from 11.2.

Preparation: Make one copy each of Worksheets 1 and 2 for every learner.

Time: 20–30 minutes

Unit 11 Self-study Pack

In the Workbook

Unit 11 of the *English Unlimited Intermediate Workbook* offers additional ways to practise the vocabulary and grammar taught in the Coursebook. There are also activities which build reading and writing skills and a whole page of listening and speaking tasks to use with the Interview video, giving your learners the opportunity to hear and react to authentic spoken English.

- **Vocabulary:** Verbs of communication; Relating a conversation; Exchanging news; Upbringing
- **Grammar:** Reporting speech
- **My English:** Using English at work
- **Explore reading:** Urban legends
- **Interview:** Family customs – Imelda, Nishadi and Darren

On the DVD-ROM

Unit 11 of the *English Unlimited Intermediate Self-study DVD-ROM* contains interactive games and activities for your learners to practise and improve their vocabulary, grammar and pronunciation, and also their speaking and listening, with the possibility for learners to record themselves, and a video of authentic spoken English to use with the Workbook.

- **Vocabulary and grammar:** Extra practice activities
- **Pronunciation:** Quoting
- **Explore speaking:** Ellipsis
- **Explore listening:** Late for work
- **Video:** Family customs

12.1

Goal: give a talk about an interest or activity

Core language:

VOCABULARY	Organising a talk
PRONUNCIATION	Groups of words 3

Stuntman

READING

1 Draw attention to the headline of the article about Rocky, the photo and caption. 👥 Then allow learners to write their questions. Walk round and suggest topics for questions if learners need help.

2 *Reading for main idea.* Learners read the article and answer as many of the questions they wrote in 1 as they can in pairs or small groups. In feedback, tell everyone to select one question that can be answered by the article, then learners take turns to ask and answer their questions in open pairs. Find out if anyone has seen any of the films mentioned in the article or caption about Rocky, and if they can remember the types of stunt in the film.

Optional extra: Further research

If learners have unanswered questions and are interested in Rocky's story, you could direct them to his website *http://www.actionstuntsrockytaylor.com/* (at the time of writing) or put his name into Google, which will direct readers to his website.

---

3 *Reading for detail.* Learners read the questions, then read the article again in more detail. They discuss the answers with a partner, then feed back as a class.

> 1 He went to teach judo to an actor in a film.
> 2 They wear special gel and a fireproof suit under their clothes. There are always two or three people there to put them out with fire extinguishers if they're on fire. For longer fire burns, they have to wear breathing apparatus, bottles called 'breathers' inside their suit.
> 3 He was doing a fire job, jumping out of an exploding building, but the crew made a mistake.
> 4 They feel anxious, but they don't try to stop him. He says he doesn't do it much any more because it's a young man's job.

4 👥 *Guessing meaning from context.* Do the first one together as an example and point out the paragraph references in red (e.g. *2*) and parts of speech (e.g. *adj*) to help learners find the words and match them with the definitions. Learners continue in pairs. Check pronunciation of *alight* /əˈlaɪt/, *extinguishers* /ɪkˈstɪŋɡwɪʃəz/, *re-ignite* /riːɪɡˈnaɪt/ and *burnt* /bɜːʳnt/.

> 1 fireproof 2 set on fire 3 alight 4 fire extinguishers
> 5 re-ignite 6 put (the fire) out 7 a bonfire 8 burnt

5 *Discussion.* Talk about the questions with the class and get their reactions to the article and their opinions about this type of job.

Giving a talk

LISTENING

1 Focus learners on the picture and caption and ask who Mike Caxton is and what he's doing. Then look at the questions with learners before they listen to the introduction to the talk. Play recording **3.11** and give them time to compare answers with a partner. Play the recording again if necessary before checking as a class.

> – To perform a fire burn safely, everything must be carefully choreographed, rehearsed and timed to the second.
> – Fire is like wind. If there is an opening, it will find its way in.
> – It's probably the most challenging course at the centre, but also very exciting.

2 a *Listening for main idea.* Let learners read the questions, then play the rest of the talk (recording **3.12**). Learners compare, then check as a class.

> There are three parts to the talk.
> People in the audience ask how long the course is and what qualifications the instructors have.

b 👥 *Listening for detail.* Play recording **3.12** again, while learners make notes of the key details of the course. Remind them not to write everything they hear (which would be impossible), but to write key words that will remind them about the important information. At the end, they discuss their notes with a partner. Play the recording again if necessary, before checking as a class.

> The first part covers everything about preparing for a fire burn, e.g. what equipment will be needed. In the second part, students will learn how to use the fire products properly. In the third part, students will practise doing a full and partial body burn.

c 👥 *Round-up.* Get learners' reactions to the course and find out if anyone would like to do it. Ask them to give reasons for their answers and extend this into a class discussion on dangerous or risky jobs if possible.

VOCABULARY Organising a talk

3 a *Focus on expressions.* Focus learners on the highlighted expressions in sentences from the talk. 👥 Learners put them in the order he says them. Don't go through the answers at this stage.

b Direct learners to the script to check their own answers.

> 4 Today, I'm going to talk about the fire courses at our training centre.
> 5 To start with, there are three things you need to know.
> 7 First of all, it's important to remember that when you watch a movie …
> 2 Secondly, fire is like wind: if there's an opening, it will find a way in.
> 3 And finally, you need to know that the fire course is our most challenging course.
> 8 I'm going to move on now to talk about the different parts of the course …
> 6 Before I move on to enrolment, are there any questions?
> 1 Any further questions?

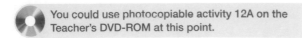

You could use photocopiable activity 12A on the Teacher's DVD-ROM at this point.

PRONUNCIATION Groups of words 3

4 **a** Learners read the two sentences from the beginning of the talk. Ask learners what the // mark indicates (where the speaker divides up groups of words, depending on meaning and emphasis). Then play recording **3.13** while learners read and notice the groups of words.

b *Practice.* Learners practise saying the sentences in groups of words.

c Look at the script with the class and project or write a few sentences onto the board. Accept learners' suggestions by marking the groups they suggest, then saying them (or inviting learners to say them) to see if they are possible. Encourage learners to contribute by pointing out that even 'wrong' suggestions are helpful in showing how incorrect divisions can change meaning. When learners are comfortable with the idea, let them continue in pairs.

d Play recording **3.14** and go through the groups of words together, marking them onto the board if possible. Play the recording again if necessary, before learners practise the talk together.

> First of all, // it's important to remember // that when you watch a movie that has a stunt performer on fire, // you're seeing exactly that, // a body that is fully on fire. // This type of stunt work // is extremely dangerous // and must be done // in the safest way possible. // The stunt performer // must use the highest-quality safety products. // But you have to remember one thing: // nothing is completely fireproof. // Everything will eventually burn // if it stays on fire long enough. // To perform a fire burn safely, // everything must be carefully choreographed, // rehearsed, // and timed to the second.

SPEAKING

5 **a** *Preparation.* Put learners into groups to prepare their talks. Walk round and help as necessary.

b Remind learners to use the language in **3a** to organise their talks and to think about how they might divide their sentences into groups of words.

c Check learners understand that they need to think of several questions to ask while listening to each talk. Monitor during the talks to see how clearly learners structure their talks and take a note of any problems for feedback at the end. Remember to give learners lots of encouragement to build up their confidence in speaking for longer turns in front of a group.

Possible answers
A full answer is given for Course A. For Courses B–D, the information could be organised logically as shown.

A Mountaineering courses
Today, I'm going to talk about the Technical Mountaineering Course (known as TMC). This is an alpine mountain climbing course that we offer in our very popular training centre in New Zealand. Lots of famous climbers have started their careers here, such as X and Y. To start with, there are three things you need to know. First of all, anyone can do the course. No previous experience of alpine mountain climbing is necessary, but participants must be fit and ready to learn and have basic rope skills, so that would include experience of rock climbing, caving or other similar activities. Secondly, you will learn all the new skills you need on the course and practise in real alpine terrain. And finally, at the end of the course, you will be able to climb almost all alpine terrain safely and with confidence. Before I move on, are there any questions? OK, I'm going to move on now to talk about the details of enrolment. It's a ten-day course and costs only NZ$3,150 per person. This includes all meals, transport, accommodation and the technical gear you'll need. Any further questions?

B Bungee jumping
– an unforgettable experience!
– bring friends, good opportunity for photos!

– professional and experienced staff
– staff do safety checks before jump

– the jump with preparation takes 30 minutes
– arrive an hour before
– weather can prevent jumping

– wear casual and comfortable clothes
– glasses and contact lenses MUST be removed
– no skirts or dresses

– participants must be in good health
– minimum age: 14
– book on website
– NZ$75 per person per jump

C Photography courses
– we will help you turn good photographs into great ones
– professional and passionate photographers to teach you all the skills you need

– learn about what camera equipment to buy
– learn how to get the most from your camera
– learn how to use Photoshop to adjust, edit and improve your photos

– never have a fuzzy picture again
– never have 'red-eye' flash photographs
– learn how moving just centimetres can turn 'dull' into 'drama'
– learn why moving yourself is better than moving your subject

– one-day courses from €50, including field trips with transport provided
– no more than ten students per tutor
– access to your own computer and work area

D Web design courses
– perfect for those who wish to learn the skills to progress into the world of web design
– locations: available internationally including the UK, the Middle East and Africa

– you need some experience of the Internet and HTML
– 16-hour course
– 7 lessons

– learn how to design and manage your own website
– introduction to the following computer software:
 • Photoshop: to learn how to create and edit images
 • Dreamweaver: to learn how to create a website
 • FrontPage: to learn how to design a web page

6 *Round-up.* Find out which activity learners found most interesting and which they would most like to do.

12.2

Goals: make polite requests
ask polite questions

Core language:

VOCABULARY	Polite requests and questions
GRAMMAR	Indirect questions

Talking to strangers

LISTENING

1 a *Listening for main idea.* Focus learners on the picture and ask if they think the people know each other or not and why / why not. Draw attention to the picture and caption of Mariama and read the questions together. Then play recording **3.15**. Learners compare their ideas, then check as a class.

> 1 It's easier to talk to strangers in Nigeria, because people are more open to speaking to people.
> 2 She mentions being in the street and waiting in a queue for a taxi.
> 3 It would be strange not to talk to someone (because everyone does).

b *Discussion.* Walk round and listen to learners' conversations so you can direct feedback at the end, or talk about the questions as a class.

2 a *Listening for main idea.* Play recording **3.16** so learners can do the matching. Give them a moment to check with a partner before going through the answers with the class.

> 1 E 2 D 3 B 4 C 5 A

b Learners share what they can remember about the requests and questions in each conversation. Then play recording **3.16** again so they can check their ideas.

> A to send them something
> B to look after something
> C to answer some questions
> D to tell them about their past
> E for an opinion

VOCABULARY Polite requests and questions

3 a Do this with the whole class, dealing with any problems as they come up.

> a 7, 8
> b 4, 5
> c 2 (send something), 3 (answer some questions), 6 (look after a case)
> d 1

Language note: Question stems

For polite questions and requests, *Could I ask you* can be used with all the endings in 3–7, but this is not the case with *Could you tell me*, which can only be followed by a noun or noun phrase (... *the time?*), a question word (... *what the time is?*) or if/whether (... *if this room is free?*).

Alternative for weaker groups

You could focus only on *Would you mind* and *Could I ask you*; learners would still be able to achieve the same communicative outcomes for the lesson.

---

b Find out if learners can remember how the people in the conversations responded, then direct them to the script to check their answers.

 You could use photocopiable activity 12B on the Teacher's DVD-ROM at this point.

SPEAKING

4 a *Preparation.* Walk round while learners are preparing their ideas and help as necessary.

b *Mini role plays.* Monitor while learners have their conversations and note down problematic uses of indirect questions for a feedback session at the end.

Survey

GRAMMAR Indirect questions

1 Ask the class what is happening in the picture (someone is doing a survey). Find out what they think the survey might be about (focus them on the rubbish in the street if necessary). Then talk about the questions as a class, asking learners why the questions in B are more polite (they are longer and less direct, which distances the speaker from the other person).

> B (indirect)

2 Project or write the questions onto the board. Give learners a moment to answer the questions in pairs, then go through 1–3 with the class, highlighting relevant information for each one.

> 1 Word order is the same as in sentences, not questions, i.e. subject, verb.
> 2 It's not used.
> 3 if

3 Focus learners on the six different survey topics and elicit a question for the first topic (shopping) with the class. Remind them to think about whether the question requires a yes/no answer or if it is asking for specific information (*wh-* question). Learners continue in pairs. Check as a class.

> Could I ask you / Could you tell me ...
> if you go shopping alone or with someone else?
> if you've had any problems with public transport?
> what your favourite café or restaurant is in your area?
> where you go in your area for entertainment?
> if you've used the local parking facilities?
> if you're happy with how clean your area is?

Note: Grammar practice

You could do the grammar practice on p143 at this point.

SPEAKING

4 👥 *Writing.* Groups choose a topic and write more questions. Remind learners to start with an indirect question but continue with direct questions. This reflects how both question types are commonly used.

5 a *Survey.* Learners mill around the class asking their questions and answering other learners' questions. Encourage them to take a note of responses so they can feed back on what they found out at the end.

   b Learners regroup and compare their findings. Allow them time to collate and plan their report.

6 *Round-up.* Go round the class and ask learners to report back on what they found out in response to different questions. Encourage learners to respond to any surprising (or incorrect) information.

 You could use photocopiable activity 12C on the Teacher's DVD-ROM at this point.

12.3 Target activity

Goals: give a talk about an interest or activity ♻
         ask polite questions ♻
         take questions in a talk

Core language:

TASK VOCABULARY	Answering questions at a talk
12.1 VOCABULARY	Organising a talk
12.2 VOCABULARY	Polite requests and questions
12.2 GRAMMAR	Indirect questions

Deal with questions in a talk

1 *Pre-listening discussion.* Ask the class what the man in the picture is doing (*he is using a metal detector to find things on the beach*). Learners then talk about the questions together or you can discuss them with the class.

TASK LISTENING

2 a *Listening for main ideas.* Read through the context and topics with the class, then play recording **3.17**. Give learners a moment to compare answers before checking as a class.

> d why Martin started treasure hunting
> a the value of a vase
> b the law about treasure hunting
> f where to start
> e finding valuable things
> c where to look for gold

   b *Listening for detail.* Focus learners on Martin's responses to the questions, then play recording **3.17** again. Learners discuss their answers first, then check as a class.

> 1 He can't answer how much the vase is worth or where to look for gold. He suggests the owner of the vase emails him a photo and more information, and for enthusiasts to join a treasure hunting club in their area if they want to look for gold.
> 2 See script on p160.

TASK VOCABULARY Answering questions at a talk

3 *Focus on expressions.* Give learners a moment to sort the questions into the three groups with a partner, then go through them with the class. Draw attention to the intonation and give learners an opportunity to repeat the questions until they can produce them fairly fluently.

> a2 b1 c3

4 a 👥 Elicit a general-knowledge question from the class or come up with an idea of your own to get learners started. Pairs then write general-knowledge questions for other people in the class. Walk round while they are writing and help as necessary.

   b *Asking and answering.* Learners take turns to ask and answer questions in open pairs. If the learner addressed doesn't know the answer, remind them to use an appropriate expression to delay answering, but then find out if anyone else in the class knows the answer.

TASK

5 👤 *Preparation.* Give learners time to prepare their talks, but point out that they only need to speak for one minute. Remind them to think about word groups and walk round and offer any help learners need with vocabulary or ideas.

6 👥 Go through the stages of the activity with the class, then learners give their talks. Monitor the question-and-answer sessions to see how learners deal with the questions.

> **Performing**
>
> If your group is not too big, this is a good opportunity for learners to give their talks to the whole class. Indicate when each speaker has talked for a minute, so that they can quickly round up their talk, and limit questions to a sensible number, e.g. three per talk. This will allow learners to perform a longer turn in front of more people while talking about a topic that is very familiar to them.

7 👥 Learners assess the question-and-answer sections of their talks with a partner. Get some feedback from different learners, then pass on any useful information you noted while monitoring their talks in **6**.

> **Optional extra: Recording talks**
>
> If you (or learners) have the facilities, suggest that learners record their talks and the questions. They can do a number of useful things with the recordings:
> - Play them back to inform their self- and peer assessment in **7**.
> - Listen to them at home and transcribe either the talk or the questions and answers (or both), and try to improve what they said (in writing). Give feedback as appropriate.
> - Rather than giving the written improvements to you to mark, learners can re-record themselves speaking and answering the questions. You can listen to learners' recordings and give feedback as appropriate.

12 Explore

Keywords: *other, another*

Goal: to use *other* and *another* in a range of expressions

Core language:

Uses of *other* and *another*
Linking expressions

Uses of *other* and *another*

1 a Focus learners on the picture and ask what the woman is doing and what problem she is having. Learners read through the speech bubbles and answer the question with a partner. Feed back as a class.

> *1, 2, 4*

b *Focus on form and meaning.* Project the sentences onto the board or use an OHT and go through the questions with the class, dealing with any problems as you go along. To answer question 2, elicit the answers from the class, then circle the words that *another one* and *others* refer to (*laptop, photos*). You could write *an other laptop* on the board and ask what the problem is, in order to draw learners' attention to the meaning of *another*.

> *1 always singular: another; singular or plural: other*
> *2 another one = the laptop; others = photos*

2 a Learners can do this in pairs or individually before comparing with a partner. Feed back as a class.

> *2 I need to look for another one.*
> *3 I haven't got any others.*
> *4 I've got other things to do which are more interesting.*
> *5 There's always another chance to do better.*

Alternative: Dictation

Read the sentences to the class, one at a time, giving them enough time to write down what you say and then to decide which word to add to each sentence. Check their ideas at the end.

b 👥 / 👥👥 *Personalisation.* Learners talk about the sentences together. In feedback, find out which sentences were true for learners.

Linking expressions

3 a *Listening for main idea.* Ask learners what they think the boy is doing (*giving a presentation*) and whether they ever had to do this at school. Learners read the questions, then listen to recording **3.18**. Check as a class.

> *Juan Carlos thinks it's a good idea. Kan doesn't.*

b 👥 Learners decide which expressions complete each extract. Check as a class, or learners can check their own answers in the script on p160. Point out that most of the expressions form clear word groups, apart from *Another point // is* and *Another thing // is that* and give learners an opportunity to practise saying the expressions.

> *1 d   2 e; a   3 b   4 c*

c Do this with the class, dealing with any problems as you go along.

> *1 d   2 b, c   3 a, e*

4 a 👤 *Preparation.* Walk round while learners are preparing their ideas and help as necessary.

Alternative for weaker groups

Learners can prepare their topics in A/A, B/B and C/C pairs. Learners do **4b** in A/B/C groups.

b 👥👥 *Discussion.* Monitor while learners are talking and take a note of their use of the new expressions for a feedback session at the end.

Round-up. Find out which topics learners couldn't agree on and why.

Explore speaking

Goal: give yourself time to think

Core language:

Sounds, words and expressions to give thinking time

1 *Listening for main ideas.* Focus learners on the picture and ask them how Jasmina might be feeling. Find out how learners would feel if they had to give a presentation to colleagues or strangers (or how they do feel if they have to do this). Then explain that they will hear a conversation between Jasmina and her husband before she gave the presentation. Play recording **3.19**. Learners discuss the answers with a partner. Then feed back as a class.

> *1 She's a bit nervous, but she thinks she's well prepared.*
> *2 be well prepared, don't get too nervous, look people in the eye at the start*

2 a Draw attention to the sounds, words and expressions in the box. Then play recording **3.19** again while learners tick items as they hear them. Ask why we use the items and point out that they're all extremely frequent (see Language note below). Ask learners why they think that is.

> *1 er (x2)   2 erm (x1)   3 like (x1)   4 sort of (x1)*
> *5 kind of (x1)   6 you know (x2)*

Optional extra

Books closed. To check answers, play the recording again, and get learners to call STOP when they hear one of the words or expressions.

Language note: Frequency

These items are all extremely frequent in spoken English. *Er* (or *uh*) is the fifth most frequent 'word', and *erm* (or *um*) is 34th. *Like* is the 14th most frequent word. *You know* is the 2nd most frequent two-word expression and *sort of* the 12th, while *kind of* is 34th (*sort of* is more frequent in British English and *kind of* in American English).

source: Cambridge International Corpus word lists (one-gram and two-gram lists)

b 👥 Look at the topics with the class, but point out to learners that they shouldn't plan their mini-talks but should use the sounds, words and expressions in **a** where necessary. Monitor while learners are talking and notice how effectively they use the language. Feed back at the end.

3 *Listening for main idea.* Learners read the question, then play recording **3.20**. Learners answer in pairs, then check as a class.

> how many people they recruited in Japan; last month's results

4 Learners mine the script in order to complete the expressions individually before checking with a partner. Remind them to record all the words and expressions in their notebooks. Check understanding of the communicative function of the expressions (to give yourself time to think).

> 2 If you hold on a minute.
> 3 Bear with me a moment.
> 4 Let me check.
> 5 Let me think.
> 6 Let me just have a look.

5 a 👤 *Writing.* Divide the class in half and tell one half they are As and the other half they are Bs. Point out the example questions and tell learners to look through the unit to write two more questions each for their section. Walk round and help as necessary.

b 👥 *Asking and answering.* Learners talk together. Point out that they can look back at relevant parts of the unit to find the answers, and that they should use the expressions to give themselves time when necessary.

12 Look again

Review

GRAMMAR Indirect questions

1 a 👥 Say the first question to the class and ask how to say it more politely to a stranger. Learners continue in pairs. Check as a class.

> **Possible answers**
> 1 Could you tell me / Could I ask you which bus I should take for the station?
> 2 Could you tell me / Could I ask you where the nearest bank is?
> 3 Could you tell me / Could I ask you if there's a post office near here?
> 4 Could you tell me / Could I ask you when the shops normally close?
> 5 Could you tell me / Could I ask you what the best way to get to the town centre is?
> 6 I was wondering if you have a map?
> 7 Could you tell me / Could I ask you where I can buy a guidebook?

> **Alternative: Question tennis with books closed**
>
> 'Serve' the questions out one at a time to different learners, who should 'volley' back an indirect question. Make sure you ask all the learners at least one question, but tell them that they can't use the same stem twice for the same question.

b 👤 Learners think of some more questions. It is not necessary for them to write them down. Walk round and help as necessary.

> **Alternative for weaker groups**
>
> Tell learners to write their questions. Walk round and help if anyone is having problems forming indirect questions.

c 👥 *Asking and answering.* Learners mill round the class asking different people their questions. Monitor to see how learners manage the indirect questions.

VOCABULARY Polite requests and questions

2 a Learners complete the expressions individually before comparing with a partner.

> 1 ask   2 favour   3 something   4 to   5 mind
> 6 sending

b 👤 *Writing.* Point out that learners should write questions that can really be responded to by other people in the class. Walk round and help as necessary while they are writing.

c 👥 *Milling.* Learners walk round the class and ask different people their questions. Encourage learners to respond and extend the conversations where possible.

CAN YOU REMEMBER? Unit 11 – Exchanging news

3 a Point out that 1–5 are in the order of an unfinished conversation. Learners do the matching. Check as a class, then learners continue the conversation together.

> 1 b   2 d   3 c   4 e   5 a

b 👥 *Writing.* Learners write their own conversations. Walk round and help as necessary.

c 👥 Put two pairs together to act out their conversations and listen to each other.

Round-up. Ask someone from each group what news people were exchanging in their conversations.

Extension

SPELLING AND SOUNDS /ɔɪ/

4 a Say two words with the /ɔɪ/ sound, e.g. *boy* and *boil*. Elicit the spellings, write both words on the board and ask which letters make the /ɔɪ/ sound. Play recording **3.21** so that learners can complete the list of words with *oi* or *oy*. Learners then check their answers in a dictionary.

> point, destroy, royal, oil, joints, noise, employer, avoid, enjoy, voyage

b Learners work out the spelling patterns with a partner. Check as a class.

> 1 oi   2 oy   3 oy

c *Spellcheck.* Play recording **3.22** or say the words yourself. Direct learners to the end of the book to check their own answers.

NOTICE Patterns with *in*

5 a Allow learners to read through the sentences, then ask them if they can remember what the first four sentences are about (1, 4: treasure hunting; 2, 3: doing fire stunts). Focus on the patterns in the first two sentences and ask the class to match them to a) or b). They continue in pairs or individually before comparing with a partner.

> *1a 2b 3b 4a 5a 6b*

b ⚇ / ⚈ *Discussion.* Walk round while learners discuss the questions and call on some learners to tell the class some interesting information about their partners in feedback to round up the lesson.

Self-assessment

Go through the list of goals, eliciting language from the unit for each one. You may need to remind learners of the contexts for the goals and let them look back through the unit if necessary. Then they circle the appropriate number for each goal. Walk round while they are doing this and talk to learners about their progress. Remind learners about the extra practice opportunities under the box, and ask where they can find things.

Unit 12 Extra activities on the Teacher's DVD-ROM

Printable worksheets, activity instructions and answer keys are on your Teacher's DVD-ROM.

12A One other thing …

Activity type: Speaking and writing – Mini-presentations – Groups / Whole class

Aim: To practise preparing and giving a short, informal talk

Language: Organising a talk – Use at any point from 12.1.

Preparation: Make one copy of the worksheet for each group of four learners. Cut up the worksheet to make a set of ten organising expressions and six sections of the talk.

Time: 20–40 minutes

12B Revenge questions

Activity type: Speaking – Pair interviews – Individuals/Pairs

Aim: To practise asking questions politely using indirect questions

Language: Polite requests and questions / Indirect questions – Use at any point from 12.2.

Preparation: Make one copy of the worksheet for every learner.

Time: 20 minutes

12C If you don't mind me asking …

Activity type: Speaking – Questionnaire – Pairs/Groups

Aim: To raise awareness of when topics or questions need to be handled sensitively and politely

Language: Polite requests and questions / Questions (direct/ indirect/'circular' and 'taboo') – Use at any point from 12.2.

Preparation: Make one copy of the questionnaire for every pair or group.

Time: 15–20 minutes

Unit 12 Self-study Pack

In the Workbook

Unit 12 of the *English Unlimited Intermediate Workbook* offers additional ways to practise the vocabulary and grammar taught in the Coursebook. There are also activities which build reading and writing skills and a whole page of listening and speaking tasks to use with the Interview video, giving your learners the opportunity to hear and react to authentic spoken English.

- **Vocabulary:** Organising a talk; Polite requests and questions; Answering questions at a talk
- **Grammar:** Indirect questions
- **Time out:** Jokes
- **Explore writing:** Preparing slides for a presentation
- **Interview:** Making presentations – Andrés and Ehinomen

On the DVD-ROM

Unit 12 of the *English Unlimited Intermediate Self-study DVD-ROM* contains interactive games and activities for your learners to practise and improve their vocabulary, grammar and pronunciation, and also their speaking and listening, with the possibility for learners to record themselves, and a video of authentic spoken English to use with the Workbook.

- **Vocabulary and grammar:** Extra practice activities
- **Pronunciation:** Groups of words
- **Explore speaking:** Respond to requests
- **Explore listening:** Town hall meeting
- **Video:** Making presentations

Looking back

13.1

Goals: talk about mistakes
criticise past actions
suggest alternatives

Core language:

VOCABULARY	Events in business
GRAMMAR	*should have, could have*
PRONUNCIATION	Common pairs of words 3

Big mistake

READING

1 *Prediction.* Focus learners on the book cover showing Gerald Ratner. Elicit ideas from the class about what type of book it might be and what it's about. Check understanding of the literal meaning of *rise and fall*.

2 *Reading for main idea.* Learners read the article and discuss their ideas with a partner. Check as a class.

> The <u>rise</u> and <u>fall</u> refers to the fact that he built up the family business into a global success, but then caused the business to fail by making a joke about how cheap some of the products were. The rise again refers to his current attempt to become successful again, this time with an online jewellery business, Gerald Online.

> **Alternative for weaker groups**
>
> If your learners need more support with the article, put this list of key events from the story on the board and ask learners to order them with a partner, then read to check.
> a He started a health club. (6)
> b He lost his job at Ratners. (4)
> c He wrote a book. (8)
> d He started working in his father's business. (1)
> e He made a joke in a speech at a business event. (3)
> f He started an online jewellery business. (7)
> g He lost all his money. (5)
> h Ratners became very successful under his leadership. (2)

> **Alternative for stronger groups**
>
> *Reading for detail.* Write these figures on the board and ask learners to scan the article to find out what they refer to.
>
> 1996   28   48   60   1991   16   27,000   6   1
>
> To raise the level of challenge, you could do this as a race, i.e. the first pair to find all the answers raises a hand.

> | | |
> |---|---|
> | 1996 | He set up a health club in 1996. |
> | 28 | He cycles 28 miles a day. |
> | 48 | He offered to resign within 48 hours of the speech. |
> | 60 | He was 60 at the time of the article. |
> | 1991 | He made the joke in a speech in 1991. |
> | 16 | The age he was when he started working in his father's business |
> | 27,000 | The number of people employed by Ratners when he ran it |
> | 6 | The number of employees at Gerald Online |
> | 1 | In his speech, Ratner said you could buy a pair of earrings for less than £1. |

3 *Discussion.* Discuss the question with the class, finding out what learners think of Ratner's story and what it reveals about him as a person.

VOCABULARY Events in business

4 a Make sure learners cover the article and read the sentences before they start writing. Walk round and monitor while they are working, offering help as necessary. Check pronunciation of *resign* /rɪˈzaɪn/ and *bankrupt* /ˈbæŋkrʌpt/, which learners may find difficult due to the consonant clusters.

> a failed   b went bankrupt   c took over   d runs
> e resign   f set up   g built up   h fired

b 👥 Encourage learners to order the sentences without looking back at the article. Check answers as a class by asking pairs to read out a sentence at a time in the correct order.

> c, g, a, e, h, b, f, d

SPEAKING

5 👥👥 *Discussion.* Give learners a few moments to think about the questions and then discuss them in pairs or with the class.

He shouldn't have …

LISTENING

1 a *Listening for main idea.* Focus learners on the picture of Debbie and Steve and explain that they will hear them talking about Ratner's story. Allow them to read the questions first, then play recording **3.23**. Feed back as a class.

> 1 Steve feels a bit sorry for Ratner. Debbie is critical of him.
> 2 They talk about the person who runs Barclaycard, who said he and his family don't use credit cards because they're too expensive.

b 👥👥 *Class discussion.* Find out who learners agree with and why. Ask if learners know any similar stories about businesspeople in their countries.

GRAMMAR *should have, could have*

2 a Elicit the modals used in the conversation from the class. Don't focus on the form yet, but come back to this after **b**.

> 1 should   2 shouldn't   3 could

b *Focus on meaning and use.* Give learners time to read the questions and think individually or with a partner. Then talk about the meaning and use with the class. Finally, focus on the form, reminding learners of the present form: *should/could* + infinitive to contrast with this past form: *should/could* + *have* + past participle. Model the sentences briefly for learners, but more time will be spent on pronunciation at a later stage.

> 1 the past
> 2 a should have, shouldn't have   b could have

3 **a** 👥 Learners read the speech bubbles and discuss what happened. Briefly check everyone understands the situations before moving on.

b 👤 *Writing.* Walk round and offer help as necessary while learners write their sentences. When they're ready, learners can discuss their sentences with a partner to see if their ideas are similar or different. Feed back as a class.

> **Possible answers**
> Derek: *He should have tried to make friends with people. He shouldn't have left so quickly. He could have given it a bit more time.*
> Alija: *She should have checked the weather forecast. She shouldn't have taken beach clothes. She could have taken warm clothes as well.*
> Kareem: *He should have practised his presentation. He could have asked for help.*
> Ian: *He shouldn't have bought cheap DVDs from the market. He should have bought them in a shop. He could have asked the stallholder to play the DVDs to check them.*

c 👥 *Discussion.* Learners discuss their opinions of each of the four situations.

> **Note: Grammar practice**
> You could do the grammar practice on p144 at this point.

 You could use photocopiable activity 13A on the Teacher's DVD-ROM at this point.

PRONUNCIATION Common pairs of words 3

4 **a** Play recording **3.24** or say the sentences yourself, focusing on the weak forms and contractions. Give learners plenty of time to practise saying the sentences and to get their mouths round these forms.

b Learners practise saying their sentences from **3b** to themselves and then to a partner.

SPEAKING

5 **a** 👤 *Preparation.* If possible, tell the learners your own story to give them a model and some ideas. Give them time to think of their own ideas and to plan how to tell their stories. Point out the framework to help learners prepare. Walk round and help as necessary.

b 👥 / 👥 *Storytelling.* Monitor while learners are telling their stories and take a note of good and incorrect uses of the modals for a feedback session later.

Round-up. Ask several learners what their partner should or could have done differently.

13.2

Goals: talk about acts of kindness and bravery
speculate about the past

Core language:

VOCABULARY	Acts of kindness and bravery
GRAMMAR	Unreal conditionals: past

A good deed

READING

1 **a** 👥 *Pre-reading discussion.* Introduce the topic by asking learners if they think they're brave or not and to say why. Read through the questions together, then learners discuss them in pairs.

b 👥 Go through each question, asking different learners what they would do and inviting a response from others in the class.

2 *Reading for main idea.* Focus learners on the questions, then they read the three news stories. In feedback, check understanding of *make it into (work)*, *impressed by the good deed*, *wealthy widow* and *grateful*.

> *Story 2 is about acts of kindness. Stories 1 and 3 are about acts of bravery.*

3 Make sure learners cover the stories before discussing the statements about the stories with a partner. They read again to check their ideas.

> 1 true   2 false   3 false   4 true   5 false   6 true

4 *Speaking.* Learners give their opinions about the people in all three stories based on their actions. Find out if they agree with each other in feedback.

VOCABULARY Acts of kindness and bravery

5 **a** Learners can complete the sentences individually before comparing with a partner. Don't check the answers yet, as this will pre-empt **b**.

b Learners check their own answers by scanning the text for the correct information.

> 2 risked   3 saved   4 left   5 thank   6 thinking
> 7 helped   8 doing

SPEAKING

6 **a** 👥 Remind learners to cover **5a**. Do the first one with the class, then learners continue together. Let them check their own answers against **5a**. Then they ask and answer the questions.

> 1 for   2 with   3 of   4 for   5 from   6 by   7 from

b 👥 *Round-up.* Find out about some of the brave or kind acts people have performed, and decide together who is the kindest person and who is the bravest person in the class.

I wouldn't have ...

GRAMMAR Unreal conditionals: past

1 Focus learners on the example sentences from the stories and do question 1 as a class. If anyone is struggling with the meaning, focus on the sentence about Rosa Flores. Ask *Did she have a family?* (no) and *Did she leave all her money to the village?* (yes), which should illustrate that the *if* sentences are imaginary. Write the pattern on the board and elicit the form from the class. You could ask the class to find another example of an unreal past conditional in the third story (*If Mr Parker hadn't got involved, then I'm sure the man would have robbed the bank*). Model the sentences for the class, and point out that it is pronounced in a similar way to *should've* and *could've*. Focus on the negative form (*wouldn't have left*), pointing out that we often say *wouldn't've* and give learners an opportunity to practise saying all the sentences.

> 1 imaginary, about the past
> 2 if + had + <u>past participle</u>, would + have + <u>past participle</u>

2 a 👥 *Listening.* Demonstrate the activity by playing the recording of the first situation, talking about it with the class and eliciting a sentence using the prompt. Then play recording **3.25**, one situation at a time; learners continue in pairs, writing a sentence for each one.

> **Possible answers**
> 1 If he hadn't crashed into the car in front, he wouldn't have met his wife.
> 2 If she'd studied harder at university, she would have got a good degree. If she'd got a good degree, it would have been easier for her to study law.
> 3 If he hadn't seen the Mexican film, he probably wouldn't have become interested in Mexico. / he probably wouldn't have moved to Mexico.
> 4 She wouldn't have become a journalist if her English teacher hadn't encouraged her at school.
> 5 She wouldn't have gone to that hotel or resort if she'd talked to her colleague first.
> 6 If he'd known more about cars, he probably wouldn't have bought that car.

Optional extra: Word groups

Learners have had several opportunities to practise saying past modals (*should've*, *would've*, etc.) and have practised putting them in longer *if* sentences in **1**. Before learners talk about their sentences from the listening, it's a good idea to spend more time focusing on the pronunciation of these unreal conditionals. In previous lessons, learners have practised breaking speech into word groups, and the pausing will help learners produce these long sentences intelligibly. Ask them to say the sentences and decide where the groups of words begin and end. Remind them to link words within word groups. Then they practise saying their sentences. Walk round and help as necessary. This will help them with **2b**.

> **Possible answers**
> 1 If he hadn't crashed // into the car in front, // he wouldn't have met his wife.
> 2 If she'd studied harder at university, // she would have got a good degree.
> If she'd got a good degree, // it would have been easier for her // to study law.
> 3 If he hadn't seen the Mexican film, // he probably wouldn't have become interested // in Mexico. / he probably wouldn't have moved // to Mexico.
> 4 She wouldn't have become a journalist // if her English teacher hadn't encouraged her // at school.
> 5 She wouldn't have gone to that hotel or resort // if she'd talked to her colleague // first.
> 6 If he'd known more about cars, // he probably wouldn't have bought that car.

b 👥 *Speaking.* Learners talk about their sentences with a new partner. In feedback, find out if learners had the same or different ideas by asking several learners to say their sentences, and asking the rest of the class to respond.

Note: Grammar practice

You could do the grammar practice on p144 at this point.

 You could use photocopiable activity 13B on the Teacher's DVD-ROM at this point.

SPEAKING

3 a 🧍 *Preparation.* Demonstrate the activity by drawing a timeline for important events in your life on the board, then explaining it to the class. Elicit questions from learners by writing *If you hadn't ..., what would you have done?* on the board, then encouraging them to ask you questions about what you should or could have done differently. Then give learners time to draw their timelines and think about which events and decisions to put on it. Explain that if they don't want to talk about something, it is best not to put it on their timelines.

b 👥 *Speaking.* Learners explain their timelines to each other.

4 a 🧍 *Writing.* Remind learners of the questions they asked you (point out the question frame on the board) and tell them to prepare about three similar questions about their partner's timeline. Walk round while they're writing and help as necessary.

b 👥 *Personalisation.* Monitor while learners ask and answer their questions and take a note of their use of real conditionals for a feedback session later.

Round-up. Ask several learners what their partners feel they should have or could have done differently in their lives.

13.3 Target activity

Goals: criticise past actions ♻

Core language:

TASK VOCABULARY	Evaluating past actions
13.1 GRAMMAR	*should have, could have*
13.2 GRAMMAR	Unreal conditionals: past

Discuss what went wrong

TASK LISTENING

1 a Focus learners briefly on the picture of the couple driving. Then learners discuss the questions together or talk about them with the class.

b Ask the class what the problem is for Debbie and Steve and how they might be feeling (probably stressed or cross). Then elicit some ideas of what they might be saying to each other. This will introduce the listening.

2 *Listening for main idea.* Learners read the questions, then play recording **3.26**. They compare answers together, then check as a class.

> 1 a map and a Greek phrase book
> 2 He's going to ask for directions in a garage.

TASK VOCABULARY Evaluating past actions

3 a *Listening for detail.* Play recording **3.26** again and tell learners to listen for these sentences and find out what Debbie and Steve are talking about in each one. They compare with a partner, then check their own ideas in the script. In feedback, give them an opportunity to practise saying the expressions.

> 1 to turn left at the roundabout
> 2 that they'd get lost
> 3 their map
> 4 their map
> 5 the phrase book

> **Alternative for stronger groups**
>
> Allow learners to discuss each sentence first with a partner, then play recording **3.26** so they can check their ideas.

b *Vocabulary expansion.* Brainstorm words or expressions to replace *better*, e.g. *helpful*, *sensible*, *a good idea*.

TASK

4 a 👥 Draw attention to the list of options for weekend breaks and make sure each group chooses a situation.

b 👥 Look at the examples with the class and ask which weekend break each one might apply to. Each group can appoint a scribe to write down the ideas suggested by the group. Walk round and help with ideas if necessary.

c 👥 *Preparation.* Learners prepare things to say, using the language from **3a**. Walk round and help learners formulate or re-formulate their ideas.

5 👥 You can place learners back to back for their phone calls, to make their conversations more realistic. Encourage learners to exaggerate their feelings in their voices and to extend the conversations as long as possible. Monitor and take a note of any problems that impede communication.

> **Optional extra: Extending conversations**
>
> Add an element of competition to encourage learners to extend their conversations. Give them a start time and challenge them to have the longest conversation in the class.

6 *Round-up.* Give learners a moment to think of their own stories about things that have gone wrong when they've been away. Then talk about this as a class.

13 Explore

Across cultures: Rules and risk

Goals: raise awareness about different attitudes to rules and risk
talk about laws and attitudes to the law in different cultures

Core language:

VOCABULARY	*make, let, be allowed to, be supposed to*

LISTENING

1 If your learners are from the same country, talk about this together, but if you have a multicultural class, give learners an opportunity to talk in pairs or small groups first, then feed back as a class.

2 *Listening for main idea.* Focus learners on the picture and check understanding of *risk*. Read the question, then play recording **3.27**.

> They talk about smoking in public and briefly about breaking speed limits.

3 a *Listening for detail.* The listening is quite long, so use the extracts in the Coursebook to provide support for learners. Make sure they read through all the sentences and pre-teach the following vocabulary: *loose manner* (= not strict, relaxed), *make a big fuss* (= complain), *interpreted* (= understood), *passer-by* (= someone who walks past), *bending the rules* (= changing them a bit) and *chaotic* (= disorganised or random). Give learners an opportunity to think about who says each statement first, before you play recording **3.27** again.

> 1 Patrizia   2 Jon   3 Jon   4 Patrizia   5 Jon   6 Patrizia
> 7 Jon   8 Patrizia   9 Patrizia   10 Patrizia

b Learners talk in pairs, then check as a class.

> Italy

4 👥 *Discussion.* Tell learners to focus on each sentence and compare their attitudes to Patrizia and Jon's. In feedback, find similarities and differences either between learners' countries and Britain or Italy, or among learners' own countries.

VOCABULARY *make, let, be allowed to, be supposed to*

5 *Focus on expressions.* Give learners a moment to think about the meaning of the four expressions with a partner before going through this with the class. Highlight the form on the board: *let/make you* + infinitive and *be supposed/allowed to* + infinitive.

Model the latter forms in sentences of your own, e.g. *You're allowed to use dictionaries* and *You're supposed to speak English*, and point out the weak form of *to* and the linking in *supposed_to* /səˈpəʊztuː/, giving learners time to practise saying the forms.

> 1 a   2 c   3 b   4 c

SPEAKING

6 a Give learners time to think of some ideas on their own, then put them in small groups to share ideas. Monitor and listen for their use of the target language, offering help to individuals as necessary, and pointing out any common problems in feedback at the end.

   b *Intercultural discussion.* Walk round while learners are talking and listen for any interesting points you can ask learners to repeat to the class in feedback.

> **Monocultural groups**
>
> If your learners are all from one country, ask them to discuss the questions and check if they agree on the answers (which they may not!). Then ask them to think about any other countries or cultures they know and think about if the laws and attitudes are different there.

> You could use photocopiable activity 13C on the Teacher's DVD-ROM at this point.

Explore writing

Goals: write a summary of information from different sources
write an email giving information

1 *Class discussion.* Brainstorm ideas as a class for question 1, then find out who in the class has organised a trip or been on a trip organised by someone else and ask them about how well their trips were organised.

2 Focus learners on the picture and caption and ask some questions to make sure learners understand the situation, e.g. *Who is Barbara? What about Zoë? Who's organising the trip? Where's Zoë travelling from/to?* Then draw attention to the different sources of information Barbara has researched for Zoë's trip and point out Barbara's notes on each one. Learners then do the task in pairs. In feedback, project the different sources of information onto the board or a screen and ask different learners to come up and circle the important information, while the rest of the class reacts by agreeing or disagreeing.

3 a *Reading for detail.* Learners read the first half of Barbara's email and locate the relevant information individually, then compare their ideas with a partner. Check as a class, referring to the texts on the board if possible.

> *The following information should be underlined in 2:*
> *timetable: Toronto, Warsaw, 13:00 and 12:30.*
> *hotel information: Hotel Bronislaw, a beautiful quiet location, The journey by car from the airport takes 15 minutes, Meeting room, flip chart and pens, data projector, internet access*
> *Barbara's notes: 2:00*

   b Give learners time to have a go at this individually, before comparing their ideas with a partner. Walk round and help as necessary before checking with the class.

> *I've booked a table at Wierzynek Restaurant for dinner at 7:30pm. We're meeting Stefan Daszkiewicz and Ela Górska there. It's right in the centre of Kraków's Old Town with tables overlooking the Market Square. The food is exquisite/traditional – it's one of the best restaurants in Kraków.*

> **Note: Goal**
>
> The goal here is for learners to practise collating information from a range of different sources so they are not expected to paraphrase or summarise the information at this level. However, if stronger learners use paraphrases, such as synonyms, or summarise information while retaining the key information, then give them praise for going beyond the task.

4 *Preparation.* Ask if learners ever go away for the weekend to celebrate things like birthdays and find out where they usually go. Then focus on the current scenario and direct learners to the appropriate information on p132. Walk round and check learners are circling appropriate information to tell their friends.

5 *Writing.* Learners can discuss and plan their emails with a partner before writing their own emails. Walk round and help as necessary.

> **Note: Drafting emails**
>
> Give learners time to improve and correct their emails and to write a final version, either in the class or for homework. If they do this at home, they can finalise their emails and send them to you to check.

6 *Round-up.* Learners exchange emails with different partners and talk about the plans together. Get learners' responses to the trip.

13 Look again

Review

VOCABULARY Events in business; Acts of kindness and bravery

1 a / Learners do the matching in pairs, or individually before comparing with a partner. Check quickly by calling out verbs and eliciting the multi-word verbs or by telling learners to cover the particles and test each other in open pairs.

> *risk (your life) by, set up, thank for, do favours for, build up, take over, rescue from, help with, resign from*

   b Learners complete the sentences with appropriate expressions. Remind them that they need to put the verbs in the correct form.

> 1 does favours for   2 resigned from   3 risk; by
> 4 helping; with   5 set up

c Learners make the sentences true for them, then talk about their ideas with a partner.

GRAMMAR Unreal conditionals: past

2 a Focus learners on the example situations and check understanding of the expressions. Give them time to think of a situation.

b *Preparation.* Learners plan how to express their ideas, using the framework provided. Walk round and help as necessary.

c *Speaking.* Monitor while learners are talking and check how and if they use unreal conditionals to express their ideas. In feedback, ask several learners to summarise their partner's situations and to say what they would have done in their place.

CAN YOU REMEMBER? Unit 12 – Polite requests and questions

3 a *Writing.* Elicit an indirect question from the class as an example, e.g. *Could I ask you what kind of music you like listening to?* Then learners continue in pairs. Walk round while they are writing and help as necessary.

b *Survey.* Learners mill round the class asking their questions and answering other learners' questions about music.

Round-up. Find out who shares the same musical tastes in the class and what those tastes are.

SPELLING AND SOUNDS /aʊ/

4 a Play recording **3.28** for learners; point out that the same sound is represented by two different letter combinations.

b Learners do this in pairs first, then check as a class.

> 1 ow   2 ou   3 ow   4 ow

c Learners can complete the words individually, then check with a partner. Let them look in a dictionary to check their answers.

> 1 about   2 row   3 council   4 mouth   5 round
> 6 doubt   7 brown   8 clown

d *Spellcheck.* Learners choose ten words from the section and test each other. Remind them to record any words they find difficult to spell in their notebooks.

NOTICE Expressions with *make*

5 a Ask learners what they remember about Gerald Ratner. Then they complete the sentences from the article and check their own answers.

> 1 speech   2 joke   3 comeback   4 profit   5 mistake

b *Vocabulary expansion.* Learners brainstorm more expressions with *make* in pairs, then call out their ideas for you to put on the board. Alternatively, you could draw a spidergram on the board like the one below and call different learners up to decide where to put the different collocations. Remind learners to record new expressions in their notebooks.

Recording high-frequency verbs

Suggest that learners make a page for *make* and pages for other very high-frequency similar verbs such as *do, have, get* and *go.* Suggest useful ways of recording these verbs and their collocations, e.g.

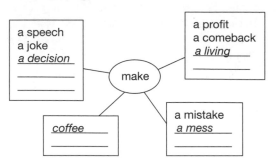

Tell learners to leave enough space to add more collocations at a later date, as they come across more uses of the verbs and to group the different uses in ways that make sense to them (which may be different from the groupings shown above).

---

c *Writing.* Walk round and help while learners write questions using expressions they have chosen.

Asking and answering. Learners can ask their questions in pairs or small groups or mill around the class asking different people.

Round-up. Ask several learners what they found out about other people in the class.

Self-assessment

Go through the list of goals, eliciting language from the unit for each one. You may need to remind learners of the contexts for the goals and let them look back through the unit if necessary. Then they circle the appropriate number for each goal. Walk round while they are doing this and talk to learners about their progress. Remind learners about the extra practice opportunities under the box, and ask where they can find things.

Unit 13 Extra activities on the Teacher's DVD-ROM

Printable worksheets, activity instructions and answer keys are on your Teacher's DVD-ROM.

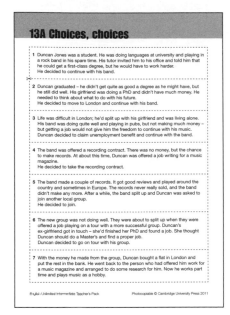

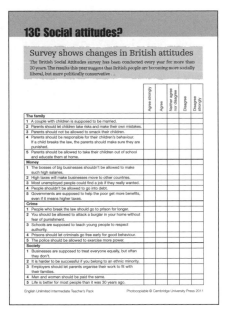

13A Choices, choices

Activity type: Reading and speaking – Dilemmas discussion – Groups / Whole class

Aim: To discuss the wisdom of choices that someone has made

Language: *should/shouldn't have / could/couldn't have* – Use at any point from 13.1.

Preparation: Make one copy of the worksheet for every three or four learners. Cut up each worksheet to make a set of seven story sections.

Time: 20–30 minutes

13B What if ...

Activity type: Speaking and grammar / Language game / Groups

Aim: To practise unreal conditionals: past in conversational contexts

Language: Unreal conditionals: past – Use at any point from 13.2.

Preparation: Make one copy of the worksheet for every five or six learners. Cut up the worksheet to make a set of ten cards.

Time: 15–20 minutes

13C Social attitudes?

Activity type: Speaking – Questionnaire/discussion – Pairs/ Groups

Aim: To practise talking about rules and obligations in society

Language: *make, let, be allowed to, be supposed to, should* – Use at any point from Across cultures, p107.

Preparation: Make one copy of the worksheet for every learner.

Time: 20 minutes

Unit 13 Self-study Pack

In the Workbook

Unit 13 of the *English Unlimited Intermediate Workbook* offers additional ways to practise the vocabulary and grammar taught in the Coursebook. There are also activities which build reading and writing skills and a whole page of listening and speaking tasks to use with the Interview video, giving your learners the opportunity to hear and react to authentic spoken English.

- **Vocabulary:** Events in business; Acts of kindness and bravery; Evaluating past actions; *make, let, be allowed to, be supposed to*
- **Grammar:** *should have*, *could have*; Unreal conditionals: past
- **My English:** Communicating in English
- **Explore reading:** Yoko Ono
- **Interview:** We all make mistakes – Nishadi and Bắc Trần

On the DVD-ROM

Unit 13 of the *English Unlimited Intermediate Self-study DVD-ROM* contains interactive games and activities for your learners to practise and improve their vocabulary, grammar and pronunciation, and also their speaking and listening, with the possibility for learners to record themselves, and a video of authentic spoken English to use with the Workbook.

- **Vocabulary and grammar:** Extra practice activities
- **Pronunciation:** Common pairs of words
- **Explore speaking:** Disagreeing politely
- **Explore listening:** Business news
- **Video:** We all make mistakes

14 In the news

14.1

Goals: understand news stories
react to the news

Core language:

VOCABULARY	Understanding news stories
	Reacting to the news
PRONUNCIATION	Groups of words and linking

Local news

LISTENING

1 Focus learners on the picture and ask what the woman's job is (*news reader* or *news presenter*). You could ask learners if they've heard any news today and how (*TV, radio, the Internet or in a newspaper*). Draw attention to the list of news stories, then allow learners to discuss what they find interesting in pairs or talk about this with the class.

2 a *Predicting from headlines*. Talk about the picture of the fire with the class, e.g. what type of fire it is, where it might be, etc. Find out who regularly listens to the news on the radio and if they listen to local or national radio stations. Then play recording **3.29**. Learners listen carefully to the radio headlines to identify the topic of each story. Don't check the answers, but give learners time to compare ideas with a partner.

   b *Listening for main ideas*. Play recording **3.30**. Learners listen to the complete stories to check their predictions from **a**.

   > See audio scripts on page 162.

VOCABULARY Understanding news stories

3 👥👥👥 Before answering the questions, learners read all the questions in small groups and help each other with the meanings of any new words and expressions. Encourage them to use dictionaries if there is an item nobody knows. Walk round and help as necessary. Then learners try to answer the questions, sharing any details that they can remember from the first listening. When everyone is ready, play recording **3.30** again. Give them a moment to compare answers with their group, before checking as a class.

   > 1 residents of the town of Tolga in North Queensland, Australia
   > 28 firefighters
   > to stay away from the area
   > 2 two police officers
   > assault (attacking the officers)
   > ten offences
   > 3 a law to ban the clearing of trees
   > a special permit
   > the LNP party, green groups (WWF)
   > 4 about 4,000
   > The number of Australians over the age of 100 will rise from 4,000 to 25,000 by 2050.
   > 5 It was run over by a car.
   > a wildlife carer (Lana Allcroft)

4 Encourage learners to make a page in their vocabulary notebooks for news stories, leaving space to add new entries and new categories. 👥 Learners categorise the words and expressions. Go through them with the class, checking pronunciation as you go.

   > *People: residents, firefighters, police, motorists, population change*
   > *Emergencies: evacuated from their homes, firefighters, injured, rescued*
   > *Crime: at the scene, police, involved in the incident, arrest … for, offences … charged with*
   > *Politics: law … introduced, oppose*

5 *Round-up*. Talk about the stories with the class, and find out what kind of stories are on learners' local news.

What's interesting is …

LISTENING

1 *Listening for main idea*. Explain that Abby and Joe are talking about two of the news stories from the radio news. Allow learners to read the two questions, then play recording **3.31**. They compare ideas with a partner, then feed back as a class.

   > *They talk about the two officers who were attacked by a boy's parents. They also talk about the fire near Tolga. Abby hadn't heard the story about the officers, but they had both heard about the fire.*

2 *Listening to understand attitudes*. Learners read through the questions with a partner, thinking about possible answers. Then play recording **3.31** again. They compare ideas, then check as a class.

   > 1 his son's birthday party
   > 2 the parents' attitude and actions
   > 3 how the fire started
   > 4 that it's a grass fire, not a forest fire
   > 5 that no one gets hurt in the fire

VOCABULARY Reacting to the news

3 a Ask the class what they remember about Luke Price (the teenager who assaulted police officers in Townsville). Point out that some items are possible more than once, but learners should try to remember the contexts from the conversation. Learners complete the sentences in pairs or individually before comparing with a partner. Learners will have an opportunity to focus on the pronunciation of the expressions a bit later.

   > 1 funny   2 important   3 interesting   4 makes
   > 5 worries   6 bothers

   b 👥 Learners discuss the context for the six extracts. Then check as a class.

   > 1, 2, 5: the fire   3, 6: Luke Price   4: Joe's son's party

   c Do this with the class and elicit more examples of sentences using *funny* and *bothers* with these meanings from learners, e.g. *She's a bit funny* or *She was being a bit funny last night* and *Does the radio bother you?*

> funny = strange / something that makes you laugh
> bother = irritate/worry

d *Vocabulary expansion.* Brainstorm more verbs and adjectives in the expressions with the class and list them in two columns on the board. Remind learners to record them in their notebooks.

Optional extra: Competition

Add an element of competition by putting learners in small teams to brainstorm more verbs and adjectives together. See which team can make the longest list.

---

4 a 👥 / 👥👥 *Writing.* Remind learners about the other three news stories in the Australian news report. Elicit a sentence about one of them using an expression from **3a**. Learners continue writing sentences together about the stories. Let them know they can refer to the scripts to jog their memories if they want.

b 👥 / 👥👥 *Discussion.* Monitor while learners discuss the stories, and check how they use the new language so you can feed back on this later. Find out if learners shared similar opinions on the stories.

Class discussion

Develop one or more of the topics which learners are most interested in into a class discussion, e.g. *Should there be laws about tree clearing? How do people feel about living to 100? Should crocodiles be kept in captivity?*

PRONUNCIATION Groups of words and linking

5 a Play recording **3.32** or say the sentence to demonstrate the word groups and linking within each group. Learners practise saying the sentence. Ask the class why it is important for news readers to use word groups rather than stringing all the words in a sentence together (*the divisions/pauses make what they are saying clearer, which helps listeners understand what they are saying*).

b 👥 Let learners do this in pairs and walk round to see how well they manage, offering help if anyone is stuck. Remind them to say the sentences out loud to each other to help them decide on the answers.

> 2 What's ‿important // is no one gets hurt.
> 3 What's ‿interesting // is the officers // were going to ‿arrest the boy ...
> 4 The thing that makes me ‿angry // is that normal kids // can't have parties ‿any more.
> 5 The thing that worries me // is how ‿it started.
> 6 The thing that bothers me // is the parents' ‿attitude, // not the boy!

c Direct learners to the script on p162, then play recording **3.33** so they can check their answers. Point out that words are not linked *across* word groups, even if a word ends in a consonant and the next word begins with a vowel, e.g. *'s // it's*. Also remind learners that word groups are not fixed, but reflect the speaker's meaning and emphasis in each case.

SPEAKING

6 👥 *Preparation.* Allow learners to discuss their own news stories, but point out that they don't have to be current, just memorable or interesting for them. Make sure they take notes to prompt them for the next stage, but tell them not to write sentences. Walk round and help as necessary with ideas or vocabulary.

7 👥👥 *Discussion.* Monitor while learners talk about their news stories and take a note of any errors which impede communication for a feedback session. *Round-up.* Ask a few people to tell the class briefly about the most interesting stories they talked about.

Following the news outside the classroom

Discuss how learners can access the news in English on the Internet outside the classroom (e.g. BBC World Service has links to current international news or past news on podcasts, or learners can listen to more Australian news on www.abc.net.au). Tell them to find a news broadcast and to listen to one or several news items that interest them as many times as they want and to select eight or ten vocabulary items to look up and record. In the next class, learners can explain their news stories to a group and teach each other the most useful vocabulary items from the stories. This can be done regularly, e.g. once a week on a Monday morning, for example, if you and your learners find this useful and interesting.

14.2

Goal: tell someone about a news story

Core language:

| GRAMMAR | Passives |
| VOCABULARY | Talking about news stories |

Fair play?

READING

1 Discuss the first question with the class, encouraging learners to give reasons for their ideas. Then focus them on the picture and dictionary entry and let them discuss the second question in pairs. Feed back as a class.

2 a 👥 *Pre-reading discussion.* Learners discuss the statements based on the article, and decide whether they're true or false. Don't go through the answers, as this will pre-empt **b**.

b Learners read the article to check their ideas. Give them an opportunity to compare ideas with a partner before checking as a class.

> 1 true   2 true   3 false   4 true   5 false

Option for weaker groups

Project the text onto a screen or use an OHT and ask learners to come up and underline the relevant parts of the text for each statement.

---

3 👥👥 *Reading for detail.* Learners read the article again and answer the questions. Check as a class.

> 1 Alain Such tested positive for drugs and so was suspended (dropped) from the Ingotel cycling team. In the 1904 Olympics, Thomas Hicks was given two injections of strychnine during the marathon. He won the race, but collapsed soon after finishing.
> 2 • It might become possible to identify 'athletic genes' in young people.
> • The World Anti-Doping Agency is taking genetic engineering in sport seriously, which probably means they think it could become a serious problem.
> • Drug testing in sport is becoming more and more frequent.
> • The main question regarding fairness is whether an advantage is available to everyone.

4 *Class discussion.* This is a good topic for a class discussion. Encourage quieter learners to contribute, as well as the more vocal people in the class.

GRAMMAR Passives

5 a Focus learners on the pairs of sentences and elicit the answers from the class. Point out that the passive is commonly used in the news, and is more common in written than spoken English.

> The B sentences are used in the article.
> The As are active; Bs are passive.

b *Focus on use.* Do this with the class. Point out that in English, you usually put the person or thing you want to talk about (the topic) at the beginning of a sentence. New information (the comment) comes after the topic. Show how the writer chooses the passive here to keep Alain Such or genetics as the topic of the sentence.

> a Alain Such   b genetics

6 *Focus on form.* Allow learners do this in pairs, then check as a class, eliciting the form for each verb tense onto the board.

> It is thought, he was given, Alain Such was suspended, Money could be invested

7 Learners read the sentences and discuss whether the verbs are passive or active. Point out that they are all in the past simple, then learners complete the sentences together. Check as a class.

> 1 were killed   2 won   3 was robbed   4 was freed
> 5 deserved   6 were stolen   7 were separated

Note: Grammar practice

You could do the grammar practice on p145 at this point.

 You could use photocopiable activity 14A on the Teacher's DVD-ROM at this point.

Talking about news stories

LISTENING

1 *Listening for main idea.* Read the questions, then play recording **3.34** so learners can identify which story from **7** in the previous section they are talking about and the connection between the two stories they mention. Play recording **3.34** again if learners

---

are unsure about the topics, then learners share any information they can remember about the articles.

> 1 7 (Sisters who were separated at birth.)
> 2 The other article was about identical twins separated at birth and about how similar they often are.

VOCABULARY Talking about news stories

2 Learners complete the sentences from the script. Direct them to the script to check their answers.

> 1c 2f 3d 4a 5g 6b 7e

SPEAKING

3 *Preparation.* Give learners plenty of time to read their articles, identify the main ideas and plan what they want to say about it. Walk round and help as necessary while they're preparing.

4 a *Talking about news stories.* Monitor while learners are talking and help out if there are any problems that impede communication. In feedback, find out if learners agree with each other.

b *Round-up.* Talk about this with the class and encourage as many learners to participate in the discussion as you can.

14.3 Target activity

Goals: react to the news ♻
tell someone about a news story ♻
evaluate options and choose one

Core language:

TASK VOCABULARY	Evaluating and selecting
14.1 VOCABULARY	Understanding news stories
14.1 VOCABULARY	Reacting to the news
14.2 GRAMMAR	Passives
14.2 VOCABULARY	Talking about news stories

Choose a story for a news programme

TASK READING AND LISTENING

1 Learners read the advert, then discuss the question with the class. Ask if anyone would be interested in going to the focus group and why / why not.

> They want people to share their views about what makes a good TV news programme to help with ideas for their new programme, The World This Week.

2 Focus learners on the pictures and ask what they think the stories might be about. Then they read the summaries and answer the question with a partner. Feed back as a class, getting learners' reactions to both stories.

3 a *Listening for main idea.* Play recording **3.35** and give learners a moment to discuss the answer before checking as a class.

> They don't agree. Melek likes the crime story. Nathan likes the Guitar Hero story. Rita's not sure about either story.

b *Listening for detail.* Play recording **3.35** again so learners can listen for what the people find most interesting about both stories. Encourage them to take brief notes as they listen to prompt their memories. Feed back as a class.

> A *That they copied the idea from the plot of a TV show.*
> B *How* Guitar Hero *can help reduce obesity.*

TASK VOCABULARY Evaluating and selecting

4 a 👥 *Focus on expressions.* Learners read the extracts and decide together which story the people are referring to. Direct learners to the script to check their own answers.

> *1A 2A 3B 4A 5B 6B 7B*

b 👥 *Vocabulary expansion.* Look at the example with the class, then learners continue to substitute the underlined words. In feedback, check understanding of all the expressions.

> *2 understand   3 seems reasonable   4 sure*
> *5 choose   6 entertaining   7 possible*

c 👥 Make sure learners cover the expressions in **a** and use the new words to help them remember the expressions. Remind them to think about their intonation and to practise 'how' they say the expressions, not just the words.

TASK

5 👥 *Preparation.* Put learners in groups, then direct them to the appropriate pages for their stories. Walk round and help while they prepare to explain their stories.

> **Alternative for weaker groups**
>
> Put learners into groups of As, Bs and Cs. Each group should read their story together and help each other with unknown vocabulary (they can use a dictionary or ask you if necessary). Then they prepare to explain their stories using language from the lesson. Give them time to practise together before moving on to **6**.

6 👥 *Talking about news stories.* Learners remain in their groups (A+B+C) from **5**. Point out that learners have to choose a story for the programme as the objective of their discussions. Monitor while learners are talking and help if there is a breakdown in communication.

7 👥 *Round-up.* Learners change groups and compare their outcomes. In feedback, find out which stories groups chose and why.

14 Explore

Keyword: *see*

Goal: use *see* to express a range of meanings
Core language:
Meanings of *see*
Patterns with *see*: *see someone do something*; *see + if*; *see + wh-* word
Expressions with *see*

Meanings of *see*

1 Learners read the sentences from previous units, then do the matching. Check as a class.

> *1C 2B 3A 4D*

2 Focus learners on the picture and ask what they think the man is doing. Elicit or teach *putting flat-pack furniture together.* Elicit a question for the first item (*Did you see the news last night?*) and write it on the board. Go through the remaining items quickly with the class, eliciting questions from different learners. Remind learners that the objective is to find someone in the class who has done or does these things by asking different people in the class. Point out that when someone says yes, learners should ask follow-up questions to find out more information. Tell them to take a note of the people who say yes so they can report back to the class at the end.

👥 Learners mill round the class asking and answering the questions. In feedback, go through the questions quickly, finding out who said yes to each one.

3 a Talk about this with the class, encouraging learners to express their opinions and to refer to specific adverts or types of adverts if they can. Point out the different forms of the word and check pronunciation of each one: *ad, advert, advertisement,*

b *Listening for main idea.* Read the questions together, then play recording **3.36**. Learners compare ideas with a partner. Play the recording again if necessary, then check as a class.

> *Rickard likes them because they're funny and you can find out about new things, like products for the house. Meninda doesn't like them because she doesn't see the point of them, often doesn't know what they're for and you can miss your programme because you're watching or talking about the ads.*

Patterns with *see*

4 a 👥 Learners read the sentences and do the matching in pairs. Go through each one with the class, highlighting the patterns on the board. Suggest learners make an entry in their notebooks for *see* as for other similar verbs like *have*, *get*, etc., and remind them to take a note of the different patterns, leaving space for new entries they may come across later.

> *Ac Bb Ca*

b 👥 *Discussion.* Monitor while learners are talking and help if they have problems with the use of *see.*

Expressions with *see*

5 a 👥 Learners read the sentences and match them to one of the meanings in **1**. In feedback, check understanding of the expressions and make sure learners have a chance to practise saying them.

> A (understand)

b 👤 *Preparation.* Walk round and help as necessary while learners are preparing their ideas.

c 👥 / 👥👥 *Discussion.* Learners talk about the statements together. In feedback, find out if they agreed with each other, and develop one or more of the points in a class discussion if you have time.

 You could use photocopiable activity 14B on the Teacher's DVD-ROM at this point.

Explore speaking

Goals: participate in a discussion
interrupt politely

Core language:
Expressions for managing a conversation, e.g. interrupting, changing topic, returning to a topic

1 *Pre-listening discussion.* Ask learners what they think is happening in the picture and how they think the woman feels. Then talk about the question with the class.

2 a *Listening for main idea.* Focus learners on the picture, caption and question, then ask some questions to check they understand the context for the listening, e.g. *Who is Celia? Who is Abby? What are Abby and her friends trying to do?* Then play recording **3.37**. Learners compare ideas with a partner, then check as a class.

> They arrange to have a surprise party for Celia because she's leaving. They agree to contact a DJ, Carlos, and mention The Meeting Point as a possible venue.

b *Listening for detail.* Ask the class if they only discuss Celia's party in the conversation (*they don't*). Draw attention to the list of topics and remind learners to take a note of important details while they listen. Then play recording **3.37** again. Let them compare with a partner before they do **c**.

c Learners check their own ideas by reading the script. Only go through this with the class if they have any problems.

3 👥 Learners categorise the highlighted expressions. In feedback, make sure learners have enough time to record the expressions in their notebooks.

> 1 interrupt: 1, 4, 8
> 2 change a topic: 2, 3, 7
> 3 return to the main topic: 5, 6, 9, 10

Alternative with books closed

Project the conversation onto a screen or the board, or use an OHP. Give the class the first function (interrupting) and get learners to work in pairs to identify the expressions in the conversation. Check as a class, then do functions 2–3 in the same way.

4 👥👥 *Practice.* Make sure learners read all the follow-up conversations between the friends before completing any gaps. Check as a class.

> 1 by the way   2 Anyway   3 by the way   4 While we're on the subject   5 can I just say something?

5 a 👥👥 Groups choose from the list of types of party.

b 👤 *Preparation.* If you think learners might need some more ideas for their interruptions, put this list on the board:
• *the football results*
• *what's on TV tonight*
• *a good restaurant to take a friend to*

Walk round and help while learners are preparing and help as necessary.

c 👥👥 *Conversation.* Encourage learners to suggest all their ideas, but remind them that they have to agree on the best option as a group. Monitor during their conversations and take a note of any problems individuals have using the strategies so that you can feed back to them at the end of their conversations.

6 *Round-up.* Find out what parties the different groups have organised and get some feedback from learners about which idea they like the best.

Note: Interrupting

For some cultures, it is very rude to interrupt other people, e.g. for the Japanese. Be sensitive to this during the lesson and show learners how they can use intonation to interrupt more or less politely. When learners have finished, put this question on the board and give them an opportunity to evaluate their conversations at the end: *How did you feel about: interrupting other people? being interrupted by other people?* Then talk about this with the class.

14 Look again

Review

GRAMMAR Passives

1 a 👤 Learners order the words individually before comparing with a partner.

> 1 My home was built in the 1970s.
> 2 My watch was given to me by my wife.
> 3 My shoes are made of plastic.
> 4 My dad was born in 1939.
> 5 Letters have been completely replaced by email.
> 6 Computers have been used in my school since 2000.

Alternative for stronger groups

Add an element of competition by making this a race and telling learners to raise their hand when they're finished. In feedback, remind learners about the weak form of *be* in *are, was* and *were*.

b 👤 *Writing.* Elicit a different sentence from the class to demonstrate the next stage, then learners continue writing true sentences. 👥 Learners talk about their sentences together.

VOCABULARY Understanding news stories

2 a Learners complete the news stories together. Check as a class.

> 1 evacuated   2 passed   3 motorists   4 arrested
> 5 firefighters; scene

b *Writing.* Walk round and help as necessary while learners are writing.

c Learners change partners and listen to each other. *Round-up.* Find out which sentences were true.

CAN YOU REMEMBER? Unit 13 – Acts of kindness

3 a Learners choose the correct words then compare with a partner. Check as a class.

> 1 to   2 for   3 for   4 of   5 with   6 with

b *Asking and answering.* Monitor while learners talk together and check how confident they are with the verbs and prepositions. Give feedback on any common problems at the end.

Extension

SPELLING AND SOUNDS /aɪ/

4 a Say a few words with the different patterns, e.g. *fine, ice, why* and *sight,* and elicit the spelling patterns for the /aɪ/ sound from the class. Then learners complete the words in each list. Play recording **3.38** so they can check their ideas, or go through this yourself with the class.

> 1 crime, decide, time, outside
> 2 idea, icy, Irish, island
> 3 by, cry, fry, July
> 4 flight, fight, light, bright

b Learners work together to work out the spelling patterns for /aɪ/.

> 1 i   2 i   3 igh   4 y

c *Spellcheck.* Play recording **3.39** while learners write down the words they hear. They can check their own spellings in script **3.39** on p163. Remind learners to record any words that they find difficult to spell correctly.

NOTICE Common passive expressions in the news

5 a Point out that these are all common expressions in news stories using the passive form. Learners choose the correct option individually, then compare with a partner. Check as a class.

> 1 investigated   2 charged   3 arrested   4 involved
> 5 given

b Give learners time to think of some recent crime stories, and to prepare to talk about them. If you have internet access or anyone has a newspaper with them, learners could scan the news briefly for ideas.

c *Speaking.* Learners work with different partners to talk about their crime stories. *Round-up.* Ask learners to tell the class any interesting stories they heard from their group.

Self-assessment

Go through the list of goals, eliciting language from the unit for each one. You may need to remind learners of the contexts for the goals and let them look back through the unit if necessary. Then they circle the appropriate number for each goal. Walk round while they are doing this and talk to learners about their progress. Remind learners about the extra practice opportunities under the box, and ask where they can find things.

 You could use photocopiable activity 14C on the Teacher's DVD-ROM at this point.

Unit 14 Extra activities on the Teacher's DVD-ROM

Printable worksheets, activity instructions and answer keys are on your Teacher's DVD-ROM.

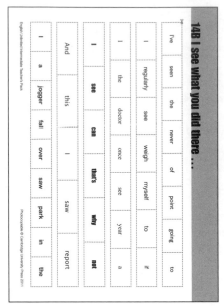

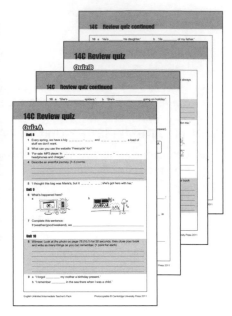

14A Run for your wife!

Activity type: Reading and writing – Completing a text / Retelling a story – Pairs/Groups

Aim: To raise awareness of when the passive is used; to react to news stories

Language: Passives – Use at any point from 14.2.

Preparation: Make one copy of the worksheet for each pair or group.

Time: 30 minutes

14B I see what you did there ...

Activity type: Reading, listening and speaking – Dictogloss with jumbled phrases – Groups

Aim: To encourage learners to internalise *see* chunks

Language: Meanings of *see* – Use at any point from Explore keyword *see*, p115.

Preparation: Make one copy of the worksheet for every three or four learners. Cut up each worksheet to make a set of six anagram strips. Do not cut up the individual words.

Alternative preparation: Make one copy of the worksheet for every three or four learners and do not cut up the anagram strips.

Time: 15–20 minutes

14C Review quiz

Activity type: Reading, speaking and writing – Competitive quiz – Pairs/Groups

Aim: To encourage learners to look back over the Coursebook and review what they have learned

Language: Various from Units 8–14

Preparation: Make one copy of Quiz A and Quiz B for each pair or group of learners.

Time: 30–40 minutes

Unit 14 Self-study Pack

In the Workbook

Unit 14 of the *English Unlimited Intermediate Workbook* offers additional ways to practise the vocabulary and grammar taught in the Coursebook. There are also activities which build reading and writing skills and two whole pages of listening and speaking tasks to use with the Documentary video, giving your learners the opportunity to hear and react to authentic spoken English.

- **Vocabulary:** Understanding news stories; Reacting to the news; Talking about news stories; Evaluating and selecting
- **Grammar:** Passives
- **Time out:** Quiz: Newspaper trivia
- **Explore writing:** Letter to a newspaper
- **Documentary:** The runner

On the DVD-ROM

Unit 14 of the *English Unlimited Intermediate Self-study DVD-ROM* contains interactive games and activities for your learners to practise and improve their vocabulary, grammar and pronunciation, and also their speaking and listening, with the possibility for learners to record themselves, and a video of authentic spoken English to use with the Workbook.

- **Vocabulary and grammar:** Extra practice activities
- **Pronunciation:** Groups of words and linking
- **Explore speaking:** Adjective synonyms
- **Explore listening:** A radio talk show
- **Video:** Documentary – The runner

Grammar Reference – Coursebook pp134–145: Answer key

Unit 1
Talking about the present
1 B relax
2 A are you doing   B 'm writing
3 A Have you been   B haven't been
4 A do you do   B watch
5 A Are you doing
6 A Have you heard
7 A Are you reading   B 'm reading
8 A do you see   B don't live
9 A Have you done   B haven't had
10 A have you seen   B 've seen

Unit 2
will, could, may, might
1a 1 'll   2 might   3 might   4 Will   5 'll   6 might   7 might
8 won't   9 might
1b 3 she may well panic
6 they may well be wrong
10 you may well be right
2a 1 <u>She might be</u> stuck in traffic.
2 <u>She's unlikely to</u> answer the phone if she's driving.
3 <u>He may well know</u> where she is.
4 He says <u>she'll definitely be here</u> soon.
5 Hm, <u>she's more likely to</u> have a lie-in!
6 <u>It could be interesting</u>.
7 Well, <u>I may have</u> a quiet evening in.
8 I know Jon <u>will definitely be cooking</u>!

Unit 3
Present perfect
2 I haven't finished the report for today's meeting <u>yet</u>.
3 He's <u>always</u> lived in the same house.
4 They've had that car <u>for</u> ten years. It's <u>never</u> broken down.
5 We've <u>just</u> come back from safari in Kenya.
6 We haven't seen each other <u>since</u> university, but it seems like yesterday.
7 I've <u>already</u> seen this film.
8 I've <u>never</u> liked spicy food.

Unit 4
Narrative verb forms
1a 1 A rang   B picked up; had put the phone down
2 A had broken   B didn't want   B was running; fell
3 A Did … have   B didn't have   B 'd/had … been
2 1 Later, we found out what had happened.
2 I didn't know what was going on.
3 We didn't realise there had been an earthquake.
4 I can't really remember what happened. / I really can't remember what happened.
5 I was on the way to the station when you called.
6 I was trying to write an email when the computer crashed.
7 Everything suddenly started shaking and the lights went out. / Everything started shaking and the lights suddenly went out.
8 Unfortunately, we hadn't heard the warnings.

Unit 5
Future forms – *will*, *going to* and present progressive
1 1 I'll
2 I'm meeting
3 I'm going to
4 's coming
5 I'm going to
6 going to watch
7 I'll
8 I'm doing
9 I'll go
10 going to call

Future in the past – *was/were supposed to*, *was/were going to*, past progressive
2 1 was going to finish / was supposed to finish
2 was eating
3 was going to call / was supposed to call
4 was getting
5 were meeting
6 was supposed to see / was going to see

Unit 6
Verb + *-ing*
Suggested answers
1 I dislike getting up early.
2 I finished my degree in psychology last year.
3 I enjoy eating out with friends.
4 I've never considered being self-employed.
5 I really want to give up smoking.
6 I fancy having something to eat right now.
7 I can't stand people who are rude.
8 I really can't face doing my filing.
9 I miss not having my parents living near me.
10 I try and avoid working at weekends, but sometimes I have to.

Unit 7
Comparing
1 1 It's <u>a lot / much</u> easier for me to read.
2 You're <u>almost</u> as fast as him.
3 It's <u>a little / a bit / marginally</u> quicker.
4 I find German <u>a bit</u> more difficult than French.
5 He's only <u>slightly</u> taller than I am.
6 My wife's <u>much / far</u> more practical than I am.
2 1 You're <u>just</u> as experienced as he is.
2 … I don't think Sally is <u>quite</u> as argumentative as her sister.
3 It's <u>slightly / marginally</u> closer if we go by the river.
4 He isn't <u>nearly</u> as difficult as he used to be.
5 My brother's <u>much / far / a lot</u> more adventurous than I am.

Unit 8
Modals of deduction and speculation
1 must   2 must   3 can't   4 might   5 must   6 might   7 must
8 can't

Unit 9
Real and unreal conditionals
1 had; 'd   2 go   3 's   4 'll; see   5 'd; didn't eat
6 worked; 'd   7 don't feel

Unit 10
Verb patterns
1 to call   2 to talk   3 talking   4 working   5 walking   6 to tell
7 to pack   8 to open

Present perfect simple and present perfect progressive
1 've been playing   2 've had   3 've been looking
4 've decorated   5 've been working   6 've finished
7 've been learning   8 've cut

Unit 11
Reporting speech
2 Bill said that he makes/made it all the time.
3 Anna asked him to help her.
4 He promised to help her. / He promised he would.
5 Anna said (that) she'd like to know how to do it.
6 They agreed to make/do it together.
7 Then Bill asked Anna to chop the veg(etables). / if she could
  chop the veg(etables).

Unit 12
Indirect questions
Suggested answers
1 a I was wondering if you always eat breakfast.
  b Could I ask you which meal of the day is the most important?
2 a Could I ask you how you get to school or work?
  b Could you tell me how long it takes?
3 a I was wondering what political party you support.
  b Could I ask you if you think it's OK not to vote in an
     election?
4 a Could I ask you how many languages you speak?
  b I was wondering if all children should learn a foreign
     language.
5 a Could you tell me if you're a member of a gym or leisure
     centre?
  b Could I ask you how much exercise you do every week?

Unit 13
should have, could have
1 shouldn't have gone
2 could have tried
3 shouldn't have stayed up
4 couldn't have worked
5 should have tidied
6 should have done
7 could have done

Unreal conditionals: past
1 wouldn't have said; 'd known
2 'd told; 'd have given
3 hadn't made; 'd have passed
4 'd have found; 'd followed
5 wouldn't have known; hadn't told me
6 'd answered; 'd have got
7 'd bought; 'd have made
8 'd come; wouldn't have enjoyed

Unit 14
Passives
1 was opened   2 are drunk   3 have been eaten   4 was written
5 were made   6 was made   7 has been seen

Acknowledgements

Theresa Clementson would like to thank Anthony, Sam and Megan for their ideas, support and unwavering confidence, and Cristina Rimini for her help and advice on all matters TEFL over the years.

Leanne Gray would like to thank colleagues and learners at Kaplan Aspect Bath for years of fun and support. Thanks to the team at Cambridge for the opportunity and Alison Bewsher for her help and support on this project.

Howard Smith would like to thank the teachers and learners he has worked with over the years for the ideas which have, no doubt, been appropriated for these activities and also the team at Cambridge, in particular Keith, Alison and Karen, for the opportunity and for their patience, encouragement and forbearance.

The authors and publishers are grateful to:

Text design and page make-up: Stephanie White at Kamae Design

Video content: all the team at Phaebus Media Group

Illustrations by Kathy Baxendale, Mark Duffin, Clare Elsom, Julian Mosedale, Vicky Woodgate

The authors and publishers acknowledge the following sources of copyright material and are grateful for the permissions granted. While every effort has been made, it has not always been possible to identify the sources of all the material used, or to trace all copyright holders. If any omissions are brought to our notice, we will be happy to include the appropriate acknowledgements on reprinting.

For the tables on the DVD-ROM and the text on pages 4 and 22 of the Teacher's book © *Common European Framework of Reference for Languages: Learning, teaching, assessment* (2001) Council of Europe Modern Languages Division, Strasbourg, Cambridge University Press